Joyce, Decadence, and Emancipation

Joyce, Decadence, and Emancipation

Vivian Heller

University of Illinois Press
Urbana and Chicago

Publication of this book was supported by a grant from Bennington College.

This book is printed on acid-free paper.

Library of Congress Cataloging-in-Publication Data

Heller, Vivian, 1954–
    Joyce, decadence, and emancipation / Vivian Heller.
        p.   cm.
    Includes bibliographical references and index.
    ISBN 0-252-06485-2 (alk. paper)
    1. Joyce, James, 1882–1941—Political and social views.
    2. Politics and literature—Ireland—History—20th century.
    3. Decadence (Literary movement)—Ireland.   4. Modernism
    (Literature)—Ireland.   5. Dublin (Ireland)—In literature.
    6. Decadence in literature.   7. Liberty in literature.   I. Title.
    PR6019.O9Z5813   1995
    823'.912—dc20   95-4398
                                                        CIP

For Peter and Christiane Heller,
with love and admiration

Contents

Acknowledgments   ix

Introduction   1

1. *Dubliners*   13

2. *A Portrait of the Artist as a Young Man*   47

3. Interchapter   78

4. "Oxen of the Sun"   95

5. "Circe"   118

6. "Penelope"   138

Conclusion   157

Epilogue   165

Bibliography   177

Index   187

Acknowledgments

I would like to thank Helen Vendler, for her superb insights and unfailing support; Maura Spiegel, for her generosity of mind and spirit; Paul Fry, for his constant encouragement; Hanna Bercovitch, for her invaluable critiques of early versions of the manuscript; Paul Royster and Lixin Shao, for hours of technical assistance; Harriet Chessman, for her excellent commentary; Rochelle Gurstein, for her wise counsel; Richard Tristman, for his wit, wisdom, and erudition; Peter, Christiane, and Stephen Heller, for helping me bring this project to completion; Alvin Feinman, for his uncompromising vision; Kenji Fujita, my husband, who has helped me to understand my subject more than he knows; and Naomi Fujita, my daughter, who has made so many things possible by coming into the world.

Introduction

This study of Joyce began as an attempt to answer a question raised by Georg Lukács, Bertolt Brecht, Walter Benjamin, and Theodor Adorno in the 1930s, namely, Is modernism a symptom of decadence or a sign of emancipation? Although the question is nearly as old as modernism itself, it shows no signs of aging; even those who are busy celebrating the advent of postmodernism resort to arguments used in modernism's defense decades ago. The exchanges of Lukács, Brecht, Benjamin, and Adorno were provoked by German expressionism, which influenced the writers of the German Left during the twenties and thirties (Jameson, "Reflections" 196). Lukács attacked expressionism in "Grosse und Verfall des Expressionismus" (1934), condemning it as romantic anticapitalism. As he saw it, the expressionists blurred social relationships by focusing on purely subjective renderings of damaged life; moreover, their aesthetic experimentation reflected a preoccupation with form at the expense of content. Brecht countered that it was Lukács who was guilty of formalism, clinging to a conventional notion of realist form as though it could address the needs of the present; his own motto was "Don't start from the good old things but the bad new ones" (qtd. in Benjamin, "Conversations" 99). Brecht's animosity was sharpened by the fact that he shared one of Lukács's most basic assumptions, as did Benjamin and Adorno; all of them believed that by analyzing decadence they were undertaking part of the labor of emancipation. Decadence was conceived as false consciousness; emancipation entailed a rigorous process of demystification. Accordingly, each participant in the debate had his own corrective or utopian aesthetic. For Lukács, critical realism was the only movement capable of representing alienation without obscuring the social totality. Adorno defended the sensuous autonomy of high art as a refuge from reification. Brecht believed that his epic theater sabotaged the bourgeois complacency encouraged by traditional, illusionistic theater. Benjamin had faith in epic theater and in cinema; both addressed audiences of relaxed or even distracted experts, restoring the authority of everyman and thereby politicizing art.

Now that so many modernist neologisms have crept into the language of advertising, the utopian aesthetics of the Frankfurt School are no longer tenable. Time has proven that nothing can resist the allure of the culture industry; Adorno's high modernism has been stripped of its autonomy, and Benjamin's popular modernism merely reinforces the status quo. Brecht argued that modernism was the realism of his day; in our day, modernism no longer demystifies reality, it decorates it, adorning corporations, enlivening commercials, aestheticizing exploitation in films. Yet the debate over modernism has not been laid to rest; on the contrary, it has come back to haunt us in a new form. Modernism has engendered postmodernism, and attempts to exalt one over the other revive the problematic of decadence and emancipation. (The word *decadence,* however, is no longer used; *neoconservatism* usually takes its place.) Jürgen Habermas has emerged as postmodernism's most formidable critic; like Lukács, he faults his contemporaries for merely reproducing the effects of alienation.[1] Other defenders of modernism echo Adorno; postmodernism is scorned for embracing the pluralism of late capitalism and surrendering to the mediocrity of consumer society; modernism is praised for its purity (despite its assimilation). Defenders of postmodernism claim that it meets the challenge of technological society instead of shying away from it, echoing the utopianism of "The Work of Art in the Age of Mechanical Reproduction," in which Benjamin envisions the emergence of an aesthetic praxis predicated on demystification. Certainly it is no accident that defenses of postmodernism sound so familiar. Although postmodernists are more acclimated to consumer society than their forbears, they still want to revolutionize perception. In this respect, they rejuvenate modernism by rebelling against it. Jean-François Lyotard, an apologist for postmodernism, acknowledges the inescapability of modernism: "A work can become modern only if it is first postmodern. Postmodernism thus understood is not modernism at its end but modernism in the nascent state, and this state is constant" (79). According to Lyotard, modernism and postmodernism share a radical insight into the limits of representation, the unattainability of meaning: the difference is that modernism is nostalgic while postmodernism is playful. Formally, modernism evokes the past; postmodernism "denies itself the solace of good forms" (81). Modernism and postmodernism are so intimately associated in Lyotard's mind that he claims Joyce as a postmodernist. Although this step muddies the waters considerably, it proves that the debate over modernism is not over; it is simply being cast in new terms.[2]

Post-structuralist readers of Joyce have made yet another contribution to the debate. Reacting against what they take to be quasi-religious models of literary interpretation, they revel in the indeterminacies of *Ulysses* and *Finnegans Wake*. Joyce, they argue, is a master of deconstruction, emancipating the reader from logocentrism through semantic ambivalence and discontinuous narration.[3] Unlike the culture critics of the Frankfurt School or their heirs, post-structuralists are not particularly political, yet their celebration of the emancipatory character of Joyce's later work betrays a utopian impulse and a belief in the cultural value of an art of demystification.

What can contemporary readers of Joyce draw from the historic debate over modernism? The problematic of decadence and emancipation is central to Joyce's work, inviting us to join the fray, and yet, if our primary motive is to arrive at a richer understanding of Joyce's work, we are finally compelled to admit that there is no "question" and no "answer" that exists apart from the all-consuming and self-preserving palimpsest that is the Joycean text.

In what sense is the question raised by the Frankfurt School central to the meaning of Joyce's work? Everything Joyce wrote was implicated in the romance of decadence and emancipation. Like his doppelgänger Stephen Dedalus, he exiled himself to forge the conscience of his race. Initially, he thought of art as a means of making the blind see their own impediment, as the following lines, written in editorial self-defense, suggest: "The points on which I have yielded are points which rivet [*Dubliners*] together. . . . I fight to retain them because I believe that in composing my chapter of moral history in exactly the way I have composed it, I have taken the first step toward the spiritual liberation of my country" (*Selected Letters* 88). Joyce's trope for decadence was paralysis. Dublin was the center of Ireland's paralysis;[4] as such, it was worthy to be presented to the world. Emancipation depended on becoming a citizen of the world, which depended, in turn, on showing that Dublin was representative. Coming from a country whose growth was stunted, Joyce treated provincialism as a form of paralysis. By making Dublin as all-encompassing as Blake's grain of sand, he escaped the confinement he feared.

Joyce's writing does not conceal its own dependence on paralysis; it dramatizes the dialectical intimacy of decadence and emancipation at every turn.[5] Cultural critics like Lukács, in their determination to translate aesthetic practice into ideology, fall short of Joyce's realization that paralysis has a language of its own and that emancipation depends, in part, on mastering that language of enervation. Consequently, Joyce's writing resists visionary closure; epiphany may illuminate paralysis, but it never dissolves it. This strategy of resistance is played out in the themes and in the structure of his fiction. Thus the concatenated narratives of *Dubliners* climax in a moment of vision at the end of "The Dead," but the closing epiphany merely confirms that paralysis, like snow, is general all over Ireland. *A Portrait of the Artist as a Young Man* never violates the thematic antinomy of Daedalus and Icarus, fabulous artificer and hubristic son. The structure of *Ulysses* is at once disjunctive and organic, leaving the seamlessness and discontinuity of the world we perceive unreconciled. Semantic boundaries become fluid in *Finnegans Wake*, yet myths and archetypes retain their shape. The open-endedness of Joyce's work is sustained by a series of structural and thematic oppositions; any attempt to interpret these oppositions out of existence is misguided. The following study is an attempt to trace the symbiotic relationship of decadence and emancipation that emerges in *Dubliners, Portrait,* and *Ulysses.* It is a study born out of the debate over modernism, a debate that Joyce engages, reformulates, and, ultimately, dissolves.

Every interpretation, however, has a hidden polemic of its own, betrayed by the textual elements stressed by the reader. My own reading is guided by the conviction that *Dubliners, Portrait,* and *Ulysses* not only dramatize the intimacy of decadence and emancipation but also constitute very different renderings of it. In order to describe these differences, I focus on Joyce's of his narrative "epiphany" (which changes from text to text) because epiphany, as Joyce conceived it, is implicated in the dialectic of decadence and emancipation. If Joyce's work represents a flowering of language, epiphany marks its peak, arresting narration in a moment of "luminous silent stasis."[6] The richness of Joyce's writing (and, by extension, the precision of epiphany) is itself a product of underdevelopment, as Jameson hypothesizes in an essay on *Ulysses:*

> Joyce's is the epic of the metropolis under imperialism, in which the development of the bourgeoisie and the proletariat alike is stunted to the benefit of a national petty bourgeoisie: indeed, precisely these rigid restraints imposed by imperialism on the development of human energies account for the symbolic displacement and flowering of the latter in eloquence, rhetoric and rhetorical language of all kinds; symbolic practices not particularly essential either to business men or the working classes but highly prized in pre-capitalist societies and preserved, as in a time capsule, in *Ulysses* itself. And this is the moment to rectify our previous account of the city and to observe that if *Ulysses* is also for us the classical, the supreme representation of something like the Platonic ideal of city life, this is due to the fact that Dublin is not exactly the full-blown capitalist metropolis, but like the Paris of Flaubert, still regressive, still distantly akin to the village, still ur- or under-developed enough to be represented, thanks to the domination of its foreign masters. ("Ulysses" 134–35)

Dublin figures in all of Joyce's writing, even in *Portrait,* where its absence is conspicuous, defining Stephen's solipsism as a flight from poverty. Joyce's literary achievement is a by-product of stagnation; correspondingly, his epiphanies are both emancipatory and decadent, at once enlightening the reader and feeding on social regression. This is particularly clear in *Dubliners,* where almost every epiphany is a disclosure of paralysis.

Before going on, I should point out that there is nothing compromised about epiphany according to Stephen Dedalus. In *Stephen Hero* and *Portrait,* he defines epiphany as the intellectual penetration of a sensuous object. The reader of *Dubliners, Portrait,* and *Ulysses* knows epiphany to be a more thoroughly mediated event, consisting of the intellectual penetration of a body of experience formed in narration. Epiphany is originally described in *Stephen Hero* as the third quality of beauty. The first quality, Stephen teaches Cranly, is integrity, "declared in a simple sudden synthesis of the faculty which apprehends" (212). The second quality is symmetry, apprehended when the mind "considers the object in whole and in part, in relation to itself and to other objects, examines the balance of its parts, contemplates the form of the object, traverses every cranny of the structure" (212). Epiphany is the final synthesis: "First we recognise that the structure is *one* integral thing, then we recognise that it is an organised composite structure, a *thing* in fact: finally, when the relation of the parts is exquisite, when the parts are adjusted to the special point, we recognise that it is *that* thing which it is. Its soul, its whatness, leaps to us from the vestment of its appearance. The soul of the commonest object, the structure of which is so adjusted, seems to us radiant. The object achieves its epiphany" (213). Epiphany, as defined by Stephen Dedalus, is a kind of aesthetic revelation. In the course of his disquisition, he uses the clock of the ballast office as an example of an object that might be epiphanized. But in *Dubliners,* the object of epiphany is not a clock or any other "item in the catalogue of Dublin's street furniture," it is Dublin itself, understood as a center of paralysis. Thus the "commonest object" is replaced by the commonest disease. Epiphany takes on new meaning, accomplishing a synthesis of decadence of subject and emancipation of mind. Through epiphany, the darkness of paralysis is made visible to the reader.

The marriage of decadence and emancipation sealed by epiphany is not sublime but emphatically mundane. Originally epiphany (i.e., the manifestation of Christ to the Gentiles in the persons of the Magi) was associated with salvation and a metaphysics of presence: in Joyce's hands, it becomes an instrument of analysis or negation. His secular epiphanies presuppose what Benjamin describes as the "contemporary decay of the aura." According to Benjamin, works of art predicated on a pre-industrial metaphysics of presence are auratic; the charged distance dividing such objects from their viewers constitutes their aura. Mechanical reproduction does away with that distance:

> Every day the urge grows stronger to get hold of an object at very close range by way of its likeness, its reproduction. Unmistakably, reproduction as offered by picture magazines and newsreels differs from the image seen by the unarmed eye. Uniqueness and perma-

nence are as closely linked in the latter as are transitoriness and reproducibility in the former. To pry an object from its shell, to destroy its
aura, is a mark of perception whose "sense of the universal equality
of things" has increased to such a degree that it extracts it from even
a unique object by means of reproduction. ("Work" 223)

Joyce had an excellent ear for the kind of changes Benjamin describes; the linguistic reverberations of mechanical reproduction
are recorded in "Aeolus," to cite the most obvious example. His
epiphanies may seem regressive by comparison, reintroducing sacral
distances into narration by interrupting its flow; after all, epiphanies do remain points of "luminous silent stasis." Yet although
epiphany illuminates the agonistic movement of the text, it does
not resolve or transcend it; that is to say, it restores sight without
shifting the reader's focus to a transcendental object. To borrow
Benjamin's terms, Joyce discards permanence but retains uniqueness; each epiphany opens its own transitory perspective.

Epiphany, like paralysis, is a condition of stasis. The difference
is that the stasis of epiphany illuminates process, whereas the stasis of paralysis arrests it. Epiphany subordinates process to vision
in its passing moment; paralysis becomes a degenerative process
in its own right. Because Joyce saw that degenerative process as a
perversion of creation and procreation, he frequently extended his
metaphor, referring to paralysis as a sexually transmitted disease.

Some critics treat Joycean modernism as though it were an exotic
strain of paralysis; others emphasize Joyce's struggle against social
and artistic constraints. Although Jameson sees the linguistic fertility of *Ulysses* as a product of Ireland's underdevelopment, he
interprets modernism in general as an "expression of the will to
overcome the commodification of late nineteenth century capitalism and to substitute for the mouldering and overstuffed bazaar of
late Victorian life the mystique and promise of some intense and
heightened, more authentic existence" (*Fables* 39).[7] Franco Moretti
describes *Ulysses* as a "long goodbye" to liberal capitalism, reading
it not only as a record but also as a symptom of social decline. Hugh
Kenner agrees with Moretti to the extent that he reads *Ulysses* as an
exercise in atrophy:

The action of the book resembles the running down of a great clock.
The sharp conflict in the sharp sunlight of the opening episode becomes slacker and slacker as the book goes on. By "Proteus" Stephen

has become immersed in himself. With "Calypso" we are transported into the mind of Mr. Bloom, and a noticeable slackening of tensions takes place. By "Wandering Rocks," the people have become discrete mechanisms; in "Cyclops," with the appearance of interspersed parodies, they are being put on display and guyed as comically animated dolls. By the "Oxen of the Sun," nobody is talking to anyone else, despite the amount of disputation; all is conveyed by indirect discourse, and external descriptive phrases like "general vacant hilarity." "Circe" is a gesticulating charade of private worlds, animated by the Locomotor Apparatus alone. "Eumaeus" immerses Stephen and Bloom into cliche; "Ithaca" is utterly depersonalized; Molly in "Penelope" has no direction but that imposed by her appetites, and no audience but herself. (*Dublin's Joyce* 244)

My own view is that the deepening reflexivity of Joyce's writing represents a limited kind of emancipation. He begins by holding the mirror up to paralysis (*Dubliners*) and ends by holding the mirror up to narration (*Ulysses, Finnegans Wake*).[8] Paralysis depends on mystification; by weaving and unweaving the material myths are made of, Joyce remains faithful to the *possibility* of emancipation. (This is not to say that he never weaves a myth without unweaving it again;[9] his own mythology is exposed in the last episode of *Ulysses,* where he reconstructs the myth of the eternally Feminine, and by the archetypes circulating through the imploded economy of *Finnegans Wake.*)

Epiphanies provide coordinate points that enable us to trace the curve of Joyce's development. Generally speaking, *Dubliners* epiphanizes paralysis, *Portrait* epiphanizes artistic self-creation, and *Ulysses* epiphanizes literary production. These differences prove that there is nothing Platonic about epiphanic form; the stasis of epiphany is necessarily colored by the narrative that it arrests. In *Dubliners,* epiphany is analytical; in *Portrait,* it is relativistic; in *Ulysses,* it is structural. The analytical epiphanies of *Dubliners* disclose an absence of meaning. Characters emerge as victims of their own blindness; epiphany allows the reader to diagnose their disease. (The exception is "The Dead," a transitional story insofar as its epiphany unfolds in the consciousness of Gabriel Conroy.) The epiphanies of *Portrait* typically reveal a fullness of meaning. Each makes an absolute claim to truth; taken together, these claims cancel one another out. Artistic self-consciousness (personified in Stephen) is formed through this process of affirmation and negation. If *Dubliners* dramatizes atrophy and *Portrait* dramatizes growth, *Ulysses* dramatizes representation itself. The subjective reflexivity of *Portrait* gives way to the narrative reflexivity of Joyce's epic. The major epiphanies of *Ulysses* provide a parting vision of its circular structure. Epiphany passes out of the consciousness of the characters; the most symphonic moments of stasis occur when the characters are fantasizing ("Penelope") or hallucinating ("Circe"). The reader is the chief beneficiary of these moments, which allow her to apprehend the shape of her own odyssey.[10]

In Joyce's writing, epiphany is played against paralysis and decadence is played against emancipation. In *Dubliners,* epiphany violates paralysis by bringing it to light. In both *Portrait* and *Ulysses,* epiphany illuminates the desire to create and the process of creation, linking art to emancipation, but unlike *Portrait, Ulysses* does not present creation as a process reserved for the artist; as we will see, art itself is secularized, becoming available to the Blooms and Mollys of "dear dirty Dublin." The result is as improbable as a perfect truce between Brecht and Adorno: the process of creation is opened to everyman within a narrative that remains self-enclosed and autonomous. *Ulysses* is an idiosyncratic pageant of literary production; by reproducing the perennial recurrence and ephemerality of literary forms, Joyce moves beyond paralysis without moving beyond this world.

To return to our opening question, it is fruitless to attempt to classify Joyce's work as decadent or emancipatory because his writing is founded on the dialectical intimacy of those terms. Joyce depended on Dublin precisely because it was, for him, the center of paralysis, challenging him to authenticate the enabling fiction of his own artistic autonomy. It is a mistake to underestimate the irony that underlies Joyce's religion of art; it is also a mistake to treat him as a master of deconstructive narration without acknowledging that he was only able to negotiate the nets of language, nationality, and religion by leaving the myth of artistic autonomy whole and intact.

Notes

1. For Habermas, specialization is a primary symptom of alienation. Drawing upon Max Weber, Habermas defines modernity as the separation

of substantive reason into the three spheres of science, morality, and art. The project of the Enlightenment was to "release the cognitive potential of each of these domains and set them free from their esoteric forms." According to Habermas, "the enlightenment philosophers wanted to utilize this accumulation of specialized culture for the enrichment of everyday life, that is to say, for the rational organization of everyday social life." Neoconservatism endorses the increasing specialization of these spheres: "The *Neoconservatives* welcome the development of modern science, as long as this only goes beyond its sphere to carry forward technical progress, capitalist growth and rational administration. Moreover, they recommend a politics of diffusing the explosive content of cultural modernity. According to one thesis, science, when properly understood, has become irrevocably meaningless for the orientation of the life-world. A further thesis is that politics must be kept as far aloof as possible from the demands of moral-practical justification. And a third thesis asserts the pure immanence of art, disputes that it has a utopian content, and points to its illusory character in order to limit the aesthetic experience to privacy. (One could name here the early Wittgenstein, Carl Schmitt of the middle period, and Gottfried Benn of the late period.) But with the decisive confinement of science, morality and art to autonomous spheres separated from the life-world and administered by experts, what remains from the project of cultural modernity is only what we would have if we were to give up the project of cultural modernity altogether. As a replacement one points to traditions, which, however, are held to be immune to demands of (normative) justification and validation" (14).

   2. Jean-Michel Rabaté also comes close to claiming Joyce as a postmodernist, but, unlike Lyotard, he does not deny him the "solace of good forms": "What I would like to argue is that Joyce's sense of being 'a modern' is inseparable from a crisis in faith, a crisis that took the very name 'modernism' and developed a debate within the Catholic and Protestant churches at the end of the nineteenth century. The debate over 'modernism' pretended to reconcile religious orthodoxy with the new dogmas of science, such as Darwinian evolutionism. It was this subversive tendency that brought about a return to Thomism as the major philosophy in Catholic schools and universities. Joyce, in that sense, can be called the heir of modernism—a modernism that was almost over as he started his career—and Aquinas the first real 'post-modern' philosopher. It is in this wider perspective that Joyce's statements on the equivalence of 'modern times' and the Middle Ages can take all their significance. His own version of Viconian cyclicity is that Europe will sooner or later return to mediaevalism: 'The old classical Europe which we knew in our youth is fast disappearing; the cycle has returned upon its tracks, and with it will come

a new consciousness which will create values returning to the mediaeval.'
Joyce felt keenly that his books would have been more appreciated in the
fourteenth and fifteenth century, and that Dublin was a privileged place
because it was still a mediaeval city" (*Authorized Reader* 187).

3. Despite their prejudice against linear narrative, which they take to
be evidence of a logocentric habit of mind, post-structuralists often treat
Finnegans Wake as the culmination of Joyce's career, approaching the rest
of his work, including *Dubliners,* as a prefiguration of the climactic text.

4. "As for my part and share in the book I have already told all I have
to tell. My intention was to write a chapter of the moral history of my
country and I chose Dublin for the scene because that city seemed to me
the centre of paralysis. I have tried to present it to the indifferent public
under four of its aspects: childhood, adolescence, maturity and public life.
The stories are arranged in this order. I have written it for the most part
in a style of scrupulous meanness and with the conviction that he is a very
bold man who dares to alter in the presentment, still more to deform,
whatever he has seen and heard" (*Selected Letters* 83).

5. Joyce's relentless diagnosis of moral paralysis in *Dubliners* suggests
that, in the beginning of his career, he had a stake in defining decadence
and emancipation in moral rather than literary terms, but by the middle
of his career, he made no secret of the emancipatory uses of literary decadence, predicating his nonlinear vision of history on the eternal recurrence of literary forms. The radical experiment of *Ulysses* thrives on the
exhaustion of the nineteenth-century novel, and *Finnegans Wake* revels
in the undoing of "wideawake language," "cutandry grammar," and the
"goahead plot."

6. "This supreme quality [of beauty] is felt by the artist when the esthetic image is first conceived in his imagination. The mind in that mysterious
instant Shelley likened beautifully to a fading coal. The instant wherein
that supreme quality of beauty, the clear radiance of the esthetic image,
is apprehended luminously by the mind which has been arrested by its
wholeness and fascinated by its harmony is the luminous silent stasis of
esthetic pleasure, a spiritual state very like to that cardiac condition which
the Italian physiologist Luigi Galvani, using a phrase almost as beautiful
as Shelley's, called the enchantment of the heart" (*Portrait* 213).

7. It is interesting to contrast Jameson's characterization of modernism in general with Wyndham Lewis's condemnation of *Ulysses* as a novel
exploding with "Victorian bric-a-brac."

8. Joyce's description of *Finnegans Wake* is relevant here: "Arabian
nights, serial stories, tales within tales, to be continued, desparate storytelling, one caps another to reproduce a rambling mockbardic tale . . .
Scharazad's feat impossible" (*James Joyce's Scribbledehobble* 25).

9. Joyce himself provides the metaphor of weaving and unweaving in *Ulysses:* "As we, or mother Dana, weave and unweave our bodies, Stephen said, from day to day, their molecules shuttled to and fro, so does the artist weave and unweave his image" (159–60).

10. In *Finnegans Wake,* epiphany occurs everywhere and nowhere; a massive condensation of meaning is found in virtually every paragraph, every sentence, and every phrase of Joyce's "night book," a characteristic that sets it apart from the works that precede it.

Dubliners

Joyce liked to say that life in his native city was a form of paralysis; he cultivated his intimacy with Dublin in exile to inoculate himself against its disease. As the following lines, written in defense of *Dubliners,* suggest, he conceived of his first major work as a kind of diagnosis: "It is not my fault that the odour of ashpits and old weeds and offal hangs round my stories. I seriously believe that you will retard the course of civilisation in Ireland by preventing the Irish people from having one good look at themselves in my nicely polished looking-glass" (*Selected Letters* 89–90). To accomplish his task, Joyce evolved a style capable of exposing the deterioration of daily life: "I have written [*Dubliners*] for the most part in a style of scrupulous meanness and with the conviction that he is a very bold man who dares to alter in the presentment, still more to deform, whatever he has seen and heard" (*Selected Letters* 83). The epiphanies of *Dubliners* strengthen its "style of scrupulous meanness," serving as instruments of negation.

Critics have often made the mistake of reading the epiphanies of *Dubliners* as disclosures of redemptive meaning. Fredric Jameson, for example, dismisses *Dubliners* as sentimental and overrated because it "suggests that epiphany or revelation is conceivable as an event within the secularized world of modern capitalism" ("Magical" 146). In fact, the epiphanies of *Dubliners* are not sentimental but relentlessly analytical, exposing the paralyzing illusions of the protagonists. With the exception of "The Dead" and "A Painful Case," epiphany does not occur as a revelatory *event* in any of the stories; epiphany may give the reader insight into the causes of a given character's blindness, but it never illuminates that character's field of vision, nor does it dispel the darkness of a benighted Dublin.

Post-structuralist critics tend to go to the opposite extreme, arguing that the muteness of *Dubliners* anticipates the unreadability of *Finnegans Wake* and that the stories are riddled, not with moments of revelation, but with moments of blankness that save the *reader* from paralysis by withholding meaning.[1] Such interpretations tend to exaggerate the obscurities of the stories and to underplay the fact that, in *Dubliners,* Joyce exposes the inner logic of paralysis, enabling the reader "to look upon its deadly work" (*Dubliners* 9).

My own view is that the epiphanies of *Dubliners* are part of a rhetoric of paralysis that includes ellipsis, repetition, and intertextuality, a rhetoric that serves to make the darkness of paralysis visible to the reader, or, to change the metaphor, a rhetoric that lends a voice to the muteness of Dublin.[2]

Stephen Dedalus's definition of *epiphany* has a direct bearing on the epiphanies of *Dubliners*. He defines *epiphany* as "a sudden spiritual manifestation, whether in the vulgarity of speech or of gesture or in a memorable phase of the mind itself." The writer's task is to "record these epiphanies with extreme care, seeing that they themselves are the most delicate and evanescent of moments" (*Stephen Hero* 211). Two distinct kinds of epiphany are implied in Stephen's definition. As A. O. Silverman points out in his introduction to Joyce's early epiphanies, those meticulously recorded manifestations fall

> into two classes which correspond, in many respects, to the two facets of Stephen Dedalus' definition in *Stephen Hero*. In one kind the mind of the writer is most important. These Epiphanies, which may be called narrative (though a case might be made for calling some of them lyric) present for the most part "memorable phases" of Joyce's mind—as he observes, reminisces or dreams. The Epiphanies of the second kind, which may be called dramatic, dispense with the narrator and focus more on "vulgarity of speech or of gesture." (13–14)

Unlike Joyce's early epiphanies, *Dubliners* cannot be spoken of as a collection of recordings, despite the wealth of realistic detail that it contains. But *Dubliners* is certainly written with "extreme care," and that care contrives the "delicate and evanescent moments" found in every story. Moreover, the stories are filled with conversations and gestures that disclose the entelechy of the plot as well as lyrical or dreamlike passages that prefigure interior monologue and give away unspoken secrets.

The first kind of epiphany is strategically humble, enlisting prosaic gestures and banal phrases to achieve its seemingly modest victory. The reader is made to believe that he is being given an unexpurgated version of the text of daily life. The second kind of epiphany is more elegant and yet, in a sense, less tactful, often employing the most refined poetic language to expose vulgarity.

The insipid yet revelatory conversation of Eliza, Nannie, and the boy's aunt at the close of "The Sisters" is an example of the first kind of epiphany. The following passage from "Araby" is another:

> Remembering with difficulty why I had come I went over to one of the stalls and examined porcelain vases and flowered tea-sets. At the door of the stall a young lady was talking and laughing with two gentlemen. I remarked their English accents and listened vaguely to their conversation.
> —O, I never said such a thing!
> —O, but you did!
> —O, but I didn't!
> —Didn't she say that?
> —Yes. I heard her.
> —O, there's a . . . fib!
> Observing me the young lady came over and asked me did I wish to buy anything. The tone of her voice was not encouraging; she seemed to have spoken to me out of a sense of duty. I looked humbly at the great jars that stood like eastern guards at either side of the dark entrance to the stall and murmured:
> —No, thank you. (35)

The saccharine exchange of a clerk and her "customers" violates the idealizing ardor of the boy's erotic monologue. To make things worse, the clerk's treatment of him is perfunctory, blocking his way to Araby even after its original charms have faded.

The second kind of epiphany, that is, the lyrical, defines and extends the symbolic structure within which it takes place. The following passage from "Two Gallants" is a prime example:

> They walked along Nassau Street and then turned into Kildare Street. Not far from the porch of the club a harpist stood in the

roadway, playing to a little ring of listeners. He plucked at the wires heedlessly, glancing quickly from time to time at the face of each new-comer and from time to time, wearily also, at the sky. His harp too, heedless that her coverings had fallen about her knees, seemed weary alike of the eyes of strangers and of her master's hands. One hand played in the bass the melody of *Silent, O Moyle,* while the other hand careered in the treble after each group of notes. The notes of the air throbbed deep and full. (54)

"Silent, O Moyle" is a nationalistic song, yet the harpist plays it heedlessly. The song is the lament of Fionnula, enchanted daughter of Lir, who has been changed into a swan and condemned to languish for as long as Erin lies in darkness. The harpist languishing over his instrument shares the fate of Fionnula. The song recurs later in the story, recalling Fionnula's doom: "Now that he [Lenehan] was alone his face looked older. His gaiety seemed to forsake him and, as he came by the railings of the Duke's lawn, he allowed his hand to run along them. *The air which the harpist had played began to control his movements.* His softly padded feet played the melody while his fingers swept a scale of variations idly along the railings after each group of notes" (56; emphasis mine). Ireland is a harp played heedlessly. The harp that is heedless of its own disgrace prefigures the slavey of "Two Gallants," who unknowingly offers herself up to exploitation. Leopold Bloom wins Molly's heart by avowing that her body is a flower (*Ulysses* 643); the body of the slavey is a betrayed country awaiting release. Lenehan, disciple of Corley, feeds off a contaminated host; Corley, his simian master, is not only host but parasite. Corley thrives upon the authority of his father, an inspector of police, fraternizing with plainclothes policemen serving British interests, who number among Ireland's "base betrayers." Lenehan is the disciple of a Judas whose crowning performance consists of opening his hand to reveal a palm crossed with gold, if not with silver. The music of the jaded harp echoes the thoughts of Lenehan, while its carelessly exposed form mirrors the body of the slavey. It is the harp that transforms both Lenehan and the slavey into embodiments of Ireland's degradation.

The difference between Stephen Dedalus's twofold definition of epiphany and the lyric and dramatic epiphanies found in *Dubliners* is self-evident; the latter are not recordings of isolated impressions but moments that take place within larger symbolic structures. The similarity is that by shedding light on those structures, the epiphanies of *Dubliners* enable the reader to grasp what Stephen would call the "quidditas," or "whatness," of the stories. The particular structure of every story carries the reader to the same general impasse, insofar as *Dubliners* consists of fifteen interlocking diagnoses of paralysis.

In *Dubliners,* epiphany, which arrests narrative movement, is offset by polyphony, which introduces the perpetual movement of intertextuality. In Joyce's later, more modernist works, paralysis is not only laid bare but dissolved in linguistic play and stylistic relativity. *Dubliners* is closer to what Lukács calls critical realism than to modernism; the critical realist text is one that contains its representations of malaise within a whole characterized by objectivity, concreteness, and a dialectical understanding of alienation. But the discreet polyphony of *Dubliners* anticipates the more extravagant experiments undertaken in *Ulysses* and *Finnegans Wake.*[3]

Polyphony is a leveling music; it silences every claim to uniqueness by underscoring its relativity. In this respect, it is the converse of epiphany, which produces an impression of uniqueness in its moment. Stephen Dedalus isolates relativism as another essential attribute of the modern spirit: "It is the essence of the modern spirit to be shy in the presence of all absolute statements. However sure you may be now of the reasonableness of your convictions, you cannot be sure that you will always think them reasonable" (*Stephen Hero* 205).[4] Relativism is written into the structure of *Dubliners,* a vertical text composed of discordant levels of literal and figurative meaning. The classical and Christian works to which Joyce pays figurative homage here cannot be used as glosses for the literal text, nor are they simply inverted. Story after story reflects the complexity of his relationship to the sources that he uses to engender his own narrative.

Although *Dubliners* is filled with stolen goods from Dante, the following passage from "Araby" constitutes one of Joyce's boldest acts of theft:

> One evening I went into the back drawing-room in which the priest had died. It was a dark rainy evening and there was no sound in the house. Through one of the broken panes I heard the rain impinge upon the earth, the fine incessant needles of water playing

in the sodden beds. Some distant lamp or lighted window gleamed below me. I was thankful that I could see so little. All my senses seemed to desire to veil themselves and, feeling that I was about to slip from them, I pressed the palms of my hands together until they trembled, murmuring: *O love! O love!* many times. (31)

The parallel passage is from the *Vita Nuova:* [5] "At that moment I say truly that the vital spirit, the one that dwells in the most secret chamber of the heart, began to tremble so violently that even the least pulses of my body were strangely affected; and trembling, it spoke these words: 'Here is a god stronger than I, who shall come to rule over me'" (2:3). Clearly, Joyce does not echo Dante merely to make his own text more resonant. Instead, he uses Dante to dramatize one moment in the tautological history of alienation. The unsublimated sexuality that fires the boy's love distinguishes it from the passion of the narrator of the *Vita Nuova.* Joyce's hypostasis of Dante's eros inspires fear of the spiritual consequences of the boy's frustration. He could easily be driven to forget the little he has known of love and to embrace the false opulence of the clerk at the fair.[6] Thus Joyce's echoes of Dante do not occasion a sentimental reunion of past and present; the disembodied sublimity of the past is only invoked as a prophecy of erotic disenchantment. In other words, polyphony is used to deepen the reader's presentiment of paralysis.

According to Stanislaus Joyce, Dante provided the ordering principle of "Grace": "There is in the story a parody of the *Divina Commedia:* in the underground lavatory *L'Inferno;* in bed at home convalescing, *Il'Purgatorio;* in church listening to a sermon, *Il'Paradiso.*" To avoid any misunderstanding of motives, Stanislaus hastens to add, "The parody in no way detracts from my brother's almost boundless admiration for the *Divina Commedia*" ("Background" 526). Dante's text is not invoked piously in "Grace," nor is it treated with simple irreverence. Instead, Joyce's use of Dante here anticipates his use of the *Odyssey* in *Ulysses.* Texts of authority are not presented as keys to the meaning of modernity but as intricate ciphers that recur again and again in its code. Canonical works are absorbed into the compromised prose of daily life. Whereas Dante itemized the corruptions of his native city according to a divine standard, Joyce honors Dublin by implicating Dante in its paralysis. In Dante's text, literal entities point to a transcendental meaning; in

Dubliners, the figurative meaning intensifies the odor of corruption already scented in the literal text.

In *Dubliners,* intertextuality often becomes a method of interrogating a treacherous past. The literal surface of texts consecrated to a transcendental meaning is designed to entrap stray phenomena, which are then stripped of their old identities and pressed into the service of an absolute; the literal text of *Dubliners,* on the other hand, displaces the Christian text to which Joyce figuratively alludes. The senile authority of the past[7] is conveyed by another aspect of the stories as well; the most memorable boys in *Dubliners* are orphans, and all of its priests are either disenfranchised or dead.[8] Youth has been betrayed by the same traditions that destroyed Parnell. If the boys accept their inheritance, it will cripple them, yet if they refuse to accept any part of it, they will be outcasts without histories or names.

Their ideological inheritance is a burden that the reader also bears. The tension between literal and figurative levels of meaning in *Dubliners* results in what Roland Barthes refers to as a "collision of codes" and in a state of revelatory blindness. Joyce's telling restriction of the reader's vision is reinforced by the fact that all the stories are told by a magisterial narrator who never fully reveals himself, even in those stories that are ostensibly told in the first person. His use of enigmatic or negative epiphanies and semiconscious characters to expose the reader to the danger of paralysis and to tease her into interpretation is best illustrated by "Clay."

In "Clay" the negative force of epiphany is particularly strong. Joyce's revision of the title from "Hallow Eve" to "Clay" not only shifts the emphasis of the story from the revisionary singing of the song to the ceremony of the three dishes[9] but it also produces a retrospective or staggered epiphany. The original title stressed the symbolic significance of the night of the festivities, thus underlining the virgin-witch theme (Magalaner and Kain 85–90) and drawing the reader's attention to the ritual wandering of people and things (corkscrews and plumcakes) from their usual places; thus Maria or Mary is banished from the household of Joe or Joseph to become a peacemaker among Magdalenes in the Dublin by Lamplight Laundry. The title, however, is a key to deeper levels of meaning. Not only does it stress the importance of Maria's first choice in the ceremony of the three dishes but it also provides a graphic corollary to Maria's fate as one who stands patiently outside life's narrative, a princeless Cinderella and a "proper mother" without a proper household of her own.

In retrospect, the title brings out the symbolic properties of clay, namely, an unwholesome malleability associated with death. Seen in the light of the following passage, it yields a staggered epiphany:[10]

> They led her up to the table amid laughing and joking and she put her hand out in the air as she was told to do. She moved her hand about here and there in the air and descended on one of the saucers. She felt a soft wet substance with her fingers and was surprised that nobody spoke or took off her bandage. There was a pause for a few seconds; and then a great deal of scuffling and whispering. Somebody said something about the garden, and at last Mrs. Donnelly said something very cross to one of the next-door girls and told her to throw it out at once: that was no play. Maria understood that it was wrong that time so she had to do it over again: and this time she got the prayer-book. (105)

In all innocence, Maria chooses death over life. Fate tricks her into it and, as usual, she is easily deceived. Her passivity is habitual and unconscious; her withdrawal from life is such an intimate fact that it is singularly undramatic. Obscure misgivings may sometimes assail her, but she is not tortured by the knowledge that she is wasting away. This is the kind of knowledge that she has never possessed. The distance between the title and this passage contributes to our sense of her ignorance; by placing the meaning of the game outside the story, Joyce also places it outside Maria's grasp. This, of course, is in keeping with her position within the story; she is always in the dark. Thus she smiles benignly at the impatient young lady who mocks her aged virginity by asking her if she wants a wedding-cake, loses her plumcake as a result of flirting with a gentleman on the tram, becomes excessively upset over the loss of the plumcake, thus canceling her moment of innocuous abandon, annoys the children whom she so yearns to please, misunderstands what happens during the ceremony of the three dishes, and omits the crucial verses from "I Dreamt that I Dwelt."

Joyce gives us the slip somewhere between the title and the event to which it refers. Momentarily left in the dark, we are in a better position to see through Maria's eyes. For a time, we become victims

of Joyce's plot, just as she is a victim of life's caprices. The following verse, elided from the song that Maria sings, has an analogous
effect:

> I dreamt that suitors besought my hand
> That knights upon bended knee,
> And with vows no maiden heart could withstand,
> That they pledged their faith to me.
> And I dreamt that one of that noble host
> Came forth my hand to claim;
> Yet I also dreamt, which charmed me most,
> That you lov'd me still the same.

The missing lines produce an epiphany. Their absence from the narrative mirrors Maria's absence; her unconsciousness of events is a
symptom of paralysis. Joyce sees to it that the same symptom threat-
ens to afflict the reader of the song's incomplete text. Joe, upon
hearing the song, is filled with a vicarious nostalgia for the life that
Maria has never known. His wistful premonition guides the reader
to the empty site of the epiphany: "When she had ended her song
Joe was very much moved. He said that there was no time like the
long ago and no music for him like poor old Balfe, whatever other
people might say; and his eyes filled up so much with tears that he
could not find what he was looking for and in the end he had to ask
his wife to tell him where the corkscrew was" (106).

Repetition, a key element in the rhetoric of paralysis developed
in *Dubliners,* makes us feel the inevitability of our arrival at this
blank conclusion. Maria can only repeat the first verse of the song
because her own growth has been arrested, reducing the movement
of her heart to a series of repetitions:

> I dreamt that I dwelt in marble halls
> With vassals and serfs at my side
> And of all who assembled within those walls
> That I was the hope and the pride.
> I had riches too great to count, could boast
> Of a high ancestral name,
> But I also dreamt, which pleased me most,
> That you loved me still the same. (106)

Maria's closing blunder is the last in a series of repetitions that serve
two related functions in "Clay," namely, to unify the story and to

dramatize the redundancy of her unfulfilled life. The ring hidden in the barmbrack and the ring hidden in one of the three dishes is another instance of repetition. Maria also suffers repeated losses in her encounters with men. Her maternal relationship to Joe ends in the loss of her place in his household; her conversation with the "colonel-looking gentleman" on the tram results in the loss of her plumcake, a mishap that disturbs her because she dimly apprehends its symbolism. Repetition also finds its way into the ceremony of the three dishes when Maria chooses a second time.

Repetition becomes a symptom of stunted growth, a disorder reflected in the kind of pleasure Maria takes in her own elfin body: "As she stood before the mirror, she thought of how she used to dress for mass on Sunday morning when she was a young girl; and she looked with quaint affection at the diminutive body which she had so often adorned" (101). Maria's body resembles the body of "Clay"; both only become visible in retrospect and both are filled with a reticence that points to death. Maria's physical compatibility with the form of the narrative that engenders her anticipates the coextensiveness of Molly's body with the text of her monologue in *Ulysses*.[11] The difference, of course, is that in "Clay" a secretive style is used to expose Maria's habitually silenced and decaying sexuality, whereas in Molly's monologue physical language is used to conjure up desires that defy the body's decline. The epiphanies that arise from these distinct states of being are entirely different. Molly's epiphany uncovers a godless poetic plenitude rich enough to compensate for life's betrayals in its moment. In the game of hide-and-go-seek that Joyce plays with the reader in "Clay," epiphany is the moment at which the equivalence of paralytic choices is revealed. Clay and the prayer-book, the invisible narrator seems to whisper, are one and the same: both confirm a denial of life.

Thus, epiphany corroborates the oblique reports of the plot without conceding the possibility of redemptive meaning. The unity of Maria's subjectivity depends on blindness; improved vision would only expose the contradiction between those countless little acts of kindness that constitute her sole raison d'être and the negative infinity to which they lead. To use Jameson's term, the "event" of revelation is not available to her; moreover, the reader's vision is restricted to the phenomena of her deepening blindness.

If epiphany points to the impotence of revelation in *Dubliners*,

repetition points to the hidden presence of a corrupt yet authorita-
tive text. Repetition belongs to the symptomatology of paralysis.[12]
The use of repetition as a sign for paralysis is particularly clear in
"An Encounter."

As Sidney Feshbach has pointed out, "An Encounter" is filled
with instances of repetition: "Joe Dillon yells, 'Ya! yaka, yaka, yaka,
yaka!' Father Butler repeats, 'This page or this page? This page? . . .
Hardly had the day . . . Hardly had the day dawned . . .' The troop
of ragged boys scream, 'Swaddlers! Swaddlers!' The sailor shouts in
measure to the falling planks, 'All right! All right!' " (86). These re-
dundancies culminate in the autoerotic monologue of the stranger,
who repeats phrases "over and over again, varying them and surrounding them with his monotonous voice" (*Dubliners* 26). The
stranger's words slowly circle "round and round in the same orbit"
(26), and although the center of his speech may seem to shift (27),
in essence it remains unchanged. The smaller instances of repetition scattered throughout the story are particles of meaning drawn
toward the same negatively charged core.

Repetition is one of several strategies used to prejudice the contest between authority and desire set up in the opening paragraph of
"An Encounter." Authority's triumph is predicted right away: the
anarchic fantasies acted out by prepubescent boys while their parents attend mass never become real enough to prevent their leader's
eventual defeat:

> It was Joe Dillon who introduced the Wild West to us. He had
> a little library made up of old numbers of *The Union Jack, Pluck* and
> *The Halfpenny Marvel.* Every evening after school we met in his back
> garden and arranged Indian battles. He and his fat young brother
> Leo the idler held the loft of the stable while we tried to carry it by
> storm; or we fought a pitched battle on the grass. But, however well
> we fought, we never won siege or battle and all our bouts ended with
> Joe Dillon's war dance of victory. His parents went to eight o'clock
> mass every morning in Gardiner Street and the peaceful odour of
> Mrs Dillon was prevalent in the hall of the house. But he played too
> fiercely for us who were younger and more timid. He looked like
> some kind of an Indian when he capered round the garden, an old
> tea-cosy on his head, beating a tin tub with his fist and yelling:
> —Ya! yaka, yaka, yaka!
> Everyone was incredulous when it was reported that he had a
> vocation for the priesthood. Nevertheless it was true. (19)

Imported tales of adventure unlock the possibility of freedom. Yet adventure flouts custom without maturing into a serious opponent; the charm of the illicit stories depends on the existence of a canon that is capable of silencing the most raucous adventurer.

The action of "An Encounter" is initially dominated by the "literature of the Wild West." Boyish impulses play across the surface of the story; however, sexuality is stirring just below: "The adventures related in the literature of the Wild West were remote from my nature but, at least, they opened doors of escape. I liked better some American detective stories which were traversed from time to time by unkempt fierce and beautiful girls" (20). Joyce makes the specter of authority hover over the text, intentionally endangering the expressions of freedom circulating there. The unequal conflict of raw desire and a Christian tradition of denial is waged in such phrases as "the literature of the Wild West" and "chronicles of disorder" (21). These phrases announce the victory of desire by dignifying the forbidden texts, but the reader is not meant to be fooled. As the case of Leo Dillon warns him, the boys have already been biased by the influences they play at rejecting. Their parochialism, for example, which teaches them that only National School boys deserve to be whipped, could easily develop into a vocation. It is against these odds that the narrator sets out with Mahony. Their adventure officially begins when they hide their school books, ritually subordinating authority to experience.

Their first sallies are quixotic imitations of "the literature of the Wild West." At noon they achieve a moment of transcendence:

It was noon when we reached the quays and, as all the labourers seemed to be eating their lunches, we bought two big currant buns and sat down to eat them on some metal piping beside the river. We pleased ourselves with the spectacle of Dublin's commerce—the barges signalled from far away by their curls of woolly smoke, the brown fishing fleet beyond Ringsend, the big white sailing-vessel which was being discharged on the opposite quay. Mahony said it would be right skit to run away to sea on one of those big ships and even I, looking at the high masts, saw, or imagined, the geography which had been scantily dosed to me at school gradually taking substance under my eyes. School and home seemed to recede from us and their influences upon us seemed to wane. (23)

Yet this vision of freedom soon recedes as well. The boys cross the Liffey and suddenly grow weary, abandoning their plan of visiting the Pigeon House. Their exhaustion proves how difficult it is for them to catch even a glimpse of liberty.

Authority returns in the guise of death, an unaccountably familiar stranger:

> When we had lain on the bank for some time without speaking I saw a man approaching from the far end of the field. I watched him lazily as I chewed one of those green stems on which girls tell fortunes. He came along by the bank slowly. He walked with one hand upon his hip and in the other hand he held a stick with which he tapped the turf lightly. He was shabbily dressed in a suit of greenish-black and wore what we used to call a jerry hat with a high crown. He seemed to be fairly old for his moustache was ashen-grey. When he passed our feet he glanced up at us quickly and then continued his way. We followed him with our eyes and saw that when he had gone on for perhaps fifty paces he turned about and began to retrace his steps. He walked towards us very slowly, always tapping the ground with his stick, so slowly that I thought he was looking for something in the grass. (24)

The stranger taps the ground with his stick as though it were a divining rod. The green stems on which girls tell fortunes are less fortuitous than they seem, strengthening our association of the stranger with prophecy. Like the clay in Maria's bowl, his appearance is a portent of death. But whereas paralysis comes to Maria as a promise, it comes to the children as a threat, tainting their adventure.

As a failed or degraded explorer, the stranger represents one possible outcome of the libidinal voyage that all boys and girls undergo. From this perspective, his resemblance to the narrator is ominous. The stranger is nameless; the narrator has no name except for "Smith," an Odyssean pseudonym. The stranger moves through the landscape like a blind man, tapping the ground with his stick; the boy wills his own blindness, refusing to look into the eyes of the stranger until the end of their encounter. However, crucial differences between the narrator and the stranger remind us that the narrator's fate is far from being sealed. The narrator blinds himself to protect his innocence, whereas the blindness of the stranger suggests sadomasochistic experience. Although both the narrator and the stranger present themselves as bookworms, the stranger only alludes to impressive-sounding titles to win the boy's favor, manipulating his literary pretensions. The narrator can dream of traveling beyond rules and regulations; the orgasm achieved by the "queer old josser" in the field has nothing to do with freedom and everything to do with Catholic prohibitions. As his monologue suggests, he is fixated on punishment; by referring to punishment as a "mystery" adored by the stranger, the narrator strengthens its as-sociation with religious repression. Thus when the stranger's sexual release passes over into postorgasmic sadism, he achieves a double consummation of authority.

The boy's full recognition of the sadism of the stranger turns into epiphany the moment he forgets to shun his gaze: "I was surprised at this sentiment and involuntarily glanced up at his face. And as I did so I met the gaze of a pair of bottle-green eyes peering at me from underneath a twitching forehead. I turned my eyes away again" (37). The color of those eyes, previously associated with "real adventure," now signals the danger of adventure's deteriora-tion into a barren inversion of religious repression. The stranger's double consummation not only reveals the intimacy of sadism and guilt-ridden abandon but also marks a climax of repetition, the most salient feature of the stranger's speech. Blind repetition is the tem-poral equivalent of living death, and the stranger savors it. The boy still possesses many consciences as opposed to one but, nonethe-less, he is in danger; after all, he is subject to the same repression that perverted the stranger's escape.

The closing epiphany reminds us that the boy is not deaf to the penitential suggestions of the stranger; in fact, he speaks the same language:

> I went up the slope calmly but my heart was beating quickly with
> fear that he would seize me by the ankles. When I reached the top of
> the slope I turned round and, without looking at him, called loudly
> across the field:
> —Murphy!
> My voice had an accent of forced bravery in it and I was ashamed
> of my paltry stratagem. I had to call the name again before Mahony
> saw me and hallooed in answer. How my heart beat as he came run-

ning across the field to me! He ran as if to bring me aid. And I was penitent; for in my heart I had always despised him a little. (28)

The biblical overtones of the closing sentence signal yet another return of repressive authority.[13] By humbling himself before Mahony in his own mind, the narrator surrenders his will to power. In a moment of crisis, his "instincts" are Christian; by sacrificing his pride, he surrenders his autonomy, opening himself up to the paralytic influence of Dublin.

The stranger's speech is incantatory, which is to say that it is repetitive and fetishistic, revolving endlessly around his unspoken fixation: "He described to me how he would whip such a boy as if he were unfolding some elaborate mystery. He would love that, he said, better than anything in this world; and his voice, as he led me monotonously through the mystery, grew almost affectionate and seemed to plead with me that I should understand him" (27).

Verbal and thematic repetition is also used to unfold a negative mystery in "The Sisters," as the remarkable opening paragraph illustrates:

> There was no hope for him this time: it was the third stroke. Night after night I had passed the house (it was vacation time) and studied the lighted square of the window: and night after night I had found it lighted in the same way, faintly and evenly. If he was dead, I thought, I would see the reflection of candles on the darkened blind for I knew that two candles must be set at the head of a corpse. He had often said to me: *I am not long for this world,* and I had thought his words idle. Now I knew they were true. Every night as I gazed up at the window I said softly to myself the word *paralysis.* It had always sounded strangely in my ears, like the word *gnomon* in the Euclid and the word *simony* in the Catechism. But now it sounded to me like the name of some maleficent and sinful being. It filled me with fear, and yet I longed to be nearer to it and to look upon its deadly work. (9)

The first line, lifted from Dante, opens the gate to Joyce's inferno. *Time,* the last word in the first phrase, is repeated in the second; *night after night* is repeated twice, as is the word *lighted.* The priest predicts his own death in a grandiloquent sentence that echoes the

Gospels (John 8:23, 14:19). The narrator admits that the words of the priest seemed idle, a judgment erased by the priest's death, only to reappear in the image of the idle chalice later in the story, a tautological image that proves, in a sense, that *all* the priest's words were idle.[14] The narrator's anticipation of the vision of the darkened blind prefigures the thematic recurrence of gnomonic imagery throughout the story. Just as a gnomon is a rectangle cut out of a larger rectangle or an internal and symmetrical division of a rectangle, the candles, once they are lit, will dissect the lighted square (Herring, "Structure" 136).[15] The narrator repeats the word *paralysis* softly, fetishizing it until it becomes a suitable signifier for enthrallment. The words *gnomon* and *simony* are mystified by the same means. Thus the three words, like the three strokes suffered by the priest, take on a force and mechanism of their own. Their negative potency depends on repetition; repetition is a means of turning words into the names of a maleficent being.

Under the priest's guidance, the narrator comes to regard the mysteries of the church as an impenetrable web of words:

> His questions showed me how complex and mysterious were certain institutions of the Church which I had always regarded as the simplest acts. The duties of the priest towards the Eucharist and towards the secrecy of the confessional seemed so grave to me that I wondered how anybody had ever found in himself the courage to undertake them; and I was not surprised when he told me that the fathers of the Church had written books as thick as the *Post Office Directory* and as closely printed as the law notices in the newspapers, elucidating all these intricate questions.[16] (13)

Here lexical density is interpreted as evidence of authority. Although the narrator suffers under the burden of that authority, he cannot bring himself to redistribute its weight in playfulness or rebellion.

Like the narrator of "An Encounter," he is dangerously attuned to the threat of punishment contained within words of power. Joyce conveys the narrator's chronic receptivity by weaving a spell of sinister words around the reader. The key words found in the opening paragraph produce thematic reverberations that lend the story its incantatory quality:

—What I mean is, said old Cotter, it's bad for children. My idea is: let a young lad run about and play with young lads of his own age and not be . . . Am I right Jack?

—That's my principle, too, said my uncle. Let him learn to box his corner. That's what I'm always saying to that Rosicrucian there: take exercise. (10–11)

The gnomon, an incomplete geometrical form, is used by Joyce as a figure of stultification; the boy's uncle vainly proposes to fill out this figure through physical education. His anti-intellectual reasoning is itself, of course, a symptom of paralysis.

Although the boy bridles at old Cotter's suggestions about his intimacy with the priest, they come back to haunt him as he is falling asleep:

In the dark of my room I imagined that I saw again the heavy grey face of the paralytic. I drew the blankets over my head and tried to think of Christmas. But the grey face still followed me. It murmured; and I understood that it desired to confess something. I felt my soul receding into some pleasant and vicious region; and there again I found it waiting for me. It began to confess to me in a murmuring voice and I wondered why it smiled continually and why the lips were so moist with spittle. But then I remembered that it had died of paralysis and I felt that I too was smiling feebly as if to absolve the simoniac of his sin. (11)

The boy resents Cotter's condescension, yet he submits to his authority, irresistibly drawn to insinuations that arouse his guilt. The heavy gray face of Father Flynn is fashioned into an indestructible icon of paralysis. The boy tries not to see his own bad faith mirrored in the face of the priest but is seduced into recognition by the priest's desire to confess, which duplicates his own. By acting as confessor to the priest, the boy takes on his sins, at once gaining the authority that adults deny him and becoming an accomplice to crimes of simony. Thus the impotent smile of Father Flynn is fully answered in the feeble smile of his confessor.[17]

The boy's secret is betrayed by a profusion of gnomonic riddles. As Phillip Herring suggests, imagery associated with one of the obsolete meanings of *gnomon* is central to the meaning of the story: "An obsolete meaning of gnomon is 'nose' (OED), the cavities of which Father Flynn attempts to fill with snuff, though the greater part of it falls on his vestments" ("Structure" 138). The snuff-box itself is associated with the theme of simony, insofar as the priest is kept in snuff for educating the boy. Later the priest is said to be *coffined,* a gnomonic word suggesting that he is *confined* or boxed in ("Structure" 138). Then pneumatic wheels are replaced by rheumatic wheels, paralytic machines designed to arrest movement ("Structure" 135). When the narrator confirms the news of the priest's death by reading a notice on the window of the drapery where he lived, his response takes gnomonic form: "The reading of the card persuaded me that he was dead and I was disturbed to find myself at check" (*Dubliners* 22). The idea of being in check suggests a chessboard composed of quadrilateral figures upon which most moves have become impossible. The gnomon also depends upon a quadrilateral figure whose geometrical development has been arrested.

Instances of repetition like those found in its opening paragraph occur throughout "The Sisters," underscoring its themes:

> —Did he . . . peacefully? she asked.
> —O, quite peacefully, ma'am, said Eliza. You couldn't tell when the breath went out of him. He had a beautiful death, God be praised.
> —And everything . . . ?
> —Father O'Rourke was in with him of a Tuesday and anointed him and prepared him and all.
> —He knew then?
> —He was quite resigned.
> —He looks quite resigned, said my aunt.
> —That's just what the woman we had in to wash him said. She said he just looked as if he was asleep, he looked that peaceful and resigned. No one would think he'd make such a beautiful corpse. (15)

The repetition of *resigned* and *peaceful* and the transformation of the cliché of a "beautiful death" into the petrified sweetness of a "beautiful corpse" advertises banality by restricting the movement of language, inducing a visceral sense of paralysis.

Repetition is a rhetorical device that helps produce the negative epiphanies of *Dubliners;* ellipsis is another. Both demonstrate paralysis by inhibiting the expressive flow of language. Ellipsis is particularly crucial in "The Sisters." The insinuating tone of old Cotter's voice, for example, depends on it:

> Old Cotter was sitting at the fire, smoking, when I came downstairs to supper. While my aunt was ladling out my stirabout he said, as if returning to some former remark of his:
> —No, I wouldn't say he was exactly . . . but there was something queer . . . there was something uncanny about him. I'll tell you my opinion. . . .
> He began to puff at his pipe, no doubt arranging his opinion in his mind. Tiresome old fool! When we knew him first he used to be rather interesting, talking of faints and worms; but I soon grew tired of him and his endless stories about the distillery.
> —I have my own theory about it, he said. I think it was one of those . . . peculiar cases. . . . But it's hard to say. . . . (9–10)

The boy's dream is an attempt to fill in the blanks that riddle old Cotter's speech. Old Cotter's significant pauses adumbrate a mystery; later, ellipsis is used to shade in its contours. The first of the ellipses found at the end of the story indicates the presence of death, always a source of linguistic embarrassment:

> My aunt waited until Eliza sighed and then said:
> —Ah, well, he's gone to a better world.
> Eliza sighed and bowed her head in assent. My aunt fingered the stem of her wine-glass before sipping a little.
> —Did he . . . peacefully? she asked. (15)

The next group of ellipses no longer point to aborted meanings but to surreptitiously delivered ones:

> —It was that chalice he broke. . . . That was the beginning of it. Of course, they say it was all right, that it contained nothing, I mean. But still. . . . They say it was the boy's fault. But poor James was so nervous, God be merciful to him!
> —And was that it? said my aunt. I heard something. . . .
> Eliza nodded.
> —That affected his mind, she said. After that he began to mope about by himself, talking to no one and wandering about by himself. So one night he was wanted for to go on a call and they couldn't find him anywhere. They looked high up and low down; and still they couldn't see a sight of him anywhere. So then the clerk suggested to try the chapel. So then they got the keys and opened the chapel

and the clerk and Father O'Rourke and another priest that was there brought in a light for to look for him. . . . And what do you think but there he was, sitting up by himself in the dark in his confession-box, wide-awake and laughing-like softly to himself? (17–18)

The closing ellipsis, whether or not it solves the riddle of the priest's sin, completes the epiphany: "—Wide-awake and laughing-like to himself. . . . So then, of course, when they saw that, that made them think that there was something gone wrong with him . . ." (18).

Ellipsis in "The Sisters" serves two different purposes. In the beginning of the story, it is used to implicate the priest in shameful mysteries; later it is used to domesticate madness and rebellion. Just as the impact of death is diffused by ellipsis at the wake, so the tragic potential of the priest's sin is destroyed by a description of his fall in sentences punctuated with pauses. Insofar as the opening ellipses only insinuate that the priest has strayed whereas the closing ellipses embellish his depravity, the latter may be seen as an answer to the question posed by the former; however, although the closing ellipses cast light on the priest's corruption, they do not reveal its causes. The closing ellipses are gestures of reluctance to complete the diagnosis. By leaving the reader with an incomplete diagnosis, and by creating an atmosphere heavy with insinuation, Joyce makes it harder for her to dismiss the disease.

Like epiphany, ellipsis in *Dubliners* indicates a dislocation of will or an atrophy of authority. Epiphany itself is often elliptical or gnomonic here, exposing an almost unspeakable absence of intelligibility. Stephen Dedalus describes epiphany as the discovery of the self-identity of an object, thus implying a fullness of sensuous meaning that language can never exhaust. The negative epiphanies of *Dubliners,* in contrast, reveal a dissolution of meaning that throws everything, including language, into question.

Joyce's style of "scrupulous meanness" is consummated in the epiphanies of *Dubliners.* All of the epiphanies are revelations of impoverishment. Thus, at the close of "Eveline," we are left with the image of a woman crippled for life: "She set her white face to him, passive, like a helpless animal. Her eyes gave him no sign of love or farewell or recognition" (41). "After the Race" ends with a devastatingly literal illumination of futility:

He knew that he would regret in the morning but at present he was glad of the rest, glad of the dark stupor that would cover up his folly. He leaned his elbows on the table and rested his head between his hands, counting the beats of his temples. The cabin door opened and he saw the Hungarian standing in a shaft of grey light:

—Daybreak, gentlemen! (48)

In "Two Gallants" the epiphany consists of a display of wealth that measures the tawdriness of its owner and his parasite: "Corley halted at the first lamp and stared grimly before him. Then with a grave gesture he extended a hand towards the light and, smiling, opened it slowly to the gaze of his disciple. A small gold coin shone in the palm" (60). The silent gesture points away from language to the decay of social exchange. "Araby" and "An Encounter" end in magniloquent despair, in keeping with the ornate disillusionments of youth, but nonetheless these epiphanies seem to point to a lack of meaning that language may reflect but never transform. "Ivy Day" belongs to the last phase of *Dubliners,* depicting the "public life of Dublin." It ends with an attempt to eulogize and resurrect the spirit of Parnell. The effort brings tears to the eyes of one of the canvassers, but the closing words of flat praise are given to Crofton, a conservative whose condescension is the kiss of death. Hynes, the author of the poem, is more deeply moved by it than the rest of the company; he is the only one who will not drink after his recitation. A refusal to drink in *Dubliners* is a refusal to be sociable; Hynes's willful alienation after his moment of political fervor is over points once again to the impotence of language.

Unlike the rest of the stories in *Dubliners,* "The Dead" is not written in a style of "scrupulous meanness." It is the most leisurely and the most musical of the stories, winding itself slowly around dialogue, description, and unspoken soliloquy. Joyce came to regret the severity of *Dubliners* before he had written "The Dead," which may account for its stylistic generosity: "Sometimes thinking of Ireland it seems to me that I have been unnecessarily harsh. I have reproduced (in *Dubliners* at least) none of the attraction of the city for I have never felt at ease in any city since I left it except in Paris. I have not reproduced its ingenuous insularity and its hospitality. The latter 'virtue' so far as I can see does not exist elsewhere in Europe" (*Selected Letters* 109–10). Joyce does finally celebrate Irish

hospitality in "The Dead," appointing Gabriel Conroy as master of
ceremonies:

> —I feel more strongly with every recurring year that our country
> has no tradition which does it so much honour and which it should
> guard so jealously as that of its hospitality. It is a tradition that is
> unique as far as my experience goes (and I have visited not a few
> places abroad) among the modern nations. Some would say, per-
> haps, that with us it is rather a failing than anything to be boasted
> of. But granted even that, it is, to my mind, a princely failing, and
> one that I trust will long be cultivated among us. (202–3)

Irony turns the homage Joyce pays into an inoculation against sentimentality. Decrepitude is constantly played against cordiality in
"The Dead"; thus when Gabriel addresses the assembled guests as
"victims of hospitality," the flattering phrase accentuates the hollow
charms of the three withered graces of Dublin. The Morkan sisters
embody the spirit of Dublin. Their "well-laden table" is a double-
edged comment on Dublin's graciousness; as critics have pointed
out, its ranks of dishes, decanters, and bottles are composed entirely
of foreign dignitaries and soldiers, with the exception of "the third
and smallest squad" of bottles, distinguished from the rest by their
white labels and "transverse green sashes."

Throughout "The Dead," the reader is given glimpses of the
hearth, yet the snow that is "general all over Ireland" always dims
his gaze. Gabriel's speech is a miniaturization of the major themes
of the story; accordingly, his praise of hospitality is endangered, if
not negated, by the passages that follow it:

> —A new generation is growing up in our midst, a generation
> actuated by new ideas and new principles. It is serious and enthu-
> siastic for these new ideas and its enthusiasm, even when it is mis-
> directed, is, I believe, in the main sincere. But we are living in a
> sceptical and, if I may use the phrase, a thought-tormented age: and
> sometimes I fear that this new generation, educated or hyperedu-
> cated as it is, will lack those qualities of humanity, of hospitality, of
> kindly humor which belonged to an older day. Listening to-night to
> the names of all those great singers of the past it seemed to me, I
> must confess, that we were living in a less spacious age. (203)

Miss Ivors belongs to the narrow new age of which Gabriel speaks;
her brand of nationalism represents the deterioration of "ingenu-

ous insularity" into fanatical isolationism. Yet Miss Ivors possesses a boldness that Gabriel lacks; his timidity has matured into pedantry and obsequiousness, prompting him to apologize for a phrase that he is proud of, namely, "thought-tormented age." The audience that applauds the conservatism and sentimentality of Gabriel would deplore the acerbity of Joyce. Although Miss Ivors is unacceptable to Joyce for different reasons, he insists that we acknowledge her youthfulness, distinguishing her from the rest of the party by having her leave after she has danced but before dinner is served.[18]

In the next movement of his speech, Gabriel warns the guests that if they live in the past, they are likely to end up entertaining the dead: "—But yet, continued Gabriel, his voice falling into a softer inflection, there are always in gatherings such as this sadder thoughts that will recur to our minds; thoughts of the past, of youth, of changes, of absent faces that we miss here to-night. Our path through life is strewn with many such sad memories: and were we to brood upon them always we could not find the heart to go on bravely with our work among the living" (204). Gabriel urges his audience to guard itself against ghosts, yet he leaves himself open by indulging his own fear of life. Consequently, when the shade of Michael Furey returns, he succumbs to its authority, lacking the conviction in his own passion that would enable him to banish it.

Gestures of sympathy freeze into images of paralysis throughout the story. Thus Gabriel's solicitude for Gretta provokes the affectionate laughter of his aunts, laughter that embarrasses Gabriel and then dies away, leaving bewilderment in its wake:

> —Goloshes! said Mrs Conroy. That's the latest. Whenever it's wet underfoot I must put on my goloshes. To-night even he wanted me to put them on, but I wouldn't. The next thing he'll buy me will be a diving suit.
> Gabriel laughed nervously and patted his tie reassuringly while Aunt Kate nearly doubled herself, so heartily did she enjoy the joke. The smile soon faded from Aunt Julia's face and her mirthless eyes were directed towards her nephew's face. After a pause she asked:
> —And what are goloshes, Gabriel? (180–81)

The joke is also on Mr. Browne, who plays the rake with two young ladies in an attempt to hide his advancing years in a cloak of gallantry; when he praises his whiskey as "the doctor's orders," he spoils the effect, drawing attention to his flushed and wizened face. Later Freddy Malins, who is, in fact, under doctor's care, explodes in "a kink of high-pitched bronchitic laughter" (185). When Gabriel remembers that his mother said that Gretta was "country-cute," he is filled with displeasure, as though his mother were not dead at all, but standing by his side. Later he suddenly exclaims that he is sick of his own country, striking the pose of an expatriate without moving an inch and thereby revealing the tenuousness of his own identity. When Aunt Julia sings "Arrayed for Bridal," her audience breaks into applause. Yet the title of the song only spotlights her spinsterhood, as does the militancy of her performance: "Her voice, strong and clear in tone, attacked with great spirit the runs which embellish the air and though she sang very rapidly she did not miss even the smallest of the grace notes" (193). To make things worse, the authenticity of the applause that follows the performance is suspect. When Miss Ivors leaves the party prematurely, Gabriel gazes "blankly down the staircase" (196), allowing his festive mask to drop; the same thing happens when he first enters the house of mirth and is greeted by the sexual disillusionment of young Lily, who seems to have passed too swiftly from innocence to experience. The monks who are said to retire to their coffins at night create such a lugubrious picture of religion that the guests are struck silent; their embarrassment itself is a parody of piety. The joke about Johnny, the old mill-horse, who falls in love with an equestrian statue of King Billy, walking around it again and again, is not only an image of life imitating death but also an allegory of Ireland's exploitation by England. Bartell D'Arcy, the only professional singer present at a party filled with talk about singers who have passed away, refuses to perform for the guests, complaining of the hoarseness of his voice; not even the cajoling of Gretta and Miss O'Callaghan can persuade him to silence the dead. Gabriel waves gaily to a "white man" as his carriage passes over O'Connell Bridge, once more blurring the distinction between the quick and the dead; his bravado is a response to Miss O'Callaghan's remark, "They say you never cross O'Connell Bridge without seeing a white horse." Edgar Allan Poe noted in his *Marginalia* that "the ancients had at least half an idea that we travelled on horseback to heaven. See a passage of Passeri, '*de anima transvectione*'—quoted by Caylus. See, also, old tombs" (36).

In short, "The Dead" is an uncanny story; as soon as the reader is ushered into the party, the familiar begins to shed its substance. And this is no wonder, given that "The Dead" consummates the three major themes of *Dubliners,* which are themselves symptoms of estrangement, namely simony, gnomon, and paralysis. The coin that Gabriel slips to Lily relates her to the slavey in "Two Gallants"; both are victims of secular simony. When the priests' motives for replacing spinsters with young boys in the choir is questioned, there is an insinuation of sexual maneuvering and of corrupt exchange. Gretta's skirt takes on gnomonic qualities in Gabriel's imaginary portrait of her: "Her blue felt hat would show off the bronze of her hair against the darkness and the dark panels of her skirt would show off the light ones" (210). Michael Furey is also a gnomonic figure, insofar as he is a vital yet missing part of Gretta's life. Gabriel, in turn, lacks "the full glory of some passion." Lily, whose curse against young men ushers us into the house of the "Three Musical Graces" of Dublin, is in danger of leading a gnomonic existence. The departure of Miss Ivors is a reminder that the spirit of youth is entirely missing from the Feast of Epiphany, a celebration of the manifestation of Christ to the gentiles in the persons of the Magi. As in all the stories comprising *Dubliners,* epiphany is transvalued here, confirming a failure of social and spiritual regeneration.

The uncanny is a revelatory shadow cast upon the characters of "The Dead." None of the characters is presented in full light; brightness would only obscure their ghostliness. Thus when Gabriel and Gretta arrive, Gretta goes into the house and is warmly received, but Gabriel lingers by the door just long enough to throw his substantiality into doubt:

> —Here I am as right as the mail, Aunt Kate! Go on up. I'll follow, called out Gabriel from the dark.
> He continued scraping his feet vigorously while the three women went upstairs, laughing, to the ladies' dressing-room. A light fringe of snow lay like a cape on the shoulders of his over-coat and like toecaps on the toes of his goloshes; and, as the buttons of his overcoat slipped with a squeaking noise through the snow-stiffened frieze, a cold fragrant air from out-of-doors escaped from crevices and folds. (177)

Lily's sarcasm throws the reality of Gabriel's marriage into question: "He waited outside the drawing-room until the waltz should finish, listening to the skirts that swept against it and to the shuffling of feet. He was still discomposed by the girl's bitter and sudden retort. It had cast a gloom over him which he tried to dispel by arranging his cuffs and the bows of his tie" (179).

Lily herself has an almost supernatural pallor: "She was a slim, growing girl, pale in complexion and with hay-coloured hair. The gas in the pantry made her look still paler" (177). Aunt Julia's face is less ghostly than corpselike: "Her hair, drawn low over the tops of her ears, was grey; and grey also, with darker shadows, was her large flaccid face" (179).

Gretta ceases to exist as Gabriel's wife in the middle of the story, suddenly changing into an apparition: "Gabriel had not gone to the door with the others. He was in a dark part of the hall gazing up the staircase. A woman was standing near the top of the first flight, in the shadow also. He could not see her face but he could see the terracotta and salmonpink panels of her skirt which the shadow made appear black and white. It was his wife" (209).

Gretta's devolution from a compelling apparition into a ghost[19] is mirrored in the changing connotations of the word *strange,* used repeatedly to describe her: "But now, after the kindling again of so many memories, the first touch of her body, musical and strange and perfumed, sent through him a keen pang of lust" (215). "To take her as she was would be brutal. No, he must see some ardour in her eyes first. He longed to be the master of her strange mood" (217). "He was in such a fever of rage and desire that he did not hear her come from the window. She stood before him for an instant, looking at him strangely. Then, suddenly raising herself on tiptoe and resting her hands lightly on his shoulders, she kissed him" (217).

Although "The Dead" is intricately related to the stories that precede it, it is also markedly different in its treatment of the past. The past does not simply feed on the present; memory can also provide access to grace, allowing the heart to reclaim long-lost and newly cherished things:

> Moments of their secret life together burst like stars upon his memory. A heliotrope envelope was lying beside his breakfast-cup and he was caressing it with his hand. Birds were twittering in the ivy and the sunny web of the curtain was shimmering along the floor: he could not eat for happiness. They were standing on the crowded

platform and he was placing a ticket inside the warm palm of her glove. He was standing with her in the cold, looking in through a grated window at a man making bottles in a roaring furnace. It was very cold. Her face, fragrant in the cold air, was quite close to his; and suddenly she called out to the man at the furnace:

—Is the fire hot, sir?

But the man could not hear her with the noise of the furnace. It was just as well. He might have answered rudely.

A wave of yet more tender joy escaped from his heart and went coursing in warm flood along his arteries. Like the tender fire of stars moments of their life together that no one knew of or would ever know of, broke upon and illumined his memory. (213)

Although Gabriel's memories are rekindled only to be extinguished by Gretta's, they are life-giving in their moment. And although Gabriel allows these memories to be taken from him, his new vision of Gretta is a tender one. The closing epiphany is filled with negative self-recognition, but it is more than a consummation of despair. Gabriel is also possessed with a desire for self-transcendence: "Better pass boldly into that other world, in the full glory of some passion, than fade and wither dismally with age" (223). He will know whether the goal of his journey westward is resurrection or death only after he has set out. Now he knows only that he has come to the last outpost of which Kafka speaks: "From a certain point onward there is no longer any turning back. That is the point that must be reached" (163).

Gabriel's marriage to Gretta is gnomonic; Michael Furey, or the romantic love that Gabriel, in his diffidence, allows him to usurp forever, is the missing part. But a second union of Gabriel and his own fate takes place at the end of the story, and it is sealed by an epiphany that is witnessed by Gabriel as well as the reader. Gabriel is not the only character to witness an epiphany in *Dubliners,* but he is the only character who does not come to an understanding too late. When Gabriel sees the light, it destroys his illusions, momentarily exalting him to almost prophetic stature; when a character like Mr. Duffy of "A Painful Case" sees the light, it only completes his isolation. Although Joyce's handling of him is ironic, Gabriel never becomes his victim; although it is true that he is a "well-meaning sentimentalist" and, in some ways, a "pitiable fatuous fellow," Joyce makes sure that it is Gabriel himself who tells us so (220). In a sense, Gabriel does exactly what Joyce wants the reader to do: he forces himself to look into Joyce's "nicely polished looking glass" twice, and he fully acknowledges the flaws reflected there the second time.[20]

The epiphanies of "The Dead" are different from the epiphanies found in other stories in *Dubliners*. They are not merely disclosures of poverty; they point to the possibility of renewal as well. Gabriel's discovery of his own solitude is a repudiation of passion. Yet, made to doubt the basis of his husbandly rights, he is able to achieve a moment of sympathy for Gretta that is more selfless than any romantic sacrifice could be; the latter, after all, is inspired by the hope of repayment in a sublime currency. The geriatric festivities arranged by the "Three Musical Graces" of Dublin are pathetic, yet they are expressions of genuine hospitality. Gabriel's former identity dissolves into an image of death at the end of the story, but without death there can be no rebirth.

The crucial difference between "The Dead" and the stories that precede it is that epiphany is an event that takes place within Gabriel's self-consciousness. Gabriel is no longer the victim of revelation but rather a seer of visions. Epiphany no longer points beyond the confines of a character's consciousness to the lack that defines it; the mind now takes possession of that emptiness. Just as Dante's vision of Cocytus at the end of the *Inferno* precedes his passage beyond hell, Gabriel's vision of snow precedes his movement westward, a movement that may carry him beyond the land of the living dead.[21]

By leaving open the possibility of redemption, a possibility that is just as terrifying, in its own way, as the possibility of paralysis, Joyce pays a fierce kind of tribute to the generosity of Dublin. Recent criticism exaggerates the final impenetrability of "The Dead." Jean-Michel Rabaté maintains, for example, that "the last oceanic silence which concludes 'The Dead' cannot be reduced by interpretation." According to Rabaté,

> The dissolution of the subject implies an infinite interpretation, not reducible to the antagonisms between East and West. The critical controversy around the value of "westward" . . . seems a little idle; what Joyce simply suggests is that a cycle has been completed, since perversion has exhausted its own possibilities. The pure annihilation of differences proposes to the subject the empty place of the other and silent listener, "playing possum," as Earwicker will have to do

to save himself in the *Wake*. The symbolic structure has been so violently fractured for Gabriel that we are left gazing at the empty mirror of the sky, in much the same way as we stand as readers metamorphosed into a horned and paralytic Shakespeare at the end of the "Circe" episode in *Ulysses*. (*Authorized Reader* 45)

Rabaté's interpretation of "The Dead" suggests that, by the end of the story, Gabriel has been brought face to face with a negative infinity, having witnessed the disintegration of the very binary oppositions that have structured his consciousness, and that the reader somehow shares in his ecstatic dislocation. In my view, it is the vital presence of antithetical possibilities that generates the powerful ambiguity of the story's final passages.

"The Dead" closes with a premonition that is larger than life, encompassing all of Ireland. In this sense, it epiphanizes every story that comes before it. Although those stories are written in a vivisective spirit, "The Dead" cuts deeper into modernity.[22] Modernism does more than diagnose paralysis; it forces us to struggle with the meaning of emancipation. Epiphany may commemorate the death of God and all his servants, but unless its witnesses are moved to strive in the world that he has left, the funeral goes on forever. If the promise inherent in those relations is passively surrendered, there can be no hope of change. Only in "The Dead" does Joyce allow one of the characters of *Dubliners* to contemplate the vast emptiness that epiphany reveals.[23] That vision forces Gabriel into exile. Although his journey is negatively inspired, there is more hope in self-conscious negation than in blind despair. In this respect, "The Dead" prepares the way for *A Portrait of the Artist as a Young Man,* in which the drama of aesthetic self-creation unfolds in the literary self-consciousness of Stephen. By resisting the ideological constraints that fetter the characters of *Dubliners,* Stephen is able to point to the ideal destination of Gabriel's journey: "Welcome, O life! I go to encounter for the millionth time the reality of experience and to forge in the smithy of my soul the uncreated conscience of my race" (252–53).

Notes

1. Stephen Heath, for example, argues that "*Dubliners* . . . extends the procedure of epiphany into a second, more general procedure within which it can be contained. This is the development of a kind of 'colourless'

writing (that zero degree of writing described by Barthes) which can be held at the same level as the repetition of fragments of discourse, framing them in an absence of any principle (of organisation, of order) or, more exactly, in the signification of its purpose to remain silent, outside commentary, interpretation, parole. Joyce, with great precision, refers to this as 'a style of scrupulous meanness'" (34–36). Heath makes much of the way in which *Dubliners* resists interpretation yet fails to acknowledge the simple fact that Joyce's withholding of meaning is a technique of insinuation. Speaking of strategies for interpreting Joyce, Hélène Cixous states that "there are two possible courses of action: the first trusting to the known facts about Joyce's work, particularly his intensive use of symbols, and his obsessive and often explicit concern to control word-order, thus pre-judging the work as a 'full' text, governed by 'the hypostasis of the signified,' a text which conceals itself but which has nothing to conceal, which is findable. This reassuring position is in fact almost necessary, granted the conscious or unconscious fashion of pushing Joyce back into the theological world from which he wanted to escape, by squeezing him 'through the back door' (cf. the versions of Joyce as Catholic, Medieval Joyce, Irish Joyce, Joyce the Jesuit in reverse and hence the right way around as well, etc.) On the other hand one can imagine a reading which would accept 'discouragement,' not in order to 'recuperate' it by taking it as a metaphor for the Joycean occult (which would, by the way, be right but would only be taking account of the formal aspect of the effect of privation), but rather by seeing in that trap which confiscates signification the sign of the willed imposture which crosses and double-crosses the *whole* of Joyce's work, making that betrayal the very breath (the breathlessness) of the subject" ("Joyce" 21). In order to adopt the second strategy outlined above, the reader of *Dubliners* must practice a strange kind of austerity, resisting the temptation to interpret the riddles posed by so many of the stories for fear of falling into a theological trap. What is one to do with the elliptical insinuations of "The Sisters," the telling repetitions of "An Encounter," the significance of the interpolated songs found in "Clay" and "Araby," and so forth?

2. Franca Ruggieri warns against ignoring the expressiveness of Joyce's silences in *Dubliners:* "There are many forms of silence in *Dubliners,* and [the] current trend to interpret those silences only as a metaphor for death and paralysis is too simplistic. Silence is always charged with meaning, just as much as the spoken word, in Conrad, Beckett, Eliot, Pinter, and in Joyce, because the absence of speech or articulate sound and the intense use of the unsaid and of silence as comment, criticism, accusation, meditation and interpretation of what has been said, can be much more meaningful than speech itself. Thus we find a clear progression from simple

aphasia towards a brief and final attempt to give verbal expression to the void. From the simple, immediate mystery in an almost realistic situation in the first stories, silence will become in the end the only metaphor for the unknowable, the sole vestige of an absolute language, mute and evocative" (53).

3. For a rich and detailed discussion of the crucial part played by popular literature in the polyphony of *Dubliners,* see Kershner 22–150.

4. Joyce's agreement with Stephen Dedalus on this score is evidenced by what Samuel Beckett characterized as "the absolute absence of the absolute" in Joyce's writing ("Dante" 22).

5. Mary T. Reynolds discusses the parallelism of these two passages in *Joyce and Dante* (165). In this particular case, Joyce does not borrow phrases from Dante, but imitates the ecstasy of his first recognition of Beatrice in the *Vita Nuova* instead.

6. In his interpretation of "Araby," Phillip Herring makes a case for the inauthenticity of the boy's emotion: "In his imagination the boy makes of the girl something she is not—an unrealistic figure of idolatry. The seven veils of mystery in which the boy cloaks her probably hide an ordinary Dublin girl of her age. Falseness resides, rather, in the voyeurism and mysticism that engender the reaction of an inexperienced lover who must learn about life the hard way, by looking for sustenance to a commercial establishment that matches his own temperament for falseness, a shabby bazaar that trades on the gullibility of wide-eyed locals by cloaking itself in the name (but not even the borrowed robes) of oriental exoticism. Neither boy nor reader mistakes the facade of Duessa's castle, realizing that falseness lies within both quester and goal, and deliverance is not from any "throng of foes," but from illusions tenaciously held" (*Uncertainty* 33–34). Herring's interpretation of "Araby" does not account for the self-betrayal enacted in the story's closing lines, nor does it acknowledge the tragic and even sinister implications of the boy's Christian-sounding renunciation of his youthful romanticism.

7. In the course of a discussion of perversity in "The Sisters" and "An Encounter," Rabaté maintains that "the pervert erects codes, maxims, laws, so as to dodge past them all the better, and to get around them. Getting around them, he also turns around in them: such is the significance of the meeting with the pervert in 'An Encounter.' In such a vicious circle, the loss of the object is atoned for by the loss of meaning. But paradoxically, perversion constantly needs the outcrop of sense, its generation as well as the reference to desire and the Law. The law of silence is merely the silence of the Law" (*Authorized Reader* 32). Speaking of Joyce's perversity, he adds that Joyce is not a "pervert" but "a neurotic who imagines himself to be a pervert in order to assure the continuity of his enjoyment" (33).

Rabaté's suggestion that Joyce derives pleasure from reanimating and resisting the dead letter of the Law is a very plausible one; however, the suggestion that there is something inherently neurotic about this form of pleasure strikes me as arbitrary.

8. The narrator of "The Sisters" is an orphan; the narrator of "An Encounter" may have parents, but he never alludes to them; the narrator of "Araby" lives with his aunt and uncle. Dead priests appear in "The Sisters" and "Araby"; Father Keon in "Ivy Day in the Committee Room" is said to resemble a "clergyman or poor actor," wears a collar that could be a layman's or a clergyman's, and is referred to as "an unfortunate man of some kind" and "a black sheep."

9. Marvin Magalaner makes this observation in "Dubliners" (89).

10. For a discussion of staggered or retrospective epiphanies cast in terms of reader-response theory, see Guerra 43.

11. R. B. Kershner notes that the text of "Clay" can be regarded as a "stylization" of Maria's "inner narrative," which is "packed with explanation, excuse, periphrasis, and even denial" (110). I would add that Maria's "inner narrative" has its visual corollary in Joyce's description of her diminutive and diminished physical form.

12. It is interesting to note that the code of symptoms devised by Joyce is antithetical to the code posited by Freud; to break the former is to master a language of repression; to break the latter is to penetrate a language of desire. The reader of "Clay" is never told what Maria really wants; he learns only what she has never allowed herself to imagine.

13. The self-betrayal enacted in the closing lines of "Araby" also takes the form of a surrender to Christian authority: "Gazing up into the darkness I saw myself as a creature driven and derided by vanity; and my eyes burned with anguish and anger" (35).

14. Rabaté links the breaking of the chalice to the etymology of *paralysis*: "*paralysis* etymologically conveys an idea of an unbinding (*para-lyein*, 'to release, to unbind') which is coupled with an anguishing immobility, while *paresis* means to 'let fall.' The priest's paralysis is both a dropping of some holy vessel (a chalice) in a parapraxis (a slip or lapsus) and the untying of the knots which paradoxically constrict the cramped movements of the protagonists" (*Authorized Reader* 29). Rabaté later points out that, according to Dante, the etymology of *author* conveys an idea of binding or tying together (160–61). It seems entirely possible that Joyce was aware that *author* and *paralysis* are etymological opposites, and that it was his consciousness of that opposition that prompted him to adopt paralysis as a key metaphor for social and spiritual decadence in *Dubliners*.

15. For a valuable discussion of Joyce's willful misuse of the word *reflection* in the opening passage of "The Sisters," see Kershner 24.

16. Joyce's delight in shredding an ideal text of authority to create a countertext that rivals the density of its mythic original is evident to any reader of *Finnegans Wake*.

17. The narrator of "An Encounter" also loses his innocence in the moment that he becomes an accomplice to "the queer old josser." Although he calls out to Mahony at the close of the story, Mahony cannot fully deliver him from the deathly world of the stranger: he is trapped between the barren alternatives of unreflecting innocence and sadomasochistic experience.

18. Earl G. Ingersoll makes an interesting comment on Molly Ivors's contribution to the eroticization of travel in "The Dead": "The metaphoric implications of travel are underscored in the interchange with Molly Ivors. After having already twitted him for being a 'West Briton,' simply because he had written the review of Browning for a Unionist paper, Molly invites him to join her and a group of Nationalists in 'an excursion to the Aran Isles this summer' and seems surprised to hear him demur, despite her 'laying her warm hand eagerly on his arm.' Certainly she has suggested that Gretta might come too—'She's from Connacht, isn't she?'—and yet she is just as certainly eroticizing this travel talk, whether that is her intent or not. As Gabriel makes clear, travel for him as a man is 'to keep in touch with the languages and partly for a change.' Her 'warmth' calls up his 'heated' reply, 'I'm sick of my own country.' Thus, when Gretta, who earlier joined in the peals of laughter at his expense, repeats Molly's enthusiastic suggestion of a 'trip to the west of Ireland,' it is understandable that he should respond 'coldly' to the very notion that raised such 'heat' in the earlier exchange with Molly. The episode concludes with Gretta repeating Molly's response and herself eroticizing the metaphor of travel when she replies, '—There's a nice husband for you, Mrs Malins'" (44–45).

19. Gabriel's vision of Gretta on the staircase is a mock epiphany, a moment of incomplete or gnomonic revelation: "He stood still in the gloom of the hall, trying to catch the air that the voice was singing and gazing up at his wife. There was grace and mystery in her attitude as if she were a symbol of something. He asked himself what is a woman standing on the stairs in the shadow, listening to distant music, a symbol of. If he were a painter he would paint her in that attitude. Her blue felt hat would show off the bronze of her hair against the darkness and the dark panels of her skirt would show off the light ones. *Distant Music* he would call the picture if he were a painter" (210).

20. Gabriel's first glimpse of his reflection reveals a chronic dissatisfaction with his own image: "As he passed in the way of the cheval-glass he caught sight of himself in full-length, his broad, well-filled shirt-front, the face whose expression always puzzled him when he saw it in a mirror and

his glimmering gilt-rimmed eyeglasses" (218). Gabriel's second glimpse constitutes a long-delayed analysis of that dissatisfaction: "A shameful consciousness of his own person assailed him. He saw himself as a ludicrous figure, acting as a pennyboy for his aunts, a nervous well-meaning sentimentalist, orating to vulgarians and idealising his own clownish lusts, the pitiable fatuous fellow he had caught glimpse of in the mirror. Instinctively he turned his back more to the light lest she might see the shame that burned on his forehead" (219–20). It is significant that in this instance, the repetition of an action is not associated with blindness but with insight. This is in keeping with the transitional character of "The Dead."

21. Ingersoll calls attention to Gretta's journey westward, treating it as a sentimental and ultimately regressive one: "As Gretta recounts her sentimental tale of Michael Furey, that frail Adonis nipped in the bud by a wintry rain, the gender associations are inverted. In a sense Gretta indicates that she has been the traveller this morning, going west through memory, regressing to the realms of romantic love; her travels are ironically pointed up in her suddenly schoolgirlish sensibility by the heavy overlay of Christian iconography. Her locution 'I was great with him at that time,' as others have noted, suggests the language of the Madonna, 'great with child,' an impression supported by her adding, 'I think he died for me.' . . . That Gabriel is willing to swallow this romantic tale of dying for love, whose subject is an unprepossessing boy in poor health who would have probably died anyway, is less a testimony to his acceptance of such tragic love as 'the real thing' and more an attestation of the need for metaphorizing travel as imaginative or spiritual rather than literal or geographic" (48). Noting the tension between irony and romanticism in "The Dead," Ingersoll comes down somewhat heavily on the side of irony. His description of "The Dead" as an affirmation of "the need for metaphorizing travel" is not altogether convincing.

22. According to Stephen Dedalus, "The modern spirit is vivisective. Vivisection is the most modern process one can conceive" (*Stephen Hero* 186).

23. For an excellent discussion of the closing of "The Dead," see Ruggieri.

2

A Portrait of the Artist as a Young Man

In *Dubliners*, Joyce devises a rhetoric of paralysis to dramatize a social disease; in *Portrait*, he undertakes a reconstruction of subjectivity. Whereas *Dubliners* epiphanizes paralysis, *Portrait* epiphanizes Stephen's linguistic gestation. The earlier work captures the domestic ways of decadence; the later one articulates the possibility of artistic emancipation.

Although it is tempting to assume that *Portrait* contains the answer to the riddle of paralysis posed in *Dubliners*, this is not the case. Stephen's struggle against paralysis is famously inconclusive. It is not clear that he will succeed in realizing his ambitions; solipsism may render him incapable of negotiating the nets of language, nationality, and religion. Moreover, Joyce's handling of the young man who inherited his own youthful pseudonym is highly problematic.[1] Granted that Joyce does not let Stephen off lightly in *Portrait*,[2] where does self-irony end and self-begetting begin?

Stephen's flight from "sordid reality" is partly inspired by the aestheticism of Pater and Wilde. His reaction to social decay owes a great deal to the literary decadence of his precursors. In his solipsism and aestheticism, Stephen personifies the decadence of modernism as described by Lukács. According to Lukács, "modernist anti-realism" brings about an identification of "man's inwardness" with an "abstract subjectivity," an identification that ultimately results in a "disintegration of personality" (*Meaning* 24, 25). Although Lukács's condemnation of what he takes to be the pathetically reflexive heroes of modernism may seem outdated, it has relevance to current discussions of *Portrait*. Critics have not

ceased to analyze Stephen's unfitness for flight. Lukács would argue
that Stephen's weakness lies in his lack of a vital connection to objective reality; current criticism, predicated on the assumption that
"objective reality" is itself a construct, often faults Stephen for being
an insufficiently ironic reader of the decentered text of the world.[3]

My own interpretation of *Portrait* is based on the premise that
solipsism constitutes a necessary stage in Stephen's movement toward artistic autonomy. The possibility of arriving at a stage beyond
solipsism is affirmed not by Stephen but by Joyce, who succeeds in
sacrificing the authorial unity of his own voice to the mutability of
his character. In the pages that follow, I will show that alienation is
essential to Stephen's incipient art and that Stephen's absoluteness
serves to bring forth the relativism of his creator. I will begin by
comparing Stephen with Gabriel Conroy, the all-too-human mes-
senger who heralds his coming.

Both Gabriel and Stephen are prone to solipsism. Gabriel's glasses
shield him from the objects of his gaze: "on his hairless face there
scintillated restlessly the polished lenses and the bright gilt rims
of the glasses which screened his delicate and restless eyes" (178).
These specular lenses are later found floating on the surface of a dis-
enchanting mirror: "[Gretta] broke loose from him and ran to the
bed and, throwing her arms across the bed-rail, hid her face. Gabriel
stood stock-still for a moment in astonishment and then followed
her. As he passed in the way of the cheval-glass he caught sight
of himself in full-length, his broad, well-filled shirt-front, the face
whose expression always puzzled him when he saw it in a mirror
and his glimmering gilt-rimmed eyeglasses" (218). Like Stephen,
Gabriel is not at home in the world; he has inherited the delicate
eyes of his creator. Although his flawed self-image is finally cor-
rected by estrangement, the medicine may prove to be too strong,
turning him into an undeceived ghost. Unlike Joyce and Stephen,
Gabriel has little use for invisibility. Stephen believes that invisibility is a virtue in an artist, but Gabriel is not caught up in the same
romance; for him, invisibility carries with it the threat of death.

Although Gabriel is a teacher and not an artist, he is touchy on
questions of sensibility. Like Stephen, he is easily embarrassed by
philistinism; unlike Stephen, he never withdraws from the world
to select his own fictive society. Gabriel's after-dinner speech is a
measure of the distance dividing them. Although it is clearly a par-

ody, only Joyce and his readers can appreciate its style of humor. Stephen may be the slave of his own sophistication, but he is never at the receiving end of a literary joke. Gabriel takes on the authority of a dying man at the moment of epiphany, but he is ineffectual in the time that precedes it. When he addresses his relatives and friends, he is carried away by the felicity of his own phrases; only later does he acknowledge that he has delivered a "foolish speech" (222). The eloquence of the epiphany at the end of "The Dead" is in excess of Gabriel's powers; only the presence of death can silence the tentative voice of his desire:

> A few light taps upon the pane made him turn to the window. It had begun to snow again. He watched sleepily the flakes, silver and dark, falling obliquely against the lamplight. The time had come for him to set out on his journey westward. Yes, the newspapers were right: snow was general all over Ireland. It was falling on every part of the dark central plain, on the treeless hills, falling softly upon the Bog of Allen and, farther westward, softly falling into the dark mutinous Shannon waves. It was falling, too, upon every part of the lonely churchyard on the hill where Michael Furey lay buried. It lay thickly drifted on the crooked crosses and headstones, on the spears of the little gate, on the barren thorns. His soul swooned slowly as he heard the snow falling faintly through the universe and faintly falling, like the descent of their last end, upon all the living and the dead. (223–24)

Unlike Gabriel, Stephen loves to linger over his reflection. Gabriel goes to the mirror only when the barrenness of his life leaves him no other choice. Stephen uses language as his mirror, inscribing his name on its surface over and over again. Words that will not "take" his image oppress him: "the nightshade of his friend's list-lessness seemed to be diffusing in the air around him a tenuous and deadly exhalation and he found himself glancing from one casual word to another on his right or left in stolid wonder that they had been so silently emptied of instantaneous sense until every mean shop legend bound his mind like the words of a spell and his soul shrivelled up, sighing with age as he walked on in a lane among heaps of dead language" (178–79).

Gabriel wakes up to the fact of his solitude just as his youth is ending; his belatedness is reversed by Stephen, who never ceases to be precocious until *Ulysses*. Stephen turns to language not to escape from solitude but to perfect it. In this respect, he confirms some of Lukács's worst suspicions about modernist subjectivity. According to Lukács, the protagonists of modernist novels suffer from a condition of ontological solitude that has its philosophical corollary in Heidegger's concept of *Geworfenheit-ins-Dasein,* or thrownness-into-being. Modernism, for Lukács, is a reactionary form of mimesis that merely reproduces alienation. Ontological solitude, a symptom of alienation, can only beget ahistoricism:

> [The] negation of history takes two different forms in modernist literature. First, the hero is strictly confined within the limits of his own experience. There is not for him—and apparently not for his creator—any pre-existent reality beyond his own self, acting upon him or being acted upon by him. Secondly, the hero himself is without personal history. He is "thrown-into-the-world": meaninglessly, unfathomably. He does not develop through contact with the world; he neither forms or is formed by it. The only "development" in this literature is the gradual revelation of the human condition. Man is now what he has always been and always will be. The narrator, the examining subject, is in motion; the examined reality is static. (*Meaning* 21)

Stephen thrives on solitude; the eventfulness of his inner life depends on it. But he is not, as Lukács would have it, sealed off from history: he knows its contradictions well enough to feel victimized by them. His early identification with Parnell, whose political career was finally destroyed by Catholic prudery, helps account for his distrust of history. Orphaned by the past, he is thrown upon the hypothetical mercy of language. But he knows he has reason to be wary of the English language as well, as the following thoughts, prompted by an English dean, indicate: "—The language in which we are speaking is his before it is mine. How different are the words *home, Christ, ale, master,* on his lips and on mine! I cannot speak or write these words without unrest of spirit. His language, so familiar and so foreign, will always be for me an acquired speech. I have not made or accepted its words. My voice holds them at bay. My soul frets in the shadow of his language" (189).

The knowledge that tyranny is written into the English language fuels Stephen's will to master it. He remains loyal to his English heroes because they serve him as teachers; at the same time, he dreams of rejuvenating his mother tongue and is offended by dialects that he considers degenerate:

> —A flaming bloody sugar, that's what he is!
>
> It was his [Cranly's] epitaph for all dead friendships and Stephen wondered whether it would ever be spoken in the same tone over his memory. The heavy lumpish phrase sank slowly out of hearing like a stone through a quagmire. Stephen saw it sink as he had seen many another, feeling its heaviness depress his heart. Cranly's speech, unlike that of Davin, had neither rare phrases of Elizabethan English nor quaintly turned versions of Irish idioms. Its drawl was an echo of the quays of Dublin given back by a bleak decaying seaport, its energy an echo of the sacred eloquence of Dublin given back flatly by a Wicklow pulpit. (195)

Cranly's speech grates on Stephen because it signals the final phase of Dublin's paralysis, namely the atrophy of its powers of persuasion. Yet his love of Davin's speech is sentimental. Parody enables Joyce to indulge and exploit his own sentimentality at the same time; Stephen must learn to distance himself from language if he wants to use it as a means of forging the "uncreated conscience of his race" (253).[4]

At best, Stephen's estrangement from England and Ireland enables him to establish that distance; at worst, it makes him a prisoner of foreign dialects.[5] For a time, he is enthralled by the paralyzing power of the past. His vulnerability is exposed by a sentimental journey to Cork, his father's birthplace. Panic is preceded by auditory alienation; the southern sound of a porter's speech suddenly disturbs him:

> By the time they had crossed the quadrangle his restlessness had risen to fever. He wondered how his father, whom he knew for a shrewd suspicious man, could be duped by the servile manners of the porter; and the lively southern speech which had entertained him all the morning now irritated his ears.
>
> They passed into the anatomy theatre where Mr Dedalus, the porter aiding him, searched the desk for his initials. Stephen remained in the background, depressed more than ever by the darkness and silence of the theatre and by the air it wore of jaded and formal study. On the desk before him he read the word *Foetus* cut several times in the dark stained wood. The sudden legend startled

his blood: he seemed to feel the absent students of the college about him and to shrink from their company. A vision of their life, which his father's words had been powerless to evoke, sprang up before him out of the word cut in the desk. A broadshouldered student with a moustache was cutting in the letters with a jackknife, seriously. Other students stood or sat near him laughing at his handiwork. One jogged his elbow. The big student turned on him, frowning. He was dressed in loose grey clothes and had tan boots.

Stephen's name was called. He hurried down the steps of the theatre so as to be as far away from the vision as he could be and, peering closely at his father's initials, hid his flushed face.

But the word and the vision capered before his eyes as he walked back across the quadrangle and towards the college gate. It shocked him to find in the outer world a trace of what he had deemed till then a brutish and individual malady of his own mind. His recent monstrous reveries came thronging into his memory. They too had sprung up before him, suddenly and furiously, out of mere words. He had soon given in to them and allowed them to sweep across and abase his intellect, wondering always where they came from, from what den of monstrous images, and always weak and humble towards others, restless and sickened of himself when they had swept over him. (89–90)

The word *foetus* is as terrible to Stephen as the idea of his own origins; both are charged with his fear of the crippling power of the past. *Foetus* belongs to the same family of words as *gnomon*, *simony*, and *paralysis*. Like those words, its potency is multiplied by repetition. Cut into the desk over and over again, it takes on an indestructible life of its own. It disfigures the present like a curse; the promise of new life withers away, leaving a stunted future in its place.

Foetus provides a point at which adolescent squeamishness and Catholic prudery intersect. The word on the desk tells a story; its "sudden legend" confirms Stephen's virginal suspicion that there is something monstrous about the "sexual myth" (Stevens, "Men Made out of Words" 335). At the same time, it drags profane mysteries down to the level of a schoolboy's prank. Stephen, who has been encouraged to repress or poeticize his sexuality, is doubly shocked.

The word carved in wood is a literal trace of the past. Stephen may be too young to make a fetish of the past, but he is just old enough to feel suffocated by it. Let us examine his horror of the word more closely. Stephen and Simon exchange places in the course of Simon's sentimental journey. While Simon relives his youth by bragging about it to his son, Stephen silently takes note of his father's puerility. The poverty of Stephen's past makes him fear for his future. Stephen comes upon the word *foetus* while his father is searching for his own initials. His revulsion is completed by Simon's success; the two inscriptions provide figurative evidence of the father's literal claim upon the life of his son. Moreover, both acts of vandalism may recall the violation of his mother's "purity" upon which his own birth depended. Catholicism conspires with oedipal impulses to produce a tragic vision of procreation. His father's sexual pride, for Stephen, is his mother's spiritual shame. Stephen destroys the significance of his father's past in order to be worthy of his mother's sacrifice. Nonetheless, his usurpation is complicated by guilt; thus the comparatively innocent word *foetus* becomes a curse.

The word carved in the desk carries a "sudden legend" to the reader as well, thematizing gestation, the ordering principle of *Portrait*. The particulars of Stephen's development translate into universal stages of artistic gestation. His birth as an artist depends on his ability to cut the cords that tie him to the past without depriving himself of its nourishment.[6]

So far, we have only discussed passages that record the damage done by alienation. These passages support Lukács's claim that modernism acquiesces in alienation by reproducing its effects without reconstructing the social totality to which the alienated subject belongs. Admittedly, Joyce does not labor to present society as an intelligible whole in *Portrait*. We see the world through Stephen's eyes, relying on his shifting negotiations with language to alert us to the changes that affect his vision. As Stephen knows full well, the language that enculturates him is the language of Ireland's oppressors. To rebel against England by mastering Gaelic strikes him as regressive; instead he resolves to free himself by making English the basis of his vocation. Historical knowledge does not bind him more closely to society, it sharpens his awareness of Ireland's impotence, moving him to empower himself as an artist by cultivating his alienation.[7] Granting that Stephen is not only an autobiographical but a representative figure typifying the artist as a young man, this is significant; it implies that Joyce regards alienation as an indispens-

able part of the structure of artistic subjectivity. The pleasure that
Stephen takes in language is a product of estrangement; his suscep-
tibility to the intoxication of words, which relates him to Daedalus
and his impetuous son, is an accident of linguistic colonization. His
poetic, which exalts the "enchantment of the heart," is simply the
theoretical corollary of his solitude.

Stephen reveals his vision of society when Davin urges him to
join the Gaelic League and he answers by renouncing all forms of
political engagement:

> —The soul is born, he said vaguely, first in those moments I told
> you of. It has a slow and dark birth, more mysterious than the birth
> of the body. When the soul of a man is born in this country there
> are nets flung at it to hold it back from flight. You talk to me of
> nationality, language, religion. I shall try to fly by those nets.
>   Davin knocked the ashes from his pipe.
> —Too deep for me, Stevie, he said. But a man's country comes
> first. Ireland first, Stevie. You can be a poet or mystic after.
> —Do you know what Ireland is? asked Stephen with cold vio-
> lence. Ireland is the old sow that eats her farrow. (203)

Stephen points to language, nationality, and religion as three contaminated sources of Irish identity: he pictures them grandly as nets
flung up to prevent the soul from realizing its autonomy in flight.
His art will come from defying the constraints imposed by Ireland;
in other words, it will exploit alienation. In *Portrait*, Joyce realizes
Stephen's dream of autonomy, fathering himself by reprojecting his
own artistic gestation. His narrative breaks off just before Stephen's
flight begins.[8] But the metaphorical union of art and flight in *Portrait* raises the following question: Can an art predicated on alienation provide a viable alternative to paralysis or, as Lukács might
argue, does it merely aestheticize the disease? The answer to this
question lies in the novel's epiphanies.

Whereas blindness generates epiphany in *Dubliners*, self-
consciousness is built into the epiphanic structure of *Portrait*. Most
of the epiphanies of *Dubliners* are only witnessed by the reader; the
epiphanies of *Portrait* literally occur to Stephen. Both Stephen and
the reader are forced into self-consciousness by the absolute claim
embodied in each epiphany. The epiphanies of *Dubliners* reveal a
deterioration of sight that cannot be repaired. (Gabriel's epiphany

is an exception: although the insight it embodies is tragic, it marks a restoration of vision nonetheless.) The youthful epiphanies of *Portrait* are revelatory and precipitous; each epiphany is uncompromising in its moment. The whole of these absolute figures is greater than the sum of its parts; the contradictory text of Stephen's life demands rereading, and self-consciousness is the implied reward. By turning against religion, Stephen not only revises his own fate but, in effect, warns the reader against accepting religious epiphanies at face value. Gabriel's single epiphany remains a tragic insight; Stephen's multiple and contradictory revelations are comical in the highest sense. Joyce suggests that if Stephen discovers that relativism is the principle of flight he may manage to overcome paralysis; self-consciousness will protect him from the blindness upon which paralysis depends. He does not give the reader the satisfaction of knowing whether Stephen succeeds, however, preserving the relativism and open-endedness of *Portrait*. By doing so, he protects the reader against paralysis as well. Mastery for Stephen will depend on his ability to distance himself from his own revelations so that he can use them as poetic material. Christa Wolf's Günderrode comments on the same principle in *No Place on Earth:* "People who are not deceived about themselves will extract something fresh out of the foment of every age, simply by lending it expression. . . . The world could not go on if this were not done" (82).

Relativism is in keeping with the organic causality that the metaphor of gestation imposes; as Richard Ellmann points out, gestation is the ordering principle of *Portrait:*

> The book begins with Stephen's father and, just before the ending, it depicts the hero's severance from his mother. From the start the soul is surrounded by liquids, urine, slime, seawater, amniotic tides, "drops of water" (as Joyce says at the end of the first chapter) "falling softly in the brimming bowl." The atmosphere of biological struggle is necessarily dark and melancholy until the light of life is glimpsed. In the first chapter the foetal soul is for a few pages only slightly individualized, the organism responds only to the most primitive sensory impressions, then the heart forms and musters its affections, the being struggles toward some unspecified uncomprehended culmination, it is flooded in ways it cannot understand or control, it gropes wordlessly toward sexual differentiation. In the third chapter shame floods Stephen's whole body as conscience develops; the

lower bestial nature is put by. Then at the end of the fourth chapter the soul discovers the goal towards which it has been mysteriously proceeding—the goal of life. It must swim no more but emerge into the air, the new metaphor being flight. The final chapter shows the soul, already fully developed, fattening itself for its journey until at last it is ready to leave. In the last few pages of the book, Stephen's diary, the soul is released from its confinement, its individuality is complete, and the style shifts with savage abruptness. ("Growth" 394–95)

Precisely because each epiphany seems to reveal the inexorable logic of events, it is essential that there be several, and that they contradict one another. Strictly sequential narration would violate the principle of gestation; Joyce's first attempt at self-portraiture contains a rejection of what he later referred to as a "goahead plot" (*Letters,* ed. Ellmann, 3:146) that applies to *Portrait* as well: "The features of infancy are not commonly reproduced in the adolescent portrait for, so capricious are we, that we cannot or will not conceive the past in any other than its iron, memorial aspect. Yet the past assuredly implies a fluid succession of presents, the development of an entity of which our actual present is a phase only" ("Portrait" 257–58).

In *Portrait,* Joyce repeats and transforms various images in order to represent Stephen's life as a "fluid succession of presents." In *Dubliners,* the repetition of certain words or phrases is associated with a rhetoric of paralysis. In *Portrait,* repetition carries no stigma; rather, it dramatizes the development of artistic subjectivity. In fact, in many cases, the recurrence of a word or trope confirms Stephen's accumulation of a poetic vocabulary that may become rich enough to compensate for his ontological solitude.

Let us turn to the text for an example of this kind of repetition. The following passage forms a nodal point in the development of a motif:

> He saw the sea of waves, long dark waves rising and falling, dark under the moonless night. A tiny light twinkled at the pierhead where the ship was entering: and he saw a multitude of people gathered by the waters' edge to see the ship that was entering their harbour. A tall man stood on the deck, looking out towards the flat dark land: and by the light at the pierhead he saw his face, the sorrowful face of Brother Michael.

He saw him lift his hand towards the people and heard him say in a loud voice of sorrow over the waters:
—He is dead. We saw him lying upon the catafalque.
A wail of sorrow went up from the people.
—Parnell! Parnell! He is dead!
They fell upon their knees, moaning in sorrow.
And he saw Dante in a maroon velvet dress and with a green velvet mantle hanging from her shoulders walking proudly and silently past the people who knelt by the waters' edge. (27)

The epic character of Stephen's dream violates his childhood.[9] Joyce does not use the dream to prove that Stephen is a precocious boy but to alert us to the part that Ireland's betrayal will play in his life. The amniotic sea that Ellmann refers to is first glimpsed here; the "cold infrahuman odour" (167) of that sea is associated with birth and with death, whereas the image of flight remains a strictly postnatal promise. The voice of Brother Michael calling to the people from across the waters and the voice of the people lamenting at the water's edge are pregnant with Ireland's betrayal. Stephen shares Joyce's identification with Parnell; in a feverish dream he takes on the weight of Ireland's losses.

Elements of the same image are scattered throughout *Portrait;* one of the most notable examples occurs at the end of the book: "The spell of arms and voices: the white arms of roads, their promises of close embraces and the black arms of tall ships that stand against the moon, their tale of distant nations. They are held out to say: We are alone. Come. And the voices say with them: We are your kinsmen. And the air is thick with their company as they call to me, their kinsman, making ready to go, shaking the wings of their exultant and terrible youth" (252). The people by the water's edge that Stephen dreamt of as a boy have grown into his kinsmen, who are no longer mourning the death of Parnell but urging him to take flight. Their voices are part of the tale told by the "white arms of roads" and the "black arms of tall ships," just as long ago the lament of the people issued from waves that talked "among themselves as they rose and fell" (26). In the time that has elapsed between the two visionary moments, Stephen's identification with Parnell has evolved into an understanding of his own vocation. The waters of conception part to reveal the inevitability of Ireland's self-betrayals and the necessity of flight.

In short, Joyce uses protean motifs and discordant epiphanies to create a "fluid succession of presents" that cancels the absolute claim of any particular moment. The closing epiphanies of *Portrait* seem final enough, but they are compromised by the vows of preceding pages. Errancy is the existential condition that Stephen chooses when he turns away from Catholicism to art. The "satanic" vocation imposes a discipline all its own, forbidding its followers to indulge in the symmetrical pleasures of eternity. Admittedly, Stephen does not give up Mariolatry when he gives up religion: all the significant females that he encounters are made in the refracted image of Mary. Mary is at once the virgin mother of his art and the archetypal temptress of his villanelle.[10] In the afterglow of inspiration, Stephen becomes one with her: "O! In the virgin womb of the imagination the word was made flesh. Gabriel the seraph had come to the virgin's chamber" (217). Nonetheless, Stephen's religion of art is rooted in time, and the nonlinear narrative of *Portrait* conforms to its rule of errancy.

Kenneth Burke has argued that errancy has its own order in *Portrait* and that the narrative is governed by a progressive "dialectic of stages":

In the *Portrait,* considered from the standpoint of "stages," the first three chapters would be like courses "prerequisite" to the choice Stephen makes in chapter IV, where he turns from priestly to artistic vocation. However, we should not overlook an intermediate stage here. After thought of "*ordination*" . . . of "a grave and *ordered* and passionless life that awaited him, a life without material cares" . . . of himself as "a being apart in every *order*" . . . of his destiny "to be elusive of social or religious *orders,*" there is talk of himself as "about to fall," then "he crossed the bridge over the stream of the Tolka," whereat he contemplates the opposite of order: "Then, bending to the left, he followed the lane which led up to his house. The faint sour stink of rotted cabbages came towards him from the kitchen-gardens on the rising ground above the river. He smiled to think it was this *disorder* . . . the misrule and confusion of his father's house and the stagnation of vegetable life, which was to win the day in his soul." Not quite. For the next episode will detail the vision of the hawklike man and the bird-girl (flight away, flight up, a *transcending* of the rotted cabbages). Hence, all told: *from* the priestly calling, *through* the dismal alternative, *to* the new exaltation, the aesthetic jesuitry that will be his purging of the alternative disorder, that will fly above it. And since the disorder had been "to the left," and since Part I should "implicitly contain" what eventuates, we might appropriately recall young Stephen's first triumph, as regards the pandybat episode, when he had gone "not to the corridor but up the staircase on the right that led up to the castle." Here is accurate writing. (444–45)

Burke's excellent analysis shows that the inner logic of Stephen's development is dialectical. Presumably, progress of some kind, given that logic, is inevitable. But Joyce does not slip the reader any hints concerning Stephen's future success or failure, leaving the possibility of arrested growth intact. Although Burke correctly points out that Stephen continues to guard his imaginative virginity after he has renounced religion, he fails to add that Stephen's virginity must eventually be sacrificed. There is a stage beyond "aesthetical jesuitry" just as there is an artist who survives the excesses of the young man. Unless Stephen attains that stage, he will go the way of Icarus, drowning in the very "amniotic tides" that he longs to fly across. Joyce may not answer the riddle of Stephen's fate, but he leaves no doubt of the danger of resisting the paradoxical flow of life itself.

But if Joyce was no longer content to diagnose Dublin's disease by the time he wrote *Portrait,* why isn't the narrative unambiguously affirmative, moving from paralysis to its cure? And if *Portrait* is a prescriptive novel rather than a diagnostic one, why doesn't the fate of its main protagonist "match" the form of the novel? Joyce suggested a correspondence between *Bildung* and narrative form in the essay that anticipated *Portrait:* "Our world . . . recognizes its acquaintance chiefly by the characters of beard and inches and is, for the most part, estranged from those of its members who seek through some art, by some process of mind as yet untabulated, to liberate from the personalized lumps of matter that which is their individuating rhythm, the first or formal relation of their parts. But for such as these a portrait is not an identificative paper but the curve of an emotion" ("Portrait" 258). Insofar as Joyce depicts the "liberation of an individuating rhythm" in *Portrait,* the novel is progressive. But although the narrative of *Portrait* is progressive, it remains open-ended. Stephen discovers a principle of individuation in literary self-consciousness, but the narrative ends before he has tested it. Given his fear of the poverty that surrounds him, can literary self-consciousness suffice? To answer that question, let us examine the narrator's relationship to Stephen.

As fictionalized autobiography, *Portrait* charts the curve of Stephen's emotion and erases the myth of the omniscient author at the same time. The most effective authors will have trouble persuading us of their omniscience once we know that they are fictionalizing their own past. In a sense, such a claim would be a confession of impotence — it would imply that they have managed to exhaust their experience.

Joyce has Stephen celebrate the omniscience of the author in a passage that echoes similar statements by Flaubert and Baudelaire:

> The personality of the artist, at first a cry or a cadence or a mood and then a fluid and lambent narrative, finally refines itself out of existence, impersonalizes itself, so to speak. The esthetic image in the dramatic form is life purified in and reprojected from the human imagination. The mystery of esthetic like that of material creation is accomplished. The artist, like the God of the creation, remains within or behind or beyond or above his handiwork, invisible, refined out of existence, indifferent, paring his fingernails. (215)

Stephen's ideal author penetrates the form of his creation so completely that he disappears. By perfecting the art of sublimation, he explodes the romantic myth of unmediated self-expression. (Stephen's contempt for this kind of mystification is shared by Joyce; for Joyce and for Stephen, Temple's assertion that Rousseau was a sincere man identifies him as a charlatan.) But although this imaginary author has mastered the form of his creation, he can never master its content, described as "life purified in and reprojected from the human imagination." He may be able to use his life as poetic material but he cannot exhaust its mysteries; indeed, the very process of turning memories into metaphors suggests that its riddles are insoluble.

The myth of the all-knowing narrator rests on an ideal of absolute authorial control that is, strictly speaking, unattainable.[11] Joyce does not even attempt to dominate his novel; in fact, he relativizes his own voice by reprojecting the past in *Portrait*. Lukács identified such willful self-effacement as one of the prerequisites of naturalism, forerunner of modernism. Eugene Lunn provides a summary of Lukács's critique in *Modernism and Marxism*:

The comprehensive vision and omniscience of the realist author is lost in naturalism. Without any real sense of the causality of events, the naturalistic author's voice is relativized to the various psychologies of his characters. Static situations with fetishized objects are described, alternating with isolated, fleeting, subjective impressions—an abstract objectivity alternating with a false subjectivity. Given this pendulum effect, we can see how Lukács might argue, as he did, that naturalism became the prototype of all modernist writing. In all of the various modernist movements, reality is perceived merely in its factual immediacy, divorced from "those mediations which connect experiences with the objective reality of society." The mechanical split between subject and object, between immediate phenomena and historical essence—instead of their actual dialectical interplay—was the thread uniting the whole variety of modernist experiment since Flaubert and Baudelaire. (81)

Joyce would seem to be guilty of Lukács's charges, yet closer inspection reveals that the laws behind those charges are unjust. First of all, Joyce manipulates the language that he appears to be ruled by. Secondly, the character made of that language is modeled on him. Although Joyce may seem to squander his authority, in fact he is being quite thrifty, saving through self-impersonation. His intimacy with Stephen does not corrupt the authority he retains: he knows his character as well as he knows himself. Stephen's weaknesses are Joyce's, which is why they cannot be separated from his strengths; the irony and ambivalence that surrounds him is the ghost of his creator's personality. The same film of personality protects the reader against the glare of the epiphanies.

Joyce invests his authority in Stephen's voice, and because that voice, acted on by other voices, changes over time, the investment yields polyphony. Unlike the discrete polyphony of *Dubliners,* which insinuates that subjectivity is deteriorating, or the strident polyphony of *Ulysses,* which heralds fragmentation, the polyphony of *Portrait* affirms the unity of a single soul's gestation. But although Stephen's subjectivity remains intact, it is not solidly grounded in the world.

Stephen is a solipsist and solipsism is an example par excellence of the disorder that Lukács might characterize as "an abstract objectivity alternating with a false subjectivity." From this vantage point, the coherence of Stephen's inner life is no more reassuring than the intelligibility of a fatal disease. Joyce's metaphor of gestation merely serves to disguise the fact of stunted growth. The organic form of the novel is deceptive, naturalizing the mischief done by alienation. Needless to say, from a Lukácsian point of view, the narrative of *Portrait* seems more wholesome than the narrative of *Ulysses:* polyphony controls the very form of the later work, whereas it obeys the logic of gestation in the earlier one. But it could be argued that Joyce only invokes the "myth of life" to conceal the frailty of his unified subject. If this is the case, *Portrait* is the more insidious work, using organic form to aestheticize decadent subjectivity. Moreover, it could be argued, *Portrait* also presents a solipsistic manifesto that defends the autonomy of the work of art and the invisibility of the author. Thus Joyce's cure for paralysis consists of promoting the growth of a degenerate and elitist form of subjectivity. The growing obscurity of his work, which consummates itself in *Finnegans Wake,* is evidence of the perversity of his proposals. In order to address these imaginary complaints, let us examine the role played by solipsism in Stephen's *Bildung.*

Stephen describes epiphany as an "enchantment of the heart" (213); according to his definition, merely self-indulgent seekers of pleasure cannot be enchanted. Aesthetic pleasure, as the Russian formalists knew, depends on estrangement. Stephen's removal from the world determines the "individuating rhythm" that shapes his life. Even in the beginning of the first chapter of *Portrait,* when phenomena are still so immediate that they appear out of focus, he is able to distance himself from his mother: "Nice mother! The first day in the hall of the castle when she had said goodbye she had put her veil double to her nose to kiss him: and her nose and eyes were red. But he had pretended not to see that she was going to cry. She was a nice mother but she was not so nice when she cried" (9). Stephen's secret refusal to play a tearful part in his mother's drama of separation is characteristic: he has already learned to resist the pressure of events by becoming their observer. Later in the same chapter, he falls ill and samples the mediated pleasures of convalescence:

> He could hear the tolling. He said over to himself the song that Brigid had taught him.
>
> *Dingdong! The castle bell!*
> *Farewell, my mother!*

> *Bury me in the old churchyard*
> *Beside my eldest brother.*
> *My coffin shall be black,*
> *Six angels at my back,*
> *Two to sing and two to pray*
> *And two to carry my soul away.*

How beautiful and sad that was! How beautiful the words were where they said *Bury me in the old churchyard!* A tremor passed over his body. How sad and how beautiful! He wanted to cry quietly but not for himself: for the words, so beautiful and sad, like music. The bell! The bell! Farewell! O farewell! (24)

Stephen at once mourns his own death and celebrates it in this passage. An intimation of death's absolute estrangement frees him to take disinterested pleasure in a familial song.

The chapter ends with an image of plenitude, a bowl almost overflowing with the praise that Stephen wins for an act of heroism. But most of the major events of succeeding chapters are so internal that even those closest to him must strain to sense their reverberations.

The moments of estrangement that Stephen experiences in the first chapter are comparatively simple; later they are overdetermined by imagination and desire. By the second chapter, his father's failures give such moments a vexed life of their own:

But the same foreknowledge which had sickened his heart and made his legs sag suddenly as he raced round the park, the same intuition that made him glance with mistrust at his trainer's flabby stubble-covered face as it bent heavily over his long stained fingers, dissipated any vision of the future. In a vague way he understood that his father was in trouble and that this was the reason why he himself had not been sent back to Clongowes. For some time he had felt the slight changes in his house; and these changes in what he had deemed unchangeable were so many slight shocks to his boyish conception of the world. The ambition which he felt astir at times in the darkness of his soul sought no outlet. A dusk like that of the outer world obscured his mind as he heard the mare's hoofs clattering along the tramtrack on the Rock Road and the great can swaying and rattling behind him. (64)

Stephen is depleted by his father's prodigality. His inner life mirrors the shabbiness of the outer world. Shame drives him inward, but he finds no refuge there; he has yet to make writing his sanctuary. On the level of the text, both trainer and track translate into symbols of

Ireland's paralysis; seen through Stephen's eyes, they become over-whelmingly particular, existing outside any poetic economy he can control.

Dumas comes to Stephen's aid; his Mercedes provides an outlet for the boy's inchoate desires, empowering him to dream of ideal intimacies:[12]

> He wanted to meet in the real world the unsubstantial image which his soul so constantly beheld. He did not know where to seek it or how; but a premonition which led him on told him that this image would, without any overt act of his, encounter him. They would meet quietly as if they had known each other and made their tryst, perhaps at one of the gates or in some more secret place. They would be alone, surrounded by darkness and silence: and in that moment of supreme tenderness he would be transfigured. He would fade into something impalpable under her eyes and then in a moment, he would be transfigured. Weakness and timidity and inexperience would fall from him in that magic moment. (65)

The seductive qualities of Mercedes are enhanced by the "squalor and insincerity" (67) that Stephen detects in his surroundings. Not only does she provide an occasion for imaginary wooing but she also encourages his narcissism and "savage indignation."

Mercedes is eventually joined by an entourage of indefinite shapes. The population of Stephen's inner world increases in proportion to society's demands upon him:

> While his mind had been pursuing its intangible phantoms and turn-ing in irresolution from such pursuit he had heard about him the constant voices of his father and of his masters, urging him to be a gentleman above all things and urging him to be a good catholic above all things. These voices had now come to be hollowsounding in his ears. When the gymnasium had been opened he had heard another voice urging him to be strong and manly and healthy and when the movement towards national revival had begun to be felt in the college yet another voice had bidden him be true to his country and help to raise up her fallen language and tradition. In the profane world, as he foresaw, a worldly voice would bid him raise up his father's fallen state by his labours and, meanwhile, the voice of his school comrades urged him to be a decent fellow, to shield others from blame or to beg them off and to do his best to get free days for the school. And it was the din of all these hollowsounding voices

that made him halt irresolutely in the pursuit of phantoms. He gave them ear only for a time but he was happy only when he was far from them, beyond their call, alone or in the company of phantasmal comrades. (83–84)

The constant voices of Stephen's masters are emptied of meaning by his father's failure. The hollow advice of his father is echoed in the hollow claims of church and state. Stephen's failure to answer is an act of defiance and an act of loyalty, a refusal to submit to authority and a refusal to usurp his father's vacant place. Silence also serves as a preventive against repeating his father's mistakes. His only happiness, namely escape, depends on ambivalence. Although the narrator's presentation of that ambivalence is ironic in this passage, it is also sympathetic, perhaps even conspiratorial; Stephen's strategy of rebellion and retreat is more than a mode of indulgence; it is an illustration of Wallace Stevens's definition of the life of the mind as a "violence from within that protects us from a violence without" ("Noble" 36).

Stephen does attempt to replace his father once, banking on the authority of a literary prize of thirty-three pounds. But the attempt is so literal that it is doomed from the start; his domestic reforms dissolve as soon as the money runs out:

> How foolish his aim had been! He had tried to build a breakwater of order and elegance against the sordid tide of life without him and to dam up, by rules of conduct and active interests and new filial relations, the powerful recurrence of the tides within him. Useless. From without as from within the water had flowed over his barriers; their tides began once more to jostle fiercely over the crumbled mole.
>
> He saw clearly too his own futile isolation. He had not gone one step nearer the lives he had sought to approach nor bridged the restless shame and rancour that divided him from mother and brother and sister. He felt that he was hardly of the one blood with them but stood to them rather in the mystical kinship of fosterage, fosterchild and fosterbrother. (98)

Stephen attempts to reenter his family by assuming the role of provider. But the wholesome system of exchange that he tries to establish is contaminated by custom, and its collapse is yet another warning of paralysis. Confronted by that sign, his new-found feelings of kinship evaporate.

He tries to square his accounts again later, this time drawing on Catholic funds.[13] Joyce parodies his efforts to become spiritually solvent:

> Every part of his day, divided by what he regarded now as the duties of his station in life, circled about its own centre of spiritual energy. His life seemed to have drawn near to eternity; every thought, word and deed, every instance of consciousness could be made to revibrate radiantly in heaven: and at times his sense of such immediate repercussion was so lively that he seemed to feel his soul in devotion pressing like fingers the keyboard of a great cash register and to see the amount of his purchase start forth immediately in heaven, not as a number but as a frail column of incense or as a slender flower. (148)

Given the terms established by the text, Stephen's efforts to see beyond estrangement are misguided; in *Portrait,* vision is a function of alienation. Lukács could use this fact to indict *Portrait* as a woefully modernist text; one of his chief complaints is that in modernist literature, "distortion becomes as inseparable a part of the portrayal of reality as the recourse to the pathological." Literature, according to Lukács, "must have a concept of the normal if it is to 'place' distortion correctly; that is to say, to see it *as* distortion" (*Meaning* 33). Although there is no "recourse to the pathological" in *Portrait,* there is solipsism, which produces distortion. The reader is made to see through the eyes of a character whose gaze is always turned inward, away from an intolerable world. But thanks to the narrator's mediation, *Portrait* does not provide sufficient ground for a related charge, namely that modernist novels abstract subjectivity from its objective context. Although our power of vision seems to be exactly equivalent to Stephen's, the external cause of his solipsism remains clearly visible. His habitual withdrawal from the world is conditioned by the social, political, and religious paralysis of Ireland. Joyce provides numerous examples of that paralysis: the church destroys Ireland's last hope by betraying Parnell, the Jesuits corrupt youths by teaching them to equate spiritual purity with sexual repression, the Irish nationalist movement enforces the parochial character of Irish life, and so forth. Even closer to home, the squandered gifts of Ireland are embodied in Stephen's father and the bleak prospects of Irish womanhood are evidenced by Stephen's mother. It could be argued that, nonetheless, when all is said and done, subjectivity takes precedence over objectivity in *Portrait*. But it cannot be denied that Joyce provides the reader with enough clues to solve the mystery of Stephen's alienation. The difference between Joyce and the realist or critical realist authors that Lukács admires is that the latter would insist on answering all the reader's questions for her.

To return to our discussion of the development of Stephen's solipsism, religion acts as a catalyst. Catholicism only inflames Stephen's desires, which are fueled by guilt. The New Testament comes to play the same part in his life as the Old Testament was said to have played in the lives of the pre-Christians: "When Law came, it was to multiply the opportunities of falling" (Romans 5:20). (The difference, of course, is that Stephen's salvation lies in poetic license.) Guilt sharpens his self-consciousness long before he turns to Imagination. His eventual escape from guilt to solipsism is simplified by the doctrine of original sin. That doctrine represents fallen man as an endless abyss of depravity, possessing a negative sublimity of his own. This godless infinity has its secular corollary in the infinite regress of solipsism.

On the other hand, the doctrine of original sin measures the finitude of the subject against a divine standard, thereby ruling out the individualistic premise upon which solipsism depends. Nonetheless, for a time Stephen manages to combine Catholicism and solipsism. Catholicism itself is partly to blame for his introversion. Ritual fails to bring him closer to others because he uses it only to aestheticize his faith. His duplicity comes to an end when he breaks away from the Jesuits. Then at last he is able to confess to himself that he is far too unworldly in his own secular way to join an ascetic community: "To merge his life in the common tide of other lives was harder for him than any fasting or prayer, and it was his constant failure to do this to his own satisfaction which caused in his soul at last a sensation of spiritual dryness together with a growth of doubts and scruples" (151–52).

After his fall from Catholic grace, he also recognizes the aestheticism of his devotion. (The intricate system of mortifications he devises for himself earlier, for example, is as refined as the symbolist experiments of Des Esseintes in Huysman's *Against Nature*.) In the following passage, Stephen, after encountering a "squad of Christian brothers," acknowledges the sensuous nature of his religiosity and his failure to achieve true humility:

> Their piety would be like their names, like their faces, like their clothes, and it was idle for him to tell himself that their humble and contrite hearts, it might be, paid a far richer tribute of devotion than his had ever been, a gift tenfold more acceptable than his elaborate adoration. It was idle for him to move himself to be generous towards them, to tell himself that if he ever came to their gates, stripped of his pride, beaten and in beggar's weeds, that they would be generous towards him, loving him as themselves. Idle and embittering, finally, to argue, against his own dispassionate certitude, that the commandment of love bade us not to love our neighbour as ourselves with the same amount and intensity of love but to love him as ourselves with the same kind of love. (166)

Catholicism treats alienation as a spiritual disease contracted through original sin; art exploits alienation as a means of achieving aesthetic distance. Stephen turns away from the idea of religion to embrace the idea of art. Catholicism, however, is still part of the air he breathes. Although his fall into aestheticism is a happy one, he envisions it as a fall nonetheless. He analyzes the pleasures that come with it after the Christian brothers have passed:

> He drew forth a phrase from his treasure and spoke it softly to himself:
> —A day of dappled seaborne clouds.
> The phrase and the day and the scene harmonized in a chord. Words. Was it their colours? He allowed them to glow and fade, hue after hue: sunrise gold, the russet and green of apple orchards, azure of waves, the greyfringed fleece of clouds. No, it was not their colours: it was the poise and balance of the period itself. Did he then love the rhythmic rise and fall of words better than their associations of legend and colour? Or was it that, being as weak of sight as he was shy of mind, he drew less pleasure from the reflection of the glowing sensible world through the prism of a language manycoloured and richly storied than from the contemplation of an inner world of individual emotions mirrored perfectly in a lucid supple periodic prose? (166)

The question that Stephen asks himself is simply this: Is he drawn to language as a means of literary self-representation or as a means of representing the world? The question itself arises from the competing claims of self and world or subject and object. The antinomies of charity versus solipsism and humility versus "elaborate adoration" are versions of the same opposition. To devote oneself to mirroring the world is to submit to it in some sense; to devote oneself to reprojecting the inner world at the expense of the outer one is an act of defiance. Although the two alternatives point to different poetics, it seems futile to try to draw an absolute distinction between them. Clearly, effective reprojection depends on some measure of objectivity and the sensible world quickly becomes lifeless and drab without an infusion of "individual emotions." The only way of fully addressing this question for Stephen would be to produce a work of art.

Portrait, however, is the story of the gestation of an artist, not the story of the conception of a work of art. One of the ironies of this story is that although solipsism leads Stephen away from religion, certain Christian virtues (i.e., charity, humility) are strengthened by his decision to become an artist. The most striking instance occurs just after he has decided to give up his religious vocation. Upon returning home, he is assailed by "the faint sour stink of rotted cabbages," and he smiles to think that it is this "disorder, the misrule and confusion of his father's house" which is "to win the day in his soul" (162). Once inside, he discovers that financial misrule has destroyed his father's claims upon his house and that his father and mother have gone to look for another transient abode. His dispossessed brothers and sisters pass the time by singing a song about lost youth:

> The voice of his younger brother from the farthest side of the fireplace began to sing the air *Oft in the Stilly Night.* One by one the others took up the air until a full choir of voices was singing. They would sing so for hours, melody after melody, glee after glee, till the last pale light died down on the horizon, till the first dark nightclouds came forth and night fell.
>
> He waited for some moments, listening, before he too took up the air with them. He was listening with pain of spirit to the overtone of weariness behind their frail fresh innocent voices. Even before they set out on life's journey they seemed weary already of the way.
>
> He heard the choir of voices in the kitchen echoed and multiplied through an endless reverberation of the choirs of endless generations

of children: and heard in all the echoes an echo also of the recurring
note of weariness and pain. All seemed weary of life even before
entering upon it. And he remembered that Newman had heard this
note also in the broken lines of Virgil *giving utterance, like the voice of
Nature herself, to that pain and weariness yet hope of better things which
had been the experience of her children in every time.* (163–64)

The secular choir in which Stephen now sings is composed of
foundlings stranded in their father's derelict house. By turning away
from Catholicism, he severs the cord that ties him to his mother;
cast out into the world, he sees his own vulnerability reflected in
the faces of his brothers and sisters. The sacrifices that they have
made for him are surpassed only by those of his mother, a debt
that Stephen came so close to repaying. Disenchantment and vulnerability bind him to his siblings; suddenly he is no longer a foster
brother because he sees that all of them are foundlings, weary before setting out on life's journey. By dedicating himself to art, a
vocation that sanctions solipsism, Stephen is able to see *Geworfen-
heit* as a condition that he shares with those around him. And in
that moment, he becomes far more capable of charity and humility
than he was before.

This epiphany, which illuminates the sufferings and hopes of
others, passes away like all the rest. Charity does not abolish solipsism; moments of pure solipsism, unadulterated by compassion,
follow in its wake. Stephen, after all, feels compelled to close himself
to the world because he is afraid of being contaminated by it:

> The lane behind the terrace was waterlogged and as he went down
> it slowly, choosing his steps amid heaps of wet rubbish, he heard a
> mad nun screeching in the nuns' madhouse beyond the wall.
> —Jesus! O Jesus! Jesus!
> He shook the sound out of his ears by an angry toss of his head
> and hurried on, stumbling through the mouldering offal, his heart
> already bitten by an ache of loathing and bitterness. His father's
> whistle, his mother's mutterings, the screech of an unseen maniac
> were to him now so many voices offending and threatening to
> humble the pride of his youth. He drove their echoes even out of
> his heart with an execration: but as he walked down the avenue and
> felt the grey morning light falling about him through the dripping
> leaves and smelt the strange wild smell of the wet leaves and bark,
> his soul was loosed of her miseries. (175–76)

But if solipsism sometimes protects Stephen against contagious miseries, it can also poison his sensibility. His defensive cultivation of cosmopolitan tastes often results in preciosity:

> The rainladen trees of the avenue evoked in him, as always, memories of the girls and women in the plays of Gerhart Hauptmann; and the memory of their pale sorrows and the fragrance falling from the wet branches mingled in a mood of quiet joy. His morning walk across the city had begun, and he foreknew that as he passed the sloblands of Fairview he would think of the cloistral silverveined prose of Newman, that as he walked along North Strand Road, glancing idly at the windows of the provision shops, he would recall the dark humour of Guido Cavalcanti and smile, that as he went by Baird's stonecutting works in Talbot Place the spirit of Ibsen would blow through him like a keen wind, a spirit of wayward boyish beauty, and that passing a grimy marinedealer's shop beyond the Liffey he would repeat the song by Ben Jonson which begins:
>
> *I was not wearier where I lay.*
>
> His mind, when wearied of its search for the essence of beauty amid the spectral words of Aristotle or Aquinas, turned often for its pleasure to the dainty songs of the Elizabethans. His mind, in the vesture of a doubting monk, stood often in shadow under the windows of that age, to hear the grave and mocking music of the lutenists or the frank laughter of waistcoateers until a laugh too low, a phrase, tarnished by time, of chambering and false honour, stung his monkish pride and drove him on from his lurkingplace. (176)

Stephen once derived aesthetic pleasure from Catholicism; now he uses his gifts to adorn the streets of Dublin. In both cases, his vision is restricted; both the character of Catholicism and the character of Dublin are blurred in the course of their appropriation. Just as aestheticism obstructed his aspiration to God, literary preciosity blocks his entry into the world, impeding the development of his art.

Stephen's aestheticism protects him against "the violence of reality"; his avoidance of intimacy with others is the emotional equivalent of that perceptual resistance. He cultivates Cranly, for example, as a secular confessor, not as a friend; Cranly, according to Stephen, has "the face of a guilty priest" who "hears the confessions of those [whom he has no] power to absolve" (178). Yet Cranly's vulnerability disturbs him. He is disturbed by the passivity that is indistinguishable from his companion's sympathy as a fallen confessor; the "dark womanish eyes" (178) of Cranly reflect his ability to "feel the sufferings of women, the weakness of their bodies and souls" and to "shield them with a strong resolute arm and bow his mind to them" (245). In short, his judgment of Cranly is confused; he is at once drawn to the "female" qualities that allow him to suffer passion and repelled by what he takes to be a sign of effeminacy. Stephen's ambivalence issues from his fear of the Other.

Although art releases Stephen from the Catholic jurisdiction of his mother, he continues to cling to her; his Mariolatry is an oblique expression of fidelity. Instead of embracing the Other, he transforms the Virgin into a poet's muse. Mariolatry in this sense is a mark of adolescence; idealization is a way of retaining one's virginity even in love. It is fitting that it is Stephen's mother who comments on his emotional underdevelopment at the end of the book, reaffirming her authority with respect to the process of gestation: "26 April: Mother is putting my new secondhand clothes in order. She prays now, she says, that I may learn in my own life and away from home and friends what the heart is and what it feels. Amen. So be it. Welcome, O life! I go to encounter for the millionth time the reality of experience and to forge in the smithy of my soul the uncreated conscience of my race" (252–53). As this passage reflects, Stephen is a very young man. His solipsism is a measure of his immaturity. Joyce does not celebrate solipsism as the epistemic equivalent of autonomous art; on the contrary, he makes Stephen share the last word with his mother to stress the importance of her son's attainment of an autonomy that can encompass mature love.

Self-consciousness per se does not result in solipsism; solipsism arises when self-consciousness becomes an end-in-itself. Stephen could cure himself of solipsism by adopting reflexivity as a strategy for making art. At the close of *Portrait* only one obstacle stands in the way. By mythologizing the artist, he runs the risk of postponing the practice of his art. His new fetish is a remnant of the old religion. Religious authority provokes the most significant negation in *Portrait;* God is replaced by imagination and confession is raised to the level of art. (Cranly, Stephen's compromised confessor, represents an intermediary stage between religion and art; although Stephen has not yet passed beyond that stage at the close of *Por-*

trait, this is precisely the journey that the narrative anticipates.) But is religious authority repudiated only to be reaffirmed in a religion of art? By fetishizing art, Stephen indulges in the very romanticism he was determined to overcome. If this is the case, then the mature artist prefigured in *Portrait* will clearly *not* be a proponent of what Eugene Lunn describes as "aggressive modernism."

The fact that Stephen mythologizes his new-found vocation is undeniable. But is this to say that Joyce does the same? Is *Portrait* simply an attempt to reconstruct his own initiation into the sacred rites of art or does it imply a critique of pure aestheticism? In order to answer this question, let us return to Stephen's conception of art.

Unlike Joyce, Stephen has not entirely given up the idea that art has the power to transform physical objects into holy things or mundane events into immutable revelations. On the level of aesthetics, Walter Benjamin will serve as a foil to Stephen. According to Benjamin, the true heir of the age of mechanical reproduction desires "to pry [the] object from its shell, to destroy its aura" ("Work" 223); Stephen prefers to keep his contemplative distance. When he does appropriate some part of his surroundings, it is to refine it and thereby confirm the uniqueness, rather than the reproducibility, of his experience.

Pure art is Stephen's consolation for the death of God. The creator should be as pure as his creation; that is to say, his work should be nothing less than the ideal sublimation of his voice. Art has no purpose beyond the attainment of beauty, and beauty, as Aquinas said, is wholeness and harmony and radiance. The subjective corollary of radiance is contemplation: "The instant wherein that supreme quality of beauty, the clear radiance of the esthetic image, is apprehended luminously by the mind which has been arrested by its wholeness and fascinated by its harmony is the luminous silent stasis of esthetic pleasure, a spiritual state very like to that cardiac condition which the Italian physiologist Luigi Galvani . . . called the enchantment of the heart" (*Portrait* 213). According to Benjamin, distraction is the modern mode of aesthetic apprehension. Nothing could be farther from his theory than Stephen's notion of the stasis induced by beauty. Benjamin heralds an art of shocks and adaptations; Stephen believes that true aesthetic experience depends on apprehending the formal integrity of the work of art.[14]

As the foetus episode illustrates. Stephen is not sentimental regarding his origins; on the contrary, he knows that the past has the power to stunt his growth. By claiming the "fabulous artificer of old" as his precursor, he uses the myth of the artist to protect him from the crippling power of the past and the squalor of modern life. Joyce indulges his whim all too kindly, using a subplot of motifs to insinuate that Stephen is not the reincarnation of Dedalus but rather the incarnation of his son. Thus watery images of gestation engender an imagination that sees itself reflected in the birdlike figure of a sensual Beatrice, an imagination poised for flight in the final pages. The myth of overreaching that Stephen unwittingly chooses ensures that the reader will not make the mistake of accepting his mythological claims at face value.

A young artist ignores historical limitations at his own peril; the mature artist takes up the burden of his own times. Stephen has not yet come of age. Thus he says to Lynch in the course of expounding his aesthetic theories, "When we come to the phenomena of artistic conception, artistic gestation and artistic reproduction I require a new terminology and a new personal experience" (209). Joyce supplies that new experience in *Portrait;* that is to say, new experience provides him with sufficient hindsight to create Stephen.

Joyce also invents a poetic terminology. Like the symbolists, he treats words as "objects in their own right" (Lunn 45). Words are not vehicles of transcendent meaning but volatile elements that comprise Stephen's inner life. Stephen's acquisition of a reflexive vocabulary is dramatized by the polyphonic structure of the text. Within this text, solipsism is the chrysallis from which a fully formed subject has yet to emerge. Solipsism itself is preceded by religious interiority, a phase that Stephen at once negates and preserves in his aspiration to become a "priest of imagination." But Joyce subverts that hypothetical priest by sacrificing the authorial unity of his own voice to the mutability of his character.

The polyphonic narrative of *Portrait* is unified by the metaphor of gestation. Joyce subordinates the myth of the artist to the myth of nature in *Portrait,* allowing the latter to order his text. Although he affirms the myth of nature again in *Ulysses,* he does not allow it to generate the kind of continuous narrative that Roland Barthes refers to as "the Book" (*Critical* 171). In *Portrait,* Stephen's mother is granted the authority to pronounce that his gestation is incomplete; in *Ulysses,* the myth of nature, embodied in Molly, is allowed to speak at greater length, becoming one voice among many, a voice that is tremendously forceful without being absolute.

Notes

1. Joyce used Stephen Daedalus as his pen name when he published "The Sisters" in *Irish Homestead* in 1904.

2. Joyce's comment to Frank Budgen regarding Stephen Dedalus as he appears in "Proteus" is well known: "I haven't let the young man off very lightly, have I? Many writers have written about themselves. I wonder if any of them has been as candid as I have?" (Budgen 51).

3. Thus, for example, Vicki Mahaffey argues that Stephen's understanding of authority is dangerously, perhaps fatally, monolithic: "What Stephen lacks is not an awareness of his own contradictory nature, but an acceptance of it. . . . What he fails to understand is the double-nature of authority, an awareness that would make him an 'artist' as well as a portrayed subject, an acceptance of the fact that, in the words of Jeremy Lane, there is 'no final authorization, no simple authority, no single author; but a relative authorization, the sanction of relation whose dual principle seeds plurality admitting and containing its contrary'" (102).

David Robinson maintains that Stephen's "flawed, fatalistic belief" in the necessary connection between names and their referents may be his downfall, noting that, by the close of *Portrait*, "It remains unclear whether [Stephen's] skill at manipulating words is sufficient to outweigh his manifest manipulation by them" (334).

R. B. Kershner argues that Stephen's artistic commitment to the Romantic concept of "an authentic and vital soul which, like God, creates *ex nihilo*" makes it "difficult and painful" for him to fully acknowledge the fact that "his mind is an amalgam of preexisting texts" (165).

David Hayman, in his excellent article "The Joycean Inset," describes the way in which insets, or interpolated passages written in a comparatively conventional manner, serve to distance readers from the very conventions that threaten to defeat Stephen: "These insets, drawing their power from our habits of reading, tease this new novel into older molds which they then twist out of shape, altering both their sources and the narrative method of the master-text which in its turn deconstructs the traditional *Bildungsroman*, being the tale not of an adjustment but of an uneasiness confirmed. *A Portrait* in part is the account of Stephen's positioning in society, but it also shows his failure to recognize his position, his potential for loss of potential. Within this context of contradictions, the insets or windows out/in are always mirrors (or even opacities), conventions self-consciously aping themselves. They are proofs of the textness of the text which occur at moments that seem most apt to expose the reader to 'reality' in the shape of distancing otherness" (149). Presumably, if Stephen could "see through" the windows provided by the insets, he would be able to understand his own position more clearly.

4. It is often said that the language of *Finnegans Wake* becomes most accessible when it is read aloud by a native Irish speaker. If it is granted that the cadences of *Finnegans Wake* are Irish, then Joyce is, in effect, subordinating the babel of his dream-book to his mother tongue, an idiosyncratic if not bizarre solution to Stephen's problem.

5. For a valuable discussion of Stephen's vexed response to his linguistic plight in *Portrait* and *Ulysses,* see Macdonald "Strength." Macdonald notes that while Stephen's linguistic displacement conforms to what poststructuralists would describe as a universal condition, Joyce's rendering of that displacement in *Portrait* is not attended by Derridean exuberance but "tempered . . . with a great deal of sadness" (n17).

6. Joyce's solution to this dilemma is well known. Although he distanced himself from Dublin, he never lost touch with it, plying relatives and friends with letters filled with the most detailed questions. Not even the imminent death of his father could bring him back to Dublin, and his father's last message to Joyce was an answer to one of his son's queries. Upon his father's death, Joyce wrote T. S. Eliot, "[My father] had an intense love for me and it adds anew to my grief and remorse that I did not go to Dublin to see him for so many years. I kept him constantly under the illusion that I would come and was always in correspondence with him but an instinct which I believed in held me back from going, much as I longed to." Although Joyce said to Pound that it was the power of his enemies that kept him from going back to Dublin, he told Philippe Soupault that going back to Dublin would prevent him from writing about it (Ellmann, *James Joyce* 643–45).

7. For a Marxist interpretation of Stephen's alienation, see Williams.

8. Mahaffey notes the irony inherent in Stephen's closing invocation of the paternal authority of the fabulous artificer: "Ironically, the book ends with Stephen asking his father, and author, to direct him by his precedent: 'Old father, old artificer, stand me now and ever in good stead.' Stephen is recording his hope that his father will continue to do what he was doing when the book opened, authoring and authorizing the story of Stephen's youth" (103). My own sense is that, at the close of *Portrait,* Stephen is not praying to a divinity but projecting a supreme fiction, and that by doing so, he is making a movement toward fathering himself.

Robinson treats Stephen's closing invocation of Daedalus as the completion of his revolt against his literal origins. According to Robinson, the ultimate success of that revolt will depend on Stephen's ability to comprehend the fact that there is no necessary relationship between words and their referents (334). Given the fact that Joyce grants Stephen the unusual privilege of consciously reflecting on the mythological meaning of his own name, Robinson's suggestion that Stephen is in danger of lapsing into a literal-minded relationship to his mythic origins is baffling.

9. For a valuable discussion of the origins of Stephen's visionary dream of Parnell, see O'Grady.

10. For a provocative discussion of Stephen's recourse to the Virgin as a means of protecting himself against the paternal authority of the church, see Restuccia 169.

11. For extensive considerations of Joyce and the problem of authority, see Mahaffey and Rabaté's *James Joyce*.

12. For a detailed discussion of Joyce's use of *The Count of Monte Cristo* in *A Portrait of the Artist as a Young Man,* see Kershner 195–209.

13. As Mahaffey points out, the priest who warns Stephen against the spiritual consequences of frequenting prostitutes by saying "As long as you commit that sin, my poor child, you will not be worth more than one farthing to God" (54) is the inspiration behind the image of a sublime cash register that occurs a few pages later. Taken together, these images point back to the theme of simony, understood as a confounding of material and spiritual values, that runs through *Dubliners*.

14. Mahaffey makes the following comments on the difference between paralysis and epiphany: "Stephen employs 'stasis' in a way that connotes rest or equilibrium, but stasis is also 'stagnation'; in *Dubliners,* the most operative meaning of 'paralysis' is 'loss of the ability to move; a state of powerlessness or incapacity to act,' yet 'paralysis' comes from the Greek *paralyein,* meaning to loosen. Both 'paralysis' and 'stasis' are paradoxically double words, and Joyce uses them, in *Dubliners* and *Portrait,* to balance one another. Stasis—which replaces the more reverent term 'epiphany' that Joyce uses to mark the moment of revelation in *Stephen Hero*—is the counterpart and opposite of paralysis, producing a different but similar effect but of different duration, its accent more liberating than deadening. Joyce presents esthetic stasis as a momentary apprehension and acceptance of contradiction rather than a battle against it, a battle that eventually reveals its opponent to be the ineluctably divided self" (*Reauthorizing Joyce* 69). I would argue that Stephen's youthfulness manifests itself as a limited ability to "accept contradiction," and that his youthfulness is still very apparent at the close of *A Portrait.* Stephen's definition of epiphany, accordingly, emphasizes harmony and not contradiction, balance and not tension.

3

Interchapter

In *Portrait,* Joyce dramatizes the slow birth of artistic subjectivity, using polyphony as a means toward this end. In *Ulysses,* polyphony takes on a life of its own, triggering an explosion of narrative possibilities. Both *Portrait* and *Ulysses* are animated by a desire for emancipation, but that desire manifests itself in different ways. In *Portrait,* the struggle toward emancipation is a central theme; in *Ulysses,* that struggle is carried out in the movement from sentence to sentence and in the leap from episode to episode. Joyce's radical reinterpretation of the challenge of narration in *Ulysses* presupposes the fact of literary decadence; the experiment of *Ulysses* depends on the exhaustion of nineteenth-century narrative norms.

By capitalizing on literary decadence, Joyce reinvents the possibility of artistic emancipation. Stephen's satanic *non serviam* dictates the form of Joyce's epic; not only does each episode cut itself loose from nineteenth-century narration but it also cuts itself loose from the narrative norm established by the episode that comes before. When Eliot remarked that in *Ulysses* Joyce had exposed the futility of all English styles (Woolf 49), he was acknowledging the victory of Joyce's odyssean narrator, a narrator who practices his own form of "silence, exile and cunning," tirelessly evading the tyranny of the past.

Joyce's sense of the heroic character of his own undertaking is reflected in the following letter to Harriet Shaw Weaver: "I understand that you may begin to regard the various styles of the episodes with dismay and prefer the initial style as much as the wanderer did who longed for the rock of Ithaca. But in the compass of one day to compress all these wanderings and clothe them in the form of this day is for me only possible by such variation which, I beg you to believe, is not capricious" (*Letters*, ed. Gilbert, 129). If the reader of *Ulysses* is asked to brave perils, Joyce demands no less of himself. In the first six episodes of *Ulysses*, he articulates the inner worlds of Stephen and Bloom, providing each character with a semiprivate language of his own. In the episodes that follow, he undertakes a variation of styles that results in the transliteration, fragmentation, or subsumption of those languages.

The initial style of *Ulysses* is an outgrowth of the style of *Portrait;* once again, Joyce strips away the detachment of the third-person narrator, cultivating a symbiotic relationship of narrator and narrated. With "Aeolus," mimesis frees itself from the consciousness of any one character; from this point on, innumerable languages infiltrate Joyce's epic, anticipating the "dividual chaos" (186) of *Finnegans Wake.*

Formally speaking, what sets *Ulysses* apart from *Portrait* and *Dubliners* is its endless questioning of narrative conventions, its insistence on overturning all rules, and its commitment to destabilizing the relationship between narrator, character, and reader. By destabilizing these relations, Joyce makes us all the more conscious of narrative process, raising aesthetic self-consciousness to a new level. By giving us an inventory of styles, Joyce relativizes style, dramatizing his own aesthetic choices. By allowing one style to cancel another out, he lays bare the endless process of creation and destruction that produces a living work of art.

Although *Ulysses* calls attention to its own narrative process from the beginning, reflexivity reaches unprecedented extremes in "Circe" and "Oxen of the Sun." In the chapters that follow, I will examine these two episodes in depth, closing my consideration of *Ulysses* with a discussion of "Penelope," an episode that gives the reader the illusion of returning to solid ground. Before turning to these three episodes, I will retrace the progression of styles found in *Ulysses* as a whole. I will not attempt to be exhaustive here, but rather to provide a context for the in-depth analyses that follow.

"Telemachus," "Nestor," "Proteus"

The initial style of *Ulysses* doesn't make strenuous demands on the reader. As in *Portrait*, the narrator is on close terms with Stephen Dedalus, and the reader reaps the rewards of their intimacy. The

opening episodes of *Ulysses* are comparatively docile, obediently reproducing the activity of a fictional mind; however, in the course
of moving from "Telemachus" to "Proteus," that mind becomes in-
creasingly taken up with its own workings, preparing the way for
the reflexivity to come, a reflexivity that will eventually lead to a
disclosure of the circular nature of fiction making itself.

But what does reflexivity have to do with artistic emancipation?
the reader may ask. A comparison of *Portrait* and *Ulysses* is instruc-
tive here. In *Portrait*, Stephen struggles against the gravitational
pull of a seemingly universal condition of social and spiritual decay;
in *Ulysses,* the burden of that struggle is shifted to the narrative.
Stephen's vision of autonomy is replaced by the reality of a relentlessly self-interrogating text, a text that dramatizes the process
whereby it weaves and unweaves its own meaning. How does Joyce
extricate himself from the nets of narrative convention? By mount-
ing an attack on readerly expectations in the form of his "usylessly
unreadable Blue Book of Eccles" (*Finnegans Wake* 179).

Obviously, expectations must be established before they can be
overturned, and this is one of the functions of "Telemachus," but
even here, there are hints of the reversals to come. As critics have
often pointed out, "Telemachus" contains an overabundance of adverbs and adjectives. Some readers have interpreted that overabundance as a calculated extravagance that serves to underscore the
youthfulness of the narrative (Lawrence 45). Other readers have interpreted the descriptive lushness of "Telemachus" as an instance of
the commingling of teller and tale that occurs throughout *Ulysses*
(Riquelme 156). Still others have interpreted it as a case of stylistic contagion, evidence of Buck Mulligan's usurpation of the scene
(Benstock, *Narrative* 22). The fact that the adjectives and adverbs
of "Telemachus" have drawn so much critical attention proves that
even here, Joyce is adopting a highly self-conscious style, a style
that forces the reader to approach it as an object of interpretation
in its own right.

"Nestor" forms a perfect bridge between "Telemachus" and "Proteus," drawing the reader more completely into the theater of
Stephen's mind. As schoolteacher and wage-slave, Stephen is made
to perform before audiences that are either too naive or too narrow-
minded to understand his words. While Stephen suffers under the
uncomprehending scrutiny of Mr. Deasy and the schoolboys, we

are made to understand that Stephen's vision is painfully acute, a disparity that contributes to our sense of being able to see through his eyes. Without breaking with the style of "Telemachus," Joyce makes the reader feel that she knows Stephen from the inside.

Of the three episodes of Joyce's Telemachiad, "Proteus" comes closest to fusing narrator and narrated. At times, the identity of the narrator seems to dissolve into the identity of Stephen, and Stephen, in turn, gives himself over to a protean reflection on the workings of his own mind. As a modern-day Telemachus, Stephen is subject to the whims of his creator, but when that creator speaks, he uses a sympathetic narrator as his medium, thereby relativizing his voice. Although we haven't left the theater of Stephen's mind, we are made to see that that theater is made of words and that the meaning of those words is fluid, contingent, and ever-changing. The reflexivity of "Proteus" is not as thoroughgoing as the reflexivity of episodes to come; nonetheless, it anticipates the doubling over of the narrative that occurs in the climactic sections of *Ulysses*.

"Calypso"

The opening of "Calypso" restores our sense of the separateness of narrator and narrated: "Mr Leopold Bloom ate with relish the inner organs of beasts and fowls. He liked thick giblet soup, nutty gizzards, a stuffed roast heart, liverslices fried with crustcrumbs, fried hencod's roes. Most of all he liked grilled mutton kidneys which gave to his palate a fine tang of faintly scented urine" (45). The amused tone of these sentences has something in common with the opening of "Telemachus": "Stately, plump Buck Mulligan came from the stairhead, bearing a bowl of lather on which a mirror and a razor lay crossed. A yellow dressinggown, ungirdled, was sustained gently behind him on the mild morning air" (3). Although these openings emphasize very different qualities (Bloom is identified by his appetites; Mulligan is identified by his irreverent contribution to the "universal language" of gesture), both episodes begin with a slightly mocking evocation of character. Joyce takes pains to establish an initial separation of narrator and narrated, only to violate that separation in the pages that follow.

The fact that Joyce uses the same narrative strategy in "Telemachus" and "Calypso" is significant; it serves as a reminder that the first two triads of *Ulysses* are mirror images of each other. In both triads, the narrator infiltrates the first person in stages, not only "alternating between the mimesis of scene and action in the third person and the mimesis of consciousness in the first person" but mixing first- and third-person perspectives (Riquelme 156). Interestingly enough, the shift from Stephen to Bloom disguises the fact that Joyce is repeating certain narrative choices; the reader may not even notice that he is on familiar ground. But although the first six episodes may unsettle the reader, "Aeolus" marks the real beginning of our exile. For the first time in *Ulysses,* character development becomes a matter of secondary importance and other agendas begin to dictate our wanderings.

"Aeolus"

"Aeolus" is designed to shock, as is evidenced by the history of its composition. The version that first appeared in the *Little Review* in 1918 was comparatively genteel, lacking headlines and rhetorical tropes. These were added in 1921, producing a radical departure from preceding episodes. The rhetorical figures scattered throughout the episode comprise an inventory of stylistic resources, displaying the technology of narration. The headlines stand out as discrete units of authorial will, dramatizing the mechanical reproduction of meaning. Both devices deconstruct the narrative, making it impossible to take the narrator for granted.

The style and action of "Aeolus" draw attention to the fact that meaning is a manufactured thing. Thus Bloom supervises the production of an ad:

> HOUSE OF KEY(E)S
>
> —Like that, see. Two crossed keys here. A circle. Then here the name. Alexander Keyes, tea, wine and spirit merchant. So on.
>
> Better not teach him his own business.
>
> —You know yourself, councillor, just what he wants. Then round the top in leaded: the house of keys. You see? Do you think that's a good idea?
>
> The foreman moved his scratching hand to his lower ribs and scratched there quietly.
>
> —The idea, Mr Bloom said, is the house of keys. You know, councillor, the Manx parliament. Innuendo of home rule. Tourists, you

know, from the isle of Man. Catches the eye, you see. Can you
do that?
   I could ask him perhaps about how to pronounce that *voglio*. But
then if he didn't know only make it awkward for him. Better not.
—We can do that, the foreman said. (99–100)

Meaning is not discovered but invented; divine order gives way to
Nannetti and his scissors. Meaning is a commodity; accordingly, it
is never above suspicion. Bloom's ad, for example, is a piece of subliminal advertising. His strategy is to manipulate his audience by
arousing their desire for freedom. The House of Keys is the name for
the twenty-four-member elective branch of the Isle of Man, which
has been under the British Crown without being subject to British
Rule since the 1820s. Bloom is bargaining on his readership's envy
of the Isle of Man. The Manx Parliament also evokes Mananaan
MacLir, founder of the Manx nation, a necromancer who could
enfold himself in mist.[1] Nannetti is linked to Mananaan in the preceding section by Bloom's play on his name: "He doesn't hear it.
Nanaan. Iron nerves" (99). Nannetti is a modern-day necromancer,
versed in the profitable obscurantism of advertising. And Bloom is
implicated in the production of persuasive illusions, subject to the
winds of rhetoric for better or worse:

A STREET CORTÉGE

   Both smiled over the crossblind at the file of capering newsboys in
Mr Bloom's wake, the last zigzagging white on the breeze a mocking
kite, a tail of white bowknots.
—Look at the young guttersnipe behind him hue and cry, Lenehan
said, and you'll kick. O, my rib risible! Taking off his flat spaugs and
the walk. Small nines. Steal upon larks. (107)

"Aeolus" links the language of advertising to the ancient art of
rhetoric. The three forms of oratory, namely, expository, forensic,
and deliberative, are represented by passages taken from Dawson,
Bushe, and Taylor. Each successive passage reaches farther back into
the past to achieve its victory. We move from Dawson's embellish-
ment of Ireland's natural beauties to Bushe's invocation of Michelangelo's Moses to Taylor's invocation of the living Moses, "bearing
in his arms the tables of the Law." Meanwhile, the titles advance
from a comparatively high style to a distinctly low style, echoing the
forward march of journalistic fashion. Just as the later titles deflate

those that precede them, Stephen's parable of the plums punctures
the three examples of oratory. Dawson's pastoral is replaced by "two
frisky frumps" spitting plum pits through the railings of Nelson's
pillar, Michelangelo's Moses is supplanted by the "onehandled adul-
terer" (121), and the vision of the promised land dwindles into a
bird's-eye view of "dear dirty Dublin."

Classical rhetoric and the language of advertising are presented as
components of a single technology in "Aeolus"; deflation is a means
of controlling that technology when it gets out of hand. The danger
of losing control is alluded to repeatedly in the text. Thus Bloom
associates the workings of the press with bodily decomposition:

> WITH UNFEIGNED REGRET IT IS WE
> ANNOUNCE THE DISSOLUTION OF A MOST
> RESPECTED DUBLIN BURGESS
>
> This morning the remains of the late Mr Patrick Dignam. Ma-
> chines. Smash a man to atoms if they got him caught. Rule the world
> today. His machineries are pegging away too. Like these, got out of
> hand: fermenting. Working away, tearing away. And that old grey
> rat tearing to get in. (98)

In the next section, he reflects on the necessity for constant vigi-
lance over the machinery of the press: "The machines clanked in
threefour time. Thump, thump, thump. Now if he got paralyzed
there and no one knew how to stop them they'd clank on and on
the same, print it over and over and up and back. Monkeydoodle
the whole thing. Want a cool head" (98).

Joyce fosters Odyssean adaptability in the reader by providing her
with an inventory of rhetorical tropes and oratorical forms within
a deflationary narrative. The effect of this preparation is to strip her
of her passivity; after "Aeolus," she cannot be innocent again.

"Lestrygonians"

With "Lestrygonians," we return to something resembling the initial style. However, the balance between first-person narration and
third-person narration that is struck in the opening episodes of
Ulysses is not maintained here. From the outset, Bloom tips the
scale: "Pineapple rock, lemon platt, butter scotch. A sugarsticky
girl shovelling scoopfuls of creams for a christian brother. Some

school treat. Bad for their tummies. Lozenge and comfit manu-
facturer to His Majesty the King. God. Save. Our. Sitting on his
throne sucking red jujubes white" (124). In the pages that follow, third-person narration is typically confined to the openings
of paragraphs, often signaling Bloom's physical location (i.e., "His
slow feet walked him riverward, reading." "From Butler's monu-
ment house corner he glanced along Bachelor's walk." "As he set
foot on O'Connell Bridge a puffball of smoke plumped up from
the parapet." "He walked along the parapet." and so forth). While
the third-person narrator guides us through the streets of Dublin,
Bloom thinks of higher (and lower) things. Joyce exploits the objectivity of the third-person narrator but limits his access to Bloom's
inner life, multiplying opportunities for interior monologue.

Why does Joyce revert to interior monologue, a crucial element
of the initial style, in "Lestrygonians"? In "Aeolus," meaning is
manufactured before our eyes; in "Lestrygonians," we return to the
spectacle of Bloom wending his way through the city, and we are
able to overhear his thoughts with a minimum of distraction. Peri-
stalsis, the technique of the episode, replaces the Aeolian machinery of the press: the problem of public dissemination becomes less
pressing than the problem of private consumption, a matter that
lends itself to interior monologue. But even though Joyce focuses
on the internal processes of Bloom, he doesn't let the reader forget
that Bloom himself is passing through the body of a larger organism
and that interiority and exteriority are relative terms. Thus, while
Bloom feeds on the sights, sounds, and smells of the city, Dublin
is quietly "digesting" Bloom. The conversation about Bloom that
takes place toward the close of "Lestrygonians" underscores the fact
that, at any given point, Bloom is at once consumer and consumed.

"Scylla and Charybdis"

In "Scylla and Charybdis," Stephen asserts that all experience is circular and that fiction making, a reenactment of experience, is, by
the same token, reflexive: "As we, or mother Dana, weave and unweave our bodies . . . from day to day, their molecules shuttled
to and fro, so does the artist weave and unweave his image. And
as the mole on my right breast is where it was when I was born,
though all my body has been woven of new stuff from time to

time, so through the ghost of the unquiet father the image of
the unliving son looks forth" (159–60). In Stephen's view, experience is the ground of all fiction making; accordingly, the ideal of
objectivity holds little value for him, leading him to claim, with
Wildean equanimity, that he doesn't believe his own interpretation
of Hamlet (175). But although he grandly dismisses his theory,
"Scylla and Charybdis" is an endorsement of its underlying principle, namely that all mental travel is circular, or, as Stephen puts it,
"We walk through ourselves, meeting robbers, ghosts, giants, old
men, young men, wives, widows, brothers-in-love, but always meeting ourselves" (175). The third-person narrator drops all pretense
of objectivity here, openly toying with various rhetorical devices;
his adoption of archaic Shakespearean terms is only one instance
of his refusal to remain detached, impartial, offstage. Correspondingly, the rarefied style of "Scylla and Charybdis" flaunts its own in-
ventiveness, weaving together mock-Platonic dialogue, blank verse,
epic allusion, dramatic form, and musical notation to create a literary tour de force that mirrors Stephen's rhetorical victory. Why is
the narrator so eager to show us that he is on Stephen's side? Joyce
obviously takes pleasure in having Stephen, a version of himself,
defend a theory that is a piece of fiction in disguise, a fiction that
reveals more about the author of *Ulysses* than it reveals about the author of *Hamlet*. In this regard, "Scylla and Charybdis" is yet another
example of the "cyclological" (*Finnegans Wake* 220) composition of
Ulysses.

Stephen's emphasis on the reflexive nature of art is a key to the
circularity of *Ulysses* as a whole. His reference to "the playwright
who wrote the folio of this world and wrote it badly (He gave
us light first and the sun two days later)" (175), is itself a piece
of deliberately flawed writing (the sun of *Genesis* was created four
days later, not two) that links God, Shakespeare, and Joyce. The
error is an inspired bit of misremembering; it shows that Joyce is
not subject to the authority of Scripture or to the authority of any
other text. Using Stephen as his proxy, he writes *Genesis* into his
own creation, and he makes a point of doing it "badly," incorpo-
rating Shakespeare and the *Old Testament* in the same breath. If it
is decadent to submit to the dead hand of the past, Joyce's idiosyncratic transposition of the words of his precursors is surely a gesture
toward emancipation.

"Wandering Rocks"

Insofar as "Wandering Rocks" combines free indirect discourse, interior monologue, and dialogue, it echoes the initial style. However, there is nothing approaching a symbiosis of narrator and narrated here; instead, the reader is cut loose from the anchor of a dominant perspective and set adrift. Father Conmee's opening ruminations create a false sense of security; in every subsequent section, perspective is violated by the incursion of foreign narrative fragments, resulting in a concatenation of disparate scenes. Some sections drop the formality of establishing a human perspective altogether; thus the closing section is taken up by the viceregal cavalcade, an empty display of pomp and circumstance that determines what we see on the street.

In "Wandering Rocks," Joyce presents the reader with an accumulation of simultaneously occurring events. Perspective is coincidental here; as Ned Lambert tells the clergyman who wants to take a picture of the council chamber of Saint Mary's abbey, "the most historic spot in all of Dublin," "Bring the camera whenever you like. I'll get those bags cleared away from the windows. You can take [the picture] from here or from here" (189). One vantage point is as good as another; there is no angle of vision that can provide us with a panoramic view of Dublin life.

The technique of "Wandering Rocks" has been described as inhuman, decentered, and inventorylike (Lawrence 82–88), and it is true that no matter how moving or arresting individual scenes may be, the reader's response is systematically short-circuited. As in "Aeolus," the narrative draws attention to its own mechanics, making it impossible for us to lose ourselves in a mirage of verisimilitude. If we leave "Wandering Rocks" with a total picture of Dublin, it is only because we have taken it upon ourselves to assemble the fragments that Joyce has laid out before us. By refusing to perform that task for us, Joyce practices a subversive form of realism, distributing the labor of narration. Perspective is not tied to necessity; the reader is made to recognize the instability of authorial will.

"Sirens"

In "Sirens," language approaches the condition of music, becoming
curiously abstract. S. L. Goldberg's impatience with "Sirens" is in-
structive here: "The attempt at a fuga per canonem form . . . is
not only unsuccessful in practise . . . it is meaningless in conception. Apart from its place in Joyce's total scheme . . . the only kind
of effect it could achieve is a specious patterning of the material,
an extrinsic imposition of casual shape" (281). The abstractness of
"Sirens" is, of course, part of Joyce's design. By making language
in the image of music, he underscores the fact that language is a
self-referential system in its own right. The famous "overture" to
"Sirens" sets the stage for a programmatic repetition of phrases that
assures the musical movement of the episode as a whole.[2] The sudden shifts of perspective that occur in "Wandering Rocks" give way
to more fluid transitions, transitions that depend on the repetition
and variation of leading phrases or motifs. Throughout the episode,
language, masquerading as music, claims the power to transcend all
divisions and differences. Moments of reconciliation are common
here, but, true to the spirit of music, they are apt to dissolve into
thin air.

By making language imitate music, Joyce amplifies the self-
echoing, self-perpetuating, self-consuming character of the Word.
As Bloom notes, everything has its own music, that is to say, its
own language: "Instruments. A blade of grass, shell of her hands,
then blow. Even comb and tissue paper you can knock a tune out
of. Molly in her shift in Lombard street west, hair down. I suppose each kind of trade made its own, don't you see? Hunter with
a horn. Haw. Have you the? *Cloche. Sonnez la.* Shepherd his pipe.
Pwee little wee. Policeman a whistle. Locks and keys! Sweep! Four
o'clock's all's well!" (237–38). It is not Bloom's consciousness of
betrayal that forms the heart of "Sirens"; it is the seductive movement of a musicalized language, a language that parodies its own
lyricism (Lawrence 98–99), creating strange bedfellows by virtue
of its promiscuous vibrations.

"Cyclops"

Interior monologue gives way to the furious ranting of the citizen
in "Cyclops." The extroverted voice of the citizen drowns out the in-

terior monologue that we have grown so accustomed to, preparing us for a return to traditional storytelling. However, the words of the citizen can't be trusted, and the prolix commentators that regularly interrupt him deliver additional blows to his authority. Cyclopean blindness and encyclopedic exhaustiveness are placed side by side; our sense of having come to a semantic impasse is compounded by the mutual exclusiveness of first-person narration and narrative digression. In "Wandering Rocks," shifts of perspective did not entail shifts of style; in "Cyclops," we are privy to a babel of voices, and, with the exception of the regulars at Barney Kiernan's Pub, everyone seems to be speaking a different language. We begin with a promise of univocal narration only to end in polyphony; true to form, Joyce invokes a convention only to subvert it.

The swollen discourse of "Cyclops" recalls the windy rhetoric of "Aeolus." However, we are no longer confined to the journalistic afflatus of the Hibernian metropolis; thanks to several of the digressions, we also have access to an epic past. Joyce's parodic invocation of an epic past in "Cyclops" underscores his ironic handling of myth in *Ulysses* as a whole. Although the Homeric parallels of *Ulysses* connect its characters to an epic past, Joyce spares the reader a sentimental journey by surrounding those parallels in irony and self-consciousness.

"Nausicaa"

The clash of discourses that resounds in "Cyclops" is replaced by a mingling of discourses (the language of romance novels, the language of advertising, the language of the Litany of the Virgin) in the first part of "Nausicaa." By combining these discourses, Joyce presents them as interlocking parts of a single ideology. The harmony that results is as treacherous as the narrator's indulgence of Gerty MacDowell. By smiling upon the unholy alliance of romance, advertising, and religion, Joyce strips all three of their mystique; by embellishing the secret hopes and fears of Gerty MacDowell, the narrator exposes the crippled composition of her fantasies.

Stylistically speaking, "Nausicaa," a narrative composed of two seamless parts, may be more welcoming than "Aeolus," "Sirens," "Cyclops," or "Wandering Rocks," but it is only a port in the storm. Some critics feel that "Nausicaa" represents a stylistic regression (Lawrence 121–22); others have argued that it anticipates the experiments undertaken in later episodes (Riquelme 213–14). My own sense is that "Nausicaa" succeeds precisely by providing the reader with a false sense of security and by failing to prepare her for the rigors of "Oxen of the Sun." Like Bloom, the reader is ready for consolation; like Bloom, she is still far from home. Whatever comfort we draw from "Nausicaa" is quickly snatched away, which teaches us to be wary of all Joycean homecomings.

"Oxen of the Sun"

In "Oxen of the Sun," we are presented with a patchwork of styles that represents the history of English prose. Stephen and Bloom remain clearly recognizable, but the whims of literary fashion compel them to speak in languages that are not their own. Although polyphony is pushed to an extreme, the segments of the episode cohere, held together by a web of analogies associated with the theme of gestation.

"Oxen of the Sun" conforms to Stephen's circular theory of art, weaving and unweaving itself at the same time. The theme of gestation serves as a common thread, joining one style to another; at the same time, every style that Joyce revives is compromised by parody and pastiche and by sheer juxtaposition. Joyce's habit of relativizing styles by juxtaposing them is familiar enough by now, but "Oxen of the Sun" links that process of relativization to the movement of literary history. Literary history depends on one style being supplanted by another; creation depends on negation. The process of relativization that has been unfolding before our eyes is now applied to literary history as a whole, and literary history, in turn, becomes a metaphor for the history of the human race, a metaphor that Joyce pushes farther in *Finnegans Wake*.

"Circe"

If "Oxen of the Sun" plunders the history of English prose, "Circe" plunders the episodes that precede it. The local history of *Ulysses* is scrambled and rearranged to yield a circular adventure; as in "Oxen of the Sun," a new narrative is born out of the fragments of the old. Although Joyce repeats phrases, images, and motifs throughout *Ulysses*, no episode recirculates old material as obsessively as

"Circe." By writing a garbled chronicle of his own narrative odyssey, Joyce shows his hand, acknowledging the fact that narration is a process of recirculation. "Circe" confirms the fact that *Ulysses* has its own history, a history that can be decomposed and recombined.

In the cracked mirror of "Circe," previous episodes lose their shape, and the same is true of characters. Bloom's adventures in Nighttown not only threaten his identity but they also destabilize the very notion of character. Joyce refracts Bloom's image until he seems past salvaging, making no secret of the fact that Bloom's identity is a composite of qualities, a "proteiform" fiction. Bloom's vision of Rudy signals that he has returned to himself; however, after "Circe," our view of Bloom is forever changed. "Circe" teaches us that there is nothing inviolate about the convention of character; Bloom can not only be taken apart, he can be put back together again.

"Eumaeus"

After the refraction of character, atomization of episodes, and splintering of style that occurs in "Circe," "Eumaeus" affords a return to "cutandry grammar and goahead plot" (*Letters*, ed. Gilbert, 146) but that return is woefully incomplete. Abounding in dead metaphors, stale witticisms, and clichés, "Eumaeus" is a showcase of conventional wisdom. The old notion that "Eumaeus" is an approximation of Bloom's frame of mind at 1:00 A.M. is misleading; as a chapter in the reader's odyssey, the comically slack language of "Eumaeus" suggests that we cannot return to the narrative conventions that we have left behind because those conventions have been exhausted.

The notion that "Eumaeus" is an approximation of Bloom's frame of mind is misleading on another level as well. In "Circe," Joyce exposes the heterogeneity of Bloom's identity; he only allows Bloom to return to himself after he has sytematically pulled him apart. In "Eumaeus," Bloom encounters a counterfeit version of himself, a Ulysses Pseudangelos by the name of Murphy.[3] Bloom's encounter with his brine-soaked double serves as a deflationary reminder of his epic identity. In the contest between Murphy and Bloom, Bloom stands for truth, accountability, and common sense, but even though Murphy is a patent liar, Bloom can never fully defeat him. Although Bloom disapproves of Murphy's habit of lying, Bloom himself is a "genuine forgery" (518), a fact that "Circe" makes it impossible to forget. If Murphy is a dreamer, as his Morpheus-like name implies, Bloom is a dreamer as well. Murphy has literally sailed the seas, and he has returned with a collection of spurious sea yarns; Bloom has negotiated the streets of Dublin, mock-heroically exploring the perils of his own mind.

The language of "Eumaeus" has a life of its own that frequently goes beyond anything that Bloom might think or say. Some passages seem to mimic Bloom's thought process; other passages conjure up a nameless third party, a hybrid of Bloom and the third-person narrator. Similarly, some of the lines of dialogue that Joyce gives Bloom seem characteristic of him, but other lines have an absurd formality that is in excess of Bloom's discreet solicitude. Such inconsistencies remind us that we have not returned to the initial style, a style designed to reveal the inner lives of the characters. As a collection of received ideas, "Eumaeus" is yet another episode in Joyce's epic inventory, an inventory that by now includes elements from previous episodes, contributing to the spectacle of textual self-perpetuation.

"Ithaca"

There are no simple homecomings in *Ulysses;* all homecomings are adventures in their own right. In "Eumaeus," Joyce stages a return to linear narration, only to display the unreliability of the narrator. In "Ithaca," he holds out the promise of objective discourse and gives us fiction instead. The question and answer format of "Ithaca" sets up the expectation of an exchange between two disinterested parties; the internal symmetries of its style conjure up a realm of reason and light; the seeming lucidity of its formulations suggest that knowledge is within our reach. These expectations are set up only to be overturned, and if we entertained any hopes of transcending the ambiguities of *Ulysses,* we are left in the dark.

How does Joyce destabilize the rationalism of "Ithaca"? For one thing, his "mathematical catechism" teases us into assuming that it will unfold according to some abstract logic and then proceeds to generate itself from within. As Benstock puts it, "the dialogo of the structural format evolves in its own directions and according to its own self-reflexive rules" (*Narrative* 96). For another, the internal symmetries of many of the questions and answers make them strangely self-sufficient, demanding that we approach them as independent units rather than as steps in a linear progression. In addition, the intricacy of many of the answers leaves us with a sense of the impossibility of getting to the bottom of the most simple question. Finally, Bloom and Stephen speak in a language that is not their own. The fact that language cannot be traced to an omniscient narrator, or to any source within the text, throws its authority into question.

The self-sabotaging rationalism of "Ithaca" confirms the impossibility of an ideal homecoming. If reason and faith form a dialectical pair that generates the "mathematical catechism" of "Ithaca," that marriage bears strange fruit. Bloom's scientism is parodied in the logical mania of "Ithaca," just as Stephen's involuted catholicism is parodied in its catechistic format; "Ithaca" is an unstable synthesis of these volatile elements. The premise of a meeting of minds yields a meandering exchange thinly disguised as rational discourse, an exchange that gives us the impression that the swirling configurations that we have come to know as Stephen and Bloom are as remote from each other as "heavenly bodies," intersecting at a few miraculous points only to drift apart again.

"Penelope"

"Penelope" holds out the deceptive promise of an uncomplicated homecoming; its apparently straightforward style teases us into expecting a simple story. Like Bloom, we are drawn to the vital principle embodied by Molly Bloom. Yet, on closer inspection, we discover that Molly's life-affirming monologue is a tissue of contradictions and that negative statements are balanced against positive ones until the very end. Stylistically, the forcefulness of Molly's silent speech presupposes a high degree of literary sophistication.

In "Penelope," Joyce creates the illusion that we are returning to the primordial ground of all being; at first glance, the episode seems to be governed by bodily functions and desires. Yet, as we will see, Molly's monologue is animated by her hunger for "the word known to all men" (474), a word that she half remembers and half creates in her closing epiphany.

Molly is Joyce's anti-Catholic muse; sensual as she may be, she exists in a state of lack, her most vivid fantasies revolving around romantically charged words. Bodily satisfaction is not enough for her; although she may confuse her lovers' names, her epiphany is triggered by the memory of something that Bloom once said. If Molly's monologue moves the reader, it does so not by affirming some principle external to the text but by consecrating the union of eros and language. As a potent rearticulation of "the word known to all men," Molly's monologue actualizes the emancipatory potential of narrative process.

Notes

1. For the legend of Mananaan MacLir as a motif in *Ulysses*, see Gilbert 169–70.

2. It is worth noting that the fuga per canonem form does not include an overture, and that the overture to "Sirens" is an example of how freely Joyce interpreted his material.

3. The name *Murphy* is associated with false identity in "An Encounter" as well. Murphy is the name given to Mahony by the narrator, who clings to his Odyssean ruse despite the shame he feels for adopting such a "paltry stratagem" (28).

4

"Oxen of the Sun"

The novel is an inherently dialogical genre: in the words of Mikhail Bakhtin, "it can be defined as a diversity of social speech types (sometimes even a diversity of languages) and a diversity of voices, artistically organized" (262). (Some novels are more obsessively dialogical than others; post-structuralists value the "infinite productivity" of such texts (Attridge and Ferrer 7). Post-structuralists appear to be undaunted by the unreadability of *Finnegans Wake,* and they are great admirers of *Ulysses,* opposing any interpretation that attempts to subordinate the fact of its diversity to the hypothesis of some overarching pattern or final meaning. In the course of developing what they consider to be corrective readings, these critics often become guilty of a kind of essentialism, defining disjunctiveness as the hidden (or not so hidden) agenda of *Ulysses.* Disjunctiveness, for such readers, is Joyce's way of banishing the ghost of logocentrism, and as such, it is a sign of strength, a technique of demystification. My own conviction is that the choice between unity and disjunctiveness is a false one for any critic who wants to do justice to the complexity of Joyce's epic, an epic that presupposes the dialectical intimacy of decadence and emancipation. In order to demonstrate this point, I will briefly discuss the relationship of *Ulysses* to *A Portrait of the Artist as a Young Man* before turning to an analysis of the most extravagantly dialogical episode in the book, namely "Oxen of the Sun."

Ulysses is more disjunctive than *Portrait;* its epic ambition is expressed in a proliferation of colliding codes. Diverse styles are used to depict a striving toward unity in *Portrait,* marking distinct stages in the development of a single voice. In *Ulysses*, multiple styles are used to refract subjects and objects; the reader is sent on an odyssey from which there can be no complete return. In *Portrait*, it is still possible to see Stephen as a figure against a ground; in *Ulysses*, that ground breaks into animated fragments. In *Portrait*, Dublin is the "sordid reality" that crystallizes a solipsist's vision; in *Ulysses*, "dear dirty Dublin" becomes one of the main protagonists. *Portrait* is more illusionistic than *Ulysses*, tricking the reader into believing that he can see the world through Stephen's eyes. The reader of *Ulysses* is taken backstage, where he sees the action from so many different angles that he feels compelled to assist in its production.

Yet although *Ulysses* is more overtly dialogical than *Portrait*, it shares one of the unifying principles of the earlier work, namely organic development. The encyclopedic heterogeneity of *Ulysses* has led post-structuralist critics to interpret it as a "pure" text, uncontaminated by logocentrism. In fact, ideal unities still have a part to play here. The coexistence of organic development and stylistic montage is only surprising if one chooses to forget that *Ulysses* is a polymorphous text. Critics of various schools have glossed over the structural ironies of *Ulysses* in order to translate it into their own critical terms. But to deny the ambivalence of *Ulysses* is to deny the very thing that makes it into a "chaffering allincluding most farraginous chronicle" (*Ulysses* 343).

The tendency to make *Ulysses* into a monolith is reflected in the introduction to *Post-Structuralist Joyce* by Derek Attridge and Daniel Ferrer. The authors inveigh against "empiricist" and "transcendentalist" approaches to Joyce's writing that give rise to "moralizing readings." Such readings, they argue, draw upon "nineteenth century notions of character and narrative" in order to represent Joyce as an author "exhibiting an affirmative and tolerant stance toward the individual, a stance so evidently worthy that it would scarcely seem to require the length and complexity of a work like *Ulysses* to justify and promote it" (4).

According to Attridge and Ferrer, the time for assimilating Joyce to premodernist modes of interpretation is past, and we are now in a position to judge Joyce's writing in its own terms. To that end, they yoke Joyce to their own post-structuralist cause. In keeping with the anti-individualistic premise underlying post-structuralist criticism, they express their impatience with humanistic readings of

Joyce. Humanism, according to them, is such a worthy stance that it hardly needs Joyce's "benefiction." Apparently a difficult author like Joyce can only write about difficult things. If this is the authors' view, then Beckett's observation that "[Joyce's writing] is not about something; it is that something itself" (qtd. in Attridge and Ferrer 4) has no place in their introduction. Beckett's words should remind us that Joyce's writing is not about ruptures or discontinuities either; it is an attempt to reinvent the order *and* the chaos of the world.

Joyce thought of *Ulysses* as an encyclopedia;[1] like all encyclopedias, it has no essence apart from its diversity. To formulate a theory of its essence is to become a victim of Joycean irony. Needless to say, Joyce invites us to do precisely this. If we try to outwit him by isolating heterogeneity as the ruling principle of *Ulysses,* our theory quickly becomes an embarrassment to us; the fact remains that the promise of unity continues to motivate the characters of the novel and, by extension, the plot. Thus, Stephen Dedalus carries the theme of organic development in *Ulysses* just as he did in *Portrait.* Joyce discretely reminds us of his embryological identity by having him appear nine times in the novel. His presence awakens memories of lost unity in Molly and Bloom. Bloom, whose identity as father and husband has been damaged by the death of Rudy, dreams of adopting him. Molly's desire for Bloom has been deflected by the loss of their son; while Bloom sleeps she dreams of becoming both mistress and mother to Stephen. Molly, Bloom, and Rudy formed a living whole before they were divided forever; now Stephen is embraced as a substitute for the missing part. In fact, he is a poor choice—as an artist he must father himself. Nonetheless, an impossible dream of homecoming graces his meetings with Bloom, meetings that the reader is made to anticipate.

The desire for organic unity is not merely the residue of old habits of reading; it is implanted by the themes and structure of *Ulysses.* Stuart Gilbert observed long ago that each episode is ruled by a different part of the body with the exception of "Telemachus," "Nestor," and "Proteus," which take place in Stephen's mind. He concluded, probably with Joyce's approval, that "together these (organs) compose the whole body, which is thus a symbol of the structure of *Ulysses,* a living organism, and of the natural interdependence of the parts between themselves" (37n). Stylistic differences may scatter those parts, but the repetition of words and phrases to form a web of motifs binds them into a single system. The intricacy and open-endedness of that system conceals its unity; like nature, it presents itself as a vast phenomenon governed by a hidden yet immanent logic.

The tension between organic development and refraction that is present throughout *Ulysses* is particularly concentrated in "Oxen of the Sun." Joyce's stylistic tour de force is a miniature *Ulysses* in this regard as well: both are composed of disparate styles connected as moments in a circular history, at once arousing and frustrating the reader's desire for organic unity. The stylistic encyclopedism of "Oxen of the Sun" is a testimony to the burden of the past; if the narrator survives, it is in spite of his belatedness, and it requires a mighty effort. Joyce's comical reenactment of literary history in "Oxen of the Sun" exploits the decadence of his own historical moment; the negation of style through its relativization opens up the possibility of a new creation, attesting to the emancipatory uses of a decadence now rendered in literary terms. In the tightly packed universe of "Oxen of the Sun," there can only be growth where there has been negation. The following discussion of "Oxen of the Sun" is an attempt to clarify the relationship between refraction and organic development that underlies *Ulysses* as a whole and to show how that relationship constitutes yet another manifestation of the dialectical interplay of decadence and emancipation in Joyce's work.

Heterogeneity seems to dominate "Oxen of the Sun." By reproducing a series of styles, Joyce levels them, destroying their respective claims to uniqueness. The reader is not granted the simpler rhetorical pleasures to which she is accustomed; instead she is forced to become a connoisseur of parodies and pastiches. At the same time, she is called on to participate in a drama of gestation. By arranging the various styles in chronological order, Joyce presents them as stages in a single evolution. Our presentiment of incremental organic change is born out by closer examination—the styles are divided into nine groups, corresponding to the nine months of gestation. Each group contains metaphorical reminders of a particular stage of embryological development. The styles themselves overlap at various points, making it impossible to regard them as aggregate parts.[2] Finally, this elaborate drama of gestation is crudely reinforced by Mina Purefoy's labor, a nonlinguistic event that takes place, appropriately, offstage. "Oxen of the Sun" is a taxing episode because it requires the reader to integrate organic development and stylistic montage. The central theme of the episode, namely the slaying of the oxen of the sun, is born of the same synthesis, as I will demonstrate below.

In a now famous letter to Frank Budgen, Joyce translates the Homeric trespass of slaying the oxen of the sun into his own terms, defining it as "a crime committed against fecundity by sterilizing the act of coition."[3] Yet slaying the oxen is only a crime from the vantage point of the Law; seen from an artistic perspective, killing the sacred animal or shattering the icon renews life. Joyce himself complicates the issue by juxtaposing the birth of modern language with the birth of Mortimer Edward Purefoy, linking biological and artistic procreation. The analogy reminds us that crimes can also be committed against *artistic* fecundity. As a "spoiled priest," Stephen deplores contraception as a nightly destruction of "God-possibled Souls" (319); his own seed is literally spilled in "Proteus" (41) and figuratively spilled in "Oxen of the Sun." In "Proteus," his spilling is solitary; in "Oxen of the Sun," his companions seduce him into spending his inspiration. In "Scylla and Charybdis" his words are potent, but in "Oxen of the Sun" he wastes his substance in "general vacant hilarity" (332). If slaying the oxen is equivalent to spilling semantic seeds as well as semen, however, Joyce is as guilty as Stephen;[4] to imitate a style and then throw it aside is to advertise its sterility. The series of deaths that take place in "Oxen of the Sun," however, are part of a larger process of growth, like sloughing off old skins. In the *Odyssey,* Odysseus' men die for slaying the oxen; in *Ulysses,* where old styles are excavated only to be abandoned again, literary creation depends on disobedience.

A fable of creation is encapsulated in the theme of slaying the oxen. That fable reflects the interdependence of growth and negation in Joyce's writing. Stylistic montage is generated by a continuous shedding of styles in "Oxen of the Sun"—the movement of the episode depends on negation. Growth is represented as the accelerated decay of authority; style issues from its own destruction.[5] Although the technique of "Oxen of the Sun" seems extravagant— rhetorical ruins are erected only to be leveled again—the episode emphasizes the difference between waste and negation. Paralysis is general all over Ireland; all the guests at the wastrels' banquet in the maternity hospital suffer from malaise. Creation is the only cure, represented in "Oxen of the Sun" as a process that combines organic development and negation. Without negation, there is no answer to *literary* decadence and the spiritual paralysis that it implies. Paralysis is produced by a passive acceptance of the burden of history; negation is a way, not of shedding that burden, but of redistributing its weight. Joyce's prodigality consummates itself in twentieth-century gibberish—a senseless spending of words and, at the same time, a celebration of unspent potential.[6]

Turning from the technique of the episode to the action it portrays, killing the oxen takes on additional significance. As in the *Odyssey*, survival depends on transgression. Both Bloom and Stephen are compelled to commit crimes against fecundity by the circumstances of their lives. Bloom's transgressions are literal; Stephen's are largely figurative. Unlike Stephen and the rest of the company, Bloom, "the meekest man and the kindest that ever laid husbandly hand under hen" (318), never uses language to slay the oxen of the sun. His secret is exposed by the Junian narrator; he has allowed himself to become "his own and his only enjoyer" (334). (The only begetter of Shakespeare's sonnets reappears in diminished form to remind us that there is a touch of the artistic in Bloom's introversion). His peccadillo, of course, is commonplace; as the Bunyan narrator indignantly observes, "spilling" is not the exception but the rule (324). But Bloom is a special case; sexual deprivation is the price he has paid for fathering a son. The loss of Rudy has made him into a compliant cuckold, doubting his rights as a husband. As the Lamb narrator reveals, he committed his first crime against fecundity when he lost his virginity: that "bridenight" was barren because his partner dared "not bear the sunnygolden babe of day" (338). In both cases, following life's dictates eventually leads to slaying the oxen; sacrifice marks the way from innocence to experience.

Slaying the oxen is also part of a rite of initiation for Stephen. Catholicism celebrates the virginity of the soul; art sanctifies (and desecrates) experience. To make experience into his vocation, he must wean himself away from Catholicism, which he has taken in with his mother's milk. By rejecting her religion, Stephen violates her memory—and, presumably, if it is a crime to "sterilize the act of coition," it is also a crime to dishonor one's mother. His refusal to pray at her deathbed is only one of a series of desecrations; defiance dictates the very language he speaks. His thoughts are always vexed by the ghost of religion. Thus at one point he argues against contraception like a good Catholic, defending the sacredness of life: "For, Sirs, he said, our lust is brief. We are means to those small creatures within us and nature has other ends than we" (319). In the same breath, he treats the maternal body as an object of contempt, claiming absurdly that only the embryo is sacred: "He said also how at the end of the second month a human soul was infused and how in all our holy mother foldeth ever souls for God's greater glory whereas that earthly mother which was but a dam to bear beastly should die by canon for so saith he that holdeth the fisherman's seal, even that blessed Peter on which rock was holy church for all ages founded" (319). The word *beastly* betrays the perversity of his argument, echoing Mulligan's quip that his mother is "beastly dead" (7). Her ghost still haunts him because his rebellion is incomplete—even his refusal to pray at her deathbed is dictated by his fear of the potency of Catholic rhetoric, a fear that fills his speech with impieties. In the passage quoted above, he takes his revenge by using Catholicism as a weapon against her. As we will see later, Catholicism is explicitly presented as a fetishized beast that deserves to be slain in the Swift passage; here the papal bull by which Pope Adrian IV granted Ireland to English King Henry II as a papal fief becomes a caricature of bondage.

For Stephen, there are still only two choices: religious submission or artistic rebellion. Freedom depends on negation—he must reinvent the present by disentangling himself from the past. The following passage suggests that he will be haunted by the past until he produces a work of art:

> You have spoken of the past and its phantoms, Stephen said. Why think of them? If I call them into life across the waters of Lethe will not the poor ghosts troop to my call? Who supposes it? I, Bous Stephanoumenos, bullockbefriending bard, am lord and giver of their life. He encircled his gadding hair with a coronal of vine-leaves, smiling at Vincent. That answer and those leaves, Vincent said to him, will adorn you more fitly when something more, and greatly more, than a capful of light odes can call your genius father. All who wish you well hope this for you. All desire to see you bring forth the work you meditate, to acclaim you Stephaneforos. I heartily wish

you may not fail them. O no, Vincent, Lenehan said, laying a hand
on the shoulder near him. Have no fear. He could not leave his
mother an orphan. The young man's face grew dark. All could see
how hard it was for him to be reminded of his promise and of his
recent loss.[7] (339)

Stephen's face grows dark in anticipation of "sinning against the
light." Despite what Lenehan says, he must make himself into an
orphan to father his art. Creation entails sacrifice; as Bloom's procreative past confirms, one potentiality cannot be realized without the
destruction of another, a truth Stephen toys with in "Nestor": "Had
Pyrrhus not fallen by a beldam's hand in Argos or Julius Caesar not
been knifed to death. They are not to be thought away. Time has
branded them and fettered they are lodged in the room of the infinite possibilities they have ousted. But can those have been possible
seeing that they never were? Or was that only possible which came
to pass? Weave, weaver of the wind" (21). Here ousted possibilities
are assigned a special room of their own. It is not surprising that
Stephen is so quick to arrange these accommodations; after all, he
is still in the process of moving from what might have been to what
must be. Slaying the oxen is a powerful way of separating the two;
as an end in itself, it is merely destructive.

Seen from this vantage point, any model of individual development that does not acknowledge the interdependence of conception
and negation becomes obsolete. It is no coincidence that Joyce's de-
piction of the third month of gestation, during which the gender of
the embryo emerges, is also an expression of the murderousness of
history. The third month is heralded with bawdy jokes in the Elizabethan chronicle style and rumors that Stephen has fathered a son.
The "embryo philosopher" denies these rumors, boasting that he is
the "eternal son and ever virgin" (321). The mention of virginity
leads to a ritual deflowering. These spurious rites (Atherton 321–
22) are followed by darker exchanges. The story of Beau Mount
and Lecher is not merely bawdy but perverse. In the lines that follow, the signs of sexual identity that appear in the third month of
gestation turn into dark ciphers of Irish history:

Remember, Erin, thy generations and thy days of old, how thou set-
tedst little by me and by my word and broughtedst in a stranger to
my gates to commit fornication in my sight and to wax fat and kick
like Jeshurum. Therefore hast thou sinned against my light and hast

made me, thy lord, to be the slave of servants. Return, return, Clan Milly: forget me not, O Milesian. Why hast thou done this abomination before me that thou didst spurn me for a merchant of jalaps and didst deny me to the Roman and to the Indian of dark speech with whom thy daughters did lie luxuriously? Look forth now, my people, upon the land of behest, even from Horeb and from Nebo and from Pisgah and from the Horns of Hatten unto a land flowing with milk and money. But thou hast suckled me with a bitter milk: my moon and my sun thou hast quenched for ever. And thou hast left me alone for ever in the dark ways of my bitterness: and with a kiss of ashes hast thou kissed my mouth. (322)

Nascent sexuality withers into a memory of violation; sexual differentiation is associated with decay. The dirty story of Beau Mount and Lecher turns into a lamentation based on the *Catholic Improperia,* in which Christ reproaches the Jews. In Joyce's version, Ireland reproaches her own people for betraying her. Ireland's lament recalls Deasy's bigoted observation that the Irish never persecuted the Jews because Ireland never let them in (30). In fact, Ireland has been seduced by the forbears of Orangemen like Deasy; the "merchant of jalaps" to whom she has succumbed is a British colonialist resembling Haines's father, who "made his tin by selling jalaps to Zulus or some bloody swindle or other."[8] The leaders of Ireland have been betrayed by the people of Ireland, who have fallen in love with their oppressors. Ireland's betrayal of her great men is a sin against the light, a crime against the fecundity of a nation.[9] Bloom and, to a lesser degree, Stephen are exalted into victims of Ireland's betrayal. The allusion to Clan Milly evokes Molly, universalizing her adultery; like Ireland, she has opened her gates to the stranger. "Bitter milk" and "kisses of ashes"[10] conjure up Stephen's mother, whose love is like a kiss of death. Ireland's betrayal of her leaders, Molly's betrayal of Bloom, and Stephen's suffocation are all associated with the first appearance of sexuality in the third month of gestation; sexuality perpetuates the "ding dong round" of history.

History for Joyce does not progress—it merely repeats itself. This is not to say that history is an infinite regress, despite the fact that the Fall occurs over and over again. The Fall itself is a moment in a larger, sublunary cycle of generation:[11]

Assuefaction minorates atrocities (as Tully saith of his darling Stoics) and Hamlet his father showeth the prince no blister of combustion. The adiaphane in the noon of life is an Egypt's plague which in

the nights of prenativity and postmortemity is their most proper
ubi and *quomodo*. And as the ends and ultimates of all things accord
in some mean and measure with their inceptions and originals, that
same multiplicit concordance which leads forth growth from birth
accomplishing by a retrogressive metamorphosis that minishing and
ablation towards the final which is agreeable unto nature so is it with
our subsolar being. The aged sisters draw us into life: we wail, bat-
ten, sport, clip, clasp, sunder, dwindle, die: over us dead they bend.
First, saved from waters of old Nile, among bulrushes, a bed of fasci-
ated wattles: at last the cavity of a mountain, an occulted sepulchre
amid the conclamation of the hillcat and the ossifrage. And as no
man knows the ubicity of his tumulus nor to what processes we
shall thereby be ushered nor whether to Tophet or to Edenville in
the like way is all hidden when we would backward see from what
region of remoteness the whatness of our whoness hath fetched his
whenceness. (322–23)

Paradoxically, the burden of the past is lightened by the fact that
history repeats itself. "Assuefaction minorates atrocities"—the repetition of an atrocity detracts from its crippling power. Moreover,
if repeated atrocities cripple the spirit of a people, they also create a need for strong leaders. Adiaphane (a word connoting both
opacity and moral indifference) is an "Egypt's plague in the noon
of life" but it may also be a harbinger of dawn. When adiaphane
obscures the noon of life, men of genius arise to banish it. Through
their labors, the world attains epiphany, momentarily shedding its
opacity and becoming transparent. But even the great men (reintroduced by the Mosaic analogy) are not great enough to convert
history into progress: bound to the cycle of creation and destruction that engenders their own gifts, they eventually disappear into
the darkness from which they came.

Adiaphane at noon is an exotic strain of a common disease known
as death-in-life. The antithesis of adiaphane is epiphany, or life-
giving illumination. Epiphany and adiaphane are interlocking moments in Joyce's circular history. Creation, because it restores sight,
is privileged within that history, but it is not idealized. Creation
feeds on loss: experience has to be destroyed to be recreated. Joyce
remarked on the cruelty of his own art in a letter to Harriet Weaver:
"The progress of the book is . . . like the progress of some sand-
blast. As soon as I mention or include any person in it I hear of

his or her death or departure or misfortune: and each successive episode, dealing with some province of artistic culture (rhetoric or music or dialectic) leaves behind it a burnt up field" (*Selected Letters* 241). The De Quincey passage in "Oxen of the Sun" also exposes the intimacy of sacrifice and creation. Parallax, one of the phrases that has passed in and out of Bloom's mind throughout the day, suddenly takes on a life of its own:

> And on the highway of the clouds they come, muttering thunder of rebellion, the ghosts of beasts. Huuh! Hark! Huuh! Parallax stalks behind and goads them, the lancinating lightnings of whose brow are scorpions. Elk and yak, the bulls of Bashan and of Babylon, mammoth and mastodon, they come trooping to the sunken sea, *Lacus Mortis.* Ominous revengeful zodiacal host! They moan, passing upon the clouds, horned and capricorned, the trumpeted with the tusked, the lionmaned, the giantantlered, snouter and crawler, rodent, ruminant and pachyderm, all their moving moaning multitude, murderers of the sun. (338)

In this passage, Joyce provides a metaphor for his own method of narration. Words and phrases that evolve into themes through repetition drive myriad tropes and styles forward.[12] Individual styles, herded together, shed their authority; the art of persuasion turns into a play of shadows. It is the ghosts of the slain oxen that eclipse the sun; the leveling of rhetorical forms becomes the basis of a new creation that celebrates the dispersion of the Logos. Without such sacrifice, there can only be blind repetition.

Joyce has no patience with fables of history that sweeten the reality of sacrifice and trivialize the act of creation, as the following parody of Darwinian logic suggests:

> The plain straightforward question why a child of normally healthy parents and seemingly a healthy child and properly looked after succumbs unaccountably in early childhood (though other children of the same marriage do not) must certainly, in the poet's words, give us pause. Nature, we may rest assured, has her own good and cogent reasons for whatever she does and in all probability such deaths are due to some law of anticipation by which organisms in which morbous germs have taken up their residence (modern science has conclusively shown that only the plasmic substance can be said to be immortal) tend to disappear at an increasingly earlier stage of development, an arrangement which, though productive of pain to

some of our feelings (notably the maternal), is nevertheless, some of
us think, in the long run beneficial to the race in general in securing
thereby the survival of the fittest. (342)

The Darwinian narrator has become disoriented as a result of his
habit of closing his eyes to the reality of loss. Thus he sees the
tragedy of a child's death as part of a greater biological comedy,
abandoning the child's parents to their grief. He can no longer distinguish their bereavement from the general good. As the passage
suggests, his rationalization of loss engenders nothing but a cruel,
self-serving optimism.

In "Oxen of the Sun," Joyce uses a false equation to sabotage the
myth of progress. By superimposing the birth of modern language
upon the birth of a child, he links embryonic and linguistic development. Embryonic development may be the most unambiguous
instance of progress we know. Joyce seems to affirm the myth of
progress by presenting an embryology of style. But the closing style,
or antistyle, of *Ulysses* reveals the paradox built into his master plan.
Biological gestation culminates in the birth of an infant; etymologically, an infant is one who cannot speak. Similarly, linguistic gestation culminates in twentieth-century gibberish. An examination of
what actually takes place between the "unfertilized ovum" (*Selected
Letters* 251) of tortuous Latinate prose and the birth of an infantine
language does not, after all, disclose a progress of styles; on the
contrary, Joyce's impersonations become sharper as he approaches
modernity, with parody frequently taking the place of pastiche.[13]
Unlike Stephen Dedalus's invisible artist, Joyce is visibly entangled
in the history he recreates. Negation is a central element of his art,
and the impulse toward negation is fueled by the decadence of his
own historical moment.

The opening passage of "Oxen of the Sun" is not parody but
pastiche; its humor depends less on stylistic excess than on occulted local reference (i.e., *deshil eamus* means *let's go;* the mysterious
word *horhorn* refers to Horne's lying-in hospital; *hoopsa* anticipates
Bloom's entry into Bella Cohen's brothel;[14] *boyaboy* announces the
imminent birth of the Purefoy boy). The Latinate passage that follows may be exceedingly convoluted, but, as Joyce said of Molly,
it is fertilizable, consisting of a series of circular constructions waiting to be penetrated by forthright words. Those words turn out

to be Anglo-Saxon ones, as the next passage reveals. Joyce imitates Saintsbury's translations of early Anglo-Saxon to produce a
sincerely plain style. The Mandevillean narrator, by contrast, is so
prone to exaggeration that he is beyond ridicule; parody in his
case would be redundant. The courtliness of the Mallorean narrator, however, is completely out of place, serving only to bring out
the knavery of the company; his gentlemanliness becomes the butt
of several jokes. The Elizabethan chronicle style that follows is a
farrago of styles, fulfilling the dictionary definition of pastiche.[15]
Peacock excluded this style from his anthology because it was too
heterogeneous; Joyce exploits its impurity, adding Blake and Yeats
to the mix. (Anachronisms like these occur throughout "Oxen of
the Sun," disrupting any sense of strict linear progression.) The
Burton-Browne passage provides an occasion to conflate several
themes of betrayal. But the bitterness orchestrated here does not
reflect back on the narrator; although he is ponderous, he is also
full of metaphysical wit, a type of eccentricity that Joyce endorses.

The narrator of the Bunyan passage is satire's victim; although
he is filled with good intentions, he fails to preserve the chastity
of his style. Christian allegory is no longer the vehicle of transcendental meaning, conveying sexual innuendo instead: "For regarding
Believe-on-me they said it was nought else but notion and they
could conceive no thought of it for, first, Two-in-the-Bush whither
she ticed them was the very goodliest grot and in it were four pil-
lows on which were four tickets with these words printed on them,
Pickaback and Topsyturvy and Shameface and Cheek by Jowl and,
second, for that foul plague Allpox and the monsters they cared not
for them for Preservative had given them a stout shield of oxen-
gut" (324). The narrator only manages to extricate himself from
the treacherous "land of Phenomenon" (323) at the close of the
passage, in an outburst of rage.

Despite the stodginess of the Pepys passage, its narrator escapes
parody—granted, he is a little too pleased with himself for being
English, but Joyce doesn't punish him for it. His bourgeois traits
are accentuated by the Defoe narrator, whose worldliness qualifies
him to represent Lenehan the leech. The Swift passage is an exercise in savage indignation, a pastiche of a self-parodying style. The
Addison-Steele passage, on the other hand, is pure parody. Joyce
reserves the subject of Irish history for Swiftian satire; the self-

satisfied and vulgar Addisonian gentleman is fit only to introduce Buck Mulligan, the "gay betrayer."

Parody, as the OED reminds us, is often produced by severing a style from its occasion. The Sterne passage is not a parody but a pastiche because its naughty and sentimental narrator is a perfect match for the inebriated young men. The narrators of the Goldsmith, Burke, "Junius," and Gibbon passages are all parodied for their self-importance. The afflatus of the Goldsmith passage is punctured by the irreverent company to which it is addressed. Bloom's "rising choler" (333), aroused by his revulsion for Costello, undermines the high dignity of the Burkean passage because he is merely suffering from an attack of peevishness. The narrator of the Junian passage is so filled with spleen that everything he says is ridiculous. The magisterial narrator of the Gibbon passage clearly cannot keep up with the ongoing "strife of tongues" (335).

Eccentric and spendthrift stylists, whose writing is always in excess of its occasion, are harder to parody. Thus, in the Gothic passage that follows Macaulay, it is Haines and not the narrator who is held up for ridicule. Similarly, the De Quincey passage is a tribute to that author's prolific imagination rather than a joke at his expense; the narrators of the Landor and Macaulay passages do not get off as easily because they are not truly extravagant, they are merely overdressed: both insist on using high style in very mixed company.

Sentimentality without self-irony is one of Joyce's favorite targets. Thus the sweetness of Lamb's voice becomes cloying at the end of the paragraph devoted to him; sentimentality is his Achilles' heel. The Dickensian narrator, the only novelist to appear in "Oxen," is treated unfairly; Joyce exploits the sentimentality of his source by stripping away his humor. As Atherton points out, the strategic naming of "young hopeful" (321–22) is the pinprick that collapses the overblown kindliness of the passage.

The narrator of the Newman passage is exquisitely detached; he is clearly immune to parody, suggesting that Joyce agrees with Stephen's description of Newman as the greatest stylist in *Portrait* (80). The Pater and Ruskin passages are characterized by a preciosity that is exploded by a single word: "Burke's!" Although the Carlyle narrator escapes parody through sheer extravagance, the language that he speaks is completely devalued by its association with drunkenness. The mimic of the closing paragraphs, described by Joyce as a "frightful jumble of Pidgin English, nigger English, Cockney, Irish, Bowery slang and broken doggerel" (*Selected Letters* 252), spreads himself so thin that he is virtually invisible; he cannot be characterized in the terms we have been using here.

In summary, "Oxen of the Sun" does not pay tribute to the progress of literary language. On the contrary, occasions for satire seem to proliferate as we approach modern times. Pastiche is predominant until the eighteenth century; from then on, parody prevails. Goldsmith, Burke, "Junius," and Gibbon are ridiculed for their high seriousness; the same is true of Landor and Macaulay in the nineteenth century. Addison is taunted for his hypocritical gentlemanliness; Lamb and Dickens are teased for their sentimentality. It is no accident that one of Joyce's sharpest parodies is directed against the nineteenth-century language of science, a language that revolves around the theory of progress. His nineteenth-century repertoire also includes Hodgson's *Book of Errors,* a reminder that although we have come a long way from the tortuous latinity of the "Sallustian-Tacitean prelude" (*Selected Letters* 251), style does not mature with age. Instead, literary language becomes more fit for satire in the fullness of time, advancing toward its own decline; as the Swift passage implies, the same is true of nations.

Satire enables the Swiftian narrator to project the nightmare of Irish history. The chimeras that populate that nightmare are hybrids of victimization and self-betrayal. The papal bull of Adrian IV, also known as Nicholas, is, of course, the prime example: it is fashioned into a false idol by the Irish people, who worship the power of their own oppressors. Their failure of will results in an insidious romance:

> That same bull . . . was sent to our island by farmer Nicholas, the bravest cattle breeder of them all, with an emerald ring in his nose. True for you, says Mr Vincent cross the table, and a bullseye into the bargain, says he, and a plumper and a portlier bull, says he, never shit on shamrock. He had horns galore, a coat of cloth of gold and a sweet smoky breath coming out of his nostrils so that the women of our island, leaving doughballs and rollingpins, followed after him hanging his bulliness in daisychains. What for that, says Mr Dixon, but before he came over farmer Nicholas that was a eunuch had him properly gelded by a college of doctors who were no better off than

himself. So be off now, says he, and do all my cousin german the lord
Harry tells you and take a farmer's blessing, and with that he slapped
his posteriors very soundly. But the slap and the blessing stood him
friend, says Mr Vincent, for to make up he taught him a trick worth
two of the other so that maid, wife, abbess and widow to this day
affirm that they would rather any time of the month whisper in his
ear in the dark of a cowhouse or get a lick on the nape from his long
holy tongue than lie with the finest strapping young ravisher in the
four fields of all Ireland. Another then put in his word: And they
dressed him, says he, in a point shift and petticoat with a tippet and
girdle and ruffles on his wrists and clipped his forelock and rubbed
him all over with spermacetic oil and built stables for him at every
turn of the road with a gold manger in each full of the best hay in
the market so that he could doss and dung to his heart's content. By
this time the father of the faithful (for so they called him) was grown
so heavy that he could scarce walk to pasture. To remedy which our
cozening dames and damsels brought him his fodder in their apron-
laps and as soon as his belly was full he would rear up on his hind
quarters to show their ladyships a mystery and roar and bellow out
of him in bulls' language and they all after him. (327)

The papal bull becomes a fetish endowed with mythical potency. Its
idolization is a symptom of the kind of self-destructiveness noted by
Joyce in "Ireland, Island of Saints and Sages," in which he observes
that the English encountered comparatively little resistance from
the Irish during the Anglo-Saxon and Norman Invasion of 1156.
Like the Burton-Browne narrator, the Swift narrator invites us to
link Ireland's self-betrayal to Molly's betrayal of Bloom; Ireland in
the act of surrendering to exploitation is depicted as an uncontrol-
lably libidinous woman, too taken with the glamor of the stranger
to cast him off. However, Ireland, unlike pagan Molly, is dazzled
by religious authority. England's power becomes absolutely irre-
sistible when Henry IV, converted to Anglicanism, discovers that
religion is not only an opiate but an aphrodisiac, joining the ranks
of the bull. Both Henry IV and the bull know how to emasculate
Ireland by mystifying their own potency, forcing all her "real men"
into exile.

Irish history, according to the Swiftian narrator, is a history of
violation and self-betrayal. His disenchantment informs the entire
episode. Although "Oxen of the Sun" is dominated by an optimistic
metaphor, namely the metaphor of gestation, the chronological

sequence of styles presented here does not add up to a particularly positive evolution. Human gestation may be the most unambiguous instance of actualized potentiality that we know, but it becomes ambiguous when Joyce transposes it to the realm of history.

Although "Oxen of the Sun" mocks the idea of progress, it is not fatalistic. History may be littered with broken promises, but those promises are rearticulated in every human gestation. Creation depends, as we have seen, on negation. Thus dead styles grow back only to wither away again, but at the end of the episode an infant language is born. (As critics have pointed out, the promise contained in that language is fulfilled in *Finnegans Wake*.) Similarly, Stephen develops the dream of his own vocation from within the nightmare of history. Literary history, providing an inexhaustible source of parodies and pastiches, suggests that all human creations are exclusionary in retrospect, restricting the creator's vision to her own idiosyncrasies. At the same time, the stylists of the past create the possibility of their own supercession, a promise fulfilled by the very series of approximations that constitute "Oxen of the Sun."

Stephen, the "embryo philosopher," dramatizes the mysteries of artistic gestation in a more specific way. His pain may be an early warning of paralysis; on the other hand, it may be a sign of growth. The second possibility is suggested by his Joycean response to the sound of thunder. His fear is awakened in the fourth month of gestation, during which the heart is formed, a fact that Joyce reminds us of by repeating the word *heart* three times in this passage.[16] A clap of thunder has the power to terrify him because it is entangled in "love's bitter mystery" (8). For a moment he believes that his heresies have aroused the wrath of God, the active form of his mother's mute reproach; in that moment, he becomes a child, delivered from "the land of Phenomenon" by "the crack of doom" (323). Bloom offers antimetaphysical words of consolation, sensing that Stephen is in the throes of an initiation. Failure to pass the test, which entails learning to love in the face of mortality, will result in the transformation of loss into paralysis.

The linguistic events that take place in Horne's lying-in hospital prove that artistic procreation is a laborious and uncertain process. After three days of struggle, Mina Purefoy finally has her baby, but she has it offstage; the emergence of the Word (Burke's) comes later, and when it does, it is not particularly healthy. The concluding babble represents raw potentiality that may or may not be actualized by Stephen. The ten years he grants himself to prove his vocation raise our hopes for him; after all, in ten years, *Ulysses* will be published. Within the confines of the novel, his coming of age is neither assured nor canceled out; similarly, literary history is not reduced to progress or devolution. Growth depends on slaying the oxen and passing beyond the site of the slaying to live out one's exile. Growth of this kind is measured only twice in *Ulysses;* the first time occurs at the end of "Circe," after Bloom and Stephen have emerged from Nighttown; the second occurs at the end of "Penelope."

The spectator of Joyce's drama of gestation is not granted the luxury of viewing the action from a distance, nor is he made to feel that the drama of gestation that Joyce enacts by recreating and destroying styles is over when the curtain falls. If the reader has made the mistake of focusing exclusively on disjunction, failing to recognize the dialectical interdependence of disjunction and organic development, of growth and negation, he will be completely in the dark when the episode comes to a close. Joyce's labor (and the reader's) consummates itself in belated infancy; the possibility of a new creation, of artistic, if not political, emancipation is salvaged from the outrageous ruins of style.

The obsessive dialogism of "Oxen of the Sun" presupposes a condition of literary decadence. The narrator seems desperately determined to triumph over the fact of his own belatedness; the pageant of styles that we have been called on to witness leaves us with the feeling that we have arrived at the end of literary history. Yet the dominant trope of gestation militates against an entirely pessimistic reading. Perhaps the narrator is safer than we had imagined him to be; perhaps, by feeding off decadence, he is reviving the promise of emancipation.

Notes

1. "(*Ulysses*) is an epic of two races (Israelite-Irish) and at the same time the cycle of the human body as well as a little story of a day (life). . . . It is also a sort of encyclopedia. My intention is to transpose the myth *sub specie temporis nostri*. Each adventure (that is, every hour, every organ, every art being interconnected and interrelated in the structural scheme of the whole) should not only condition but even create its own technique. Each

adventure is so to say one person although it is composed of persons — as Aquinas relates of the angelic hosts" (*Letters,* ed. Gilbert, 146–47).

2. John Porter Houston warns against approaching "Oxen" as a history of English prose: "Any attempt to maintain that 'Oxen' is a history of English prose because the latter is an allegory of gestation will inevitably result in the discomfiture so often displayed by commentators of *Ulysses.*" Although Joyce's letters confirm the fact that he conceived of "Oxen of the Sun" as a "history of English prose," Houston argues that "most of us have a sufficiently ironic attitude toward advertising in general that I see no reason why we must except Joyce's publication efforts on behalf of his novels, which were at least undertaken in the sound cause of getting himself read" (131). Houston bases his argument on the chronological inconsistencies with which the episode abounds, failing to acknowledge the fact that such inconsistencies are very much a part of Joyce's design in "Oxen," a design that depends, after all, on linking literary history with the overlapping and interpenetrating phases of organic development.

3. "Am working hard at 'Oxen of the Sun,' the idea being the crime committed against fecundity by sterilizing the act of coition. Scene, lying-in hospital. Technique: a nineparted episode without divisions introduced by a Sallustian-Tacitean prelude (the unfertilized ovum), then by way of earliest English alliterative and monosyllabic and Anglo-Saxon ('Before born the babe had bliss. Within the womb he won worship.' 'Bloom dull dreamy heard: in held hat stony staring') then by way of Mandeville ('there came forth a scholar of medicine that men clepen etc') then Malory's *Morte d' Arthur* ('but that franklin Lenehan was prompt ever to pour them so that at the least way mirth should not lack'), then the Elizabethan chronicle style ('about that present time young Stephen filled all cups'), then a passage solemn, as of Milton, Taylor, Hooker, followed by a choppy Latin-gossipy bit, style of Burton-Browne, then a passage Bunyanesque ('the reason was that in the way he fell in with a certain whore whose name she said is Bird in the Hand') after a diarystyle bit Pepys-Evelyn ('Bloom sitting snug with a party of wags, among them Dixon Jun., Ja. Lynch, Doc. Madden and Stephen D. for a languor he had before and was now better, he having dreamed tonight a strange fancy and Mistress Purefoy there to be delivered, poor body, two days past her time and the midwives hard put to it, God send her quick issue') and so on through Defoe-Swift and Steele-Addison-Sterne and Landor-Pater-Newman until it ends in a frightful jumble of Pidgin English, nigger English, Cockney, Irish, Bowery slang and broken doggerel. This progression is also linked back at each part subtly with some forgoing episode of the day and, besides this, with the natural stages of development in the embryo and the periods of faunal evolution in general. The double-thudding Anglo-Saxon motive recurs

from time to time ('Loth to move from Horne's house') to give the sense of the hoofs of oxen. Bloom is the spermatozoon, the hospital the womb, the nurse the ovum, Stephen the embryo" (*Selected Letters* 252).

4. For another instance of spilt semen as a metaphor for a ruined poetic potentiality, see the execution of the Croppy Boy in "Circe" (481–85); the Croppy Boy embodies Stephen's fate (poetic death) should he fail in his resolve to mentally "kill the priest and the king" (481).

5. In the conclusion of her excellent study of "Oxen," Karen Lawrence argues that "one of the functions of all this discipline and craft in the chapter is to provide a veritable anatomy of style and a classic demonstration of the provisional nature of any one style. Referring to *Ulysses* in general and probably to 'Oxen of the Sun' in particular, T.S. Eliot said that Joyce had exposed 'the futility of all the English styles,' a judgement that suggests that style has failed to live up to its claims. For Eliot, who himself had demonstrated the desire to find 'le mot juste,' Joyce's inventories of style revealed the failure of such a stylistic absolute. Indeed, 'Oxen of the Sun' does show the naivete of assuming that any one style can convey the way things really are, but I would prefer to regard it as a demonstration of the inevitable *limitations* rather than the *failure* or futility of style." Lawrence goes on to suggest that destroying the authority of previous styles becomes a method of creation in "Oxen of the Sun": "Even the word 'limitation,' however, tends to ignore the other aspect of Joyce's stylistic tour de force in the chapter. For in treating the styles of the past as fuel for the modern writer, he makes capital of the styles while revealing their limitations. Eliot said that bad poets borrow and good poets steal—Joyce was an expert thief who could create something new out of old materials. To borrow a phrase from *Finnegans Wake*, 'Oxen of the Sun' is 'the last word in stolentelling,' a chapter fashioned out of the signature style of other writers. In 'Oxen,' Joyce attempted to outdo his predecessors by encompassing them and to expand the limits of his own text by importing, cataloguing, and displaying others. 'Oxen' is the last stand for literary plagiarism in *Ulysses*. From now on the book will pillage most mercilessly its own resources" (144–45).

6. Zack Bowen reads the final pages of "Oxen" as an instance of stylistic distortion run wild. Readers of these pages, according to Bowen, find themselves in a "purgatory of narrative confusion," but Dowie's speech provides a measure of comic relief. Dowie's speech "doesn't really afford much in terms of improving the readers' spiritual well-being, but it does indeed provide a cough mixture for linguistic inflammation, a concluding burst of understandable comic exuberance to reinforce the episode's murky comic prognostication that little meaning can come from either literature or language in general" (63). I would argue, or perhaps merely

add, that there is something celebratory about "Oxen," an episode that revels in the inexhaustibility of linguistic resources.

7. The passage itself demonstrates Stephen's subjection to the past insofar as it is a parody of the dinner at Leigh Hunt's at which Keats was crowned poet laureate.

8. In the same passage, Mulligan refers to Haines as the "oxy chap downstairs." Given Joyce's penchant for wordplay and for contriving "retrospective arrangements" within his narratives, it may not be too farfetched to read *oxy* as a pun on *oxen* and *Oxford*.

9. According to Deasy, of course, it is the Jews who have sinned against the light: he tells Stephen, "You can see the darkness in their eyes. And that is why they are wanderers on the earth to this day" (28). Stephen replies, "Who has not (sinned against the light)?" confirming the inevitability of slaying the oxen of the sun.

10. "Bitter milk" evokes "Fergus' Song," which Stephen sang while his mother was on her deathbed ("And no more turn aside and brood / Upon love's bitter mystery / For Fergus rules the brazen cars," 8). "Kisses of ashes" evokes Stephen's dream of his mother: "In a dream, silently, she had come to him, her wasted body within its loose graveclothes giving off an odour of wax and rosewood, her breath, bent over him with mute secret words, a faint odour of wetted ashes" (9).

11. Karen Lawrence rightly points out that "as in 'Cyclops,' the compendium of styles makes it impossible to identify the one which tells the truth—all the styles offer different versions of the story. As many critics have observed, 'Oxen' provides a microcosm of the method of the book: the notion of the relativity and potentiality of all styles that informs the succession of styles in the book as a whole provides the principle for this most literary of chapters. As Hugh Kenner says, 'Pastiche and parody, these are modes which test the limits of someone else's perception. Any 'style' is a system of limits; pastiche ascribes the system to another person, and invites us to attend to its recirculating habits and its exclusions.' Stylistic and dramatic possibilities are mined, but the actual significance of any one event becomes impossible to state given the constant shifting of ground rules and mediation" (137–38). Strictly speaking, Lawrence's statement should hold true not only for the movement of the plot, such as it is, and for the rendering of character, but also for the opinions advanced in individual passages of "Oxen." Nonetheless, the circular and nonprogressive vision of history presented in the Browne passage has too much relevance to the form and content of *Ulysses* and *Finnegans Wake* to be discounted.

12. John Gordon describes the way in which this forward-driving impetus acts on the episode as a whole: "From the thrice-repeated 'Let us

go' of the first paragraph to the thrice-repeated 'Come on' of the last, the characters are 'wenders' and 'marchers' continuously arriving at doors and leaving by them in a journey which at the end accelerates to a headlong race: 'All off for a buster, armstrong, hollering down the street.' Their lives are like the programmed pilgrimage of the foetus from conception to birth. In fact the whole chapter is the exfoliation of one continuous forward movement, that of the spermatozoon, which according to Joyce's notes defies gravity, turns men and women into its instruments, and even 'obliges God to create.'" In the course of describing the larger movement of "Oxen," Gordon notes that "the Teufeldrockhian argument" of the "Carlyle passage," namely, that "we are all ghosts in transit" is "the chapter's own," a point also borne out by the De Quincey passage (91–92).

13. Houston inveighs against the use of the terms *parody* and *pastiche* in analyses of "Oxen." One of Houston's chief objections to the discussion of "Oxen" in terms of parody and pastiche is that it suggests a departure, on Joyce's part, from the "stylistic allusions" and "imitations of styles" found in preceding episodes (124). The implication is that by describing a passage in "Oxen" as a parody or a pastiche, we are denying that it is related to any other passage in *Ulysses,* a suspicion that seems unwarranted. Elsewhere, Houston argues that when we refer to a passage as a parody of its original, we are claiming that we know how Joyce felt about a particular stylist (135). My own sense is that asserting that Joyce parodies a certain author is not necessarily the same thing as asserting that we know what he thinks of that author; it is merely an observation on what use he makes of a given style in a given context.

14. Zoe says, "(her lucky hand instantly saving him) Hoopsa! Don't fall upstairs" (409).

15. According to the OED, the initial meaning of *pastiche* (*pasticcio*) is "a medley of different ingredients; a hotchpotch, farrago, jumble."

16. "A black crack of noise in the street here, alack, bawled back. Loud on left Thor thundered: in anger awful the hammerhurler. Came now the storm that hist his *heart*. And Master Lynch bade him have a care to flout and witwanton as the god self was angered for his hellprate and paganry. And he that had erst challenged to be so doughty waxed wan as they might all mark and shrank together and his pitch that was before so haught uplift was now of a sudden quite plucked down and his *heart* shook within the cage of his breast as he tasted the rumour of that storm. Then did some mock and some jeer and Punch Costello fell hard again to his yale which Master Lenehan vowed he would do after and he was indeed but a word and a blow on any the least colour. But the braggart boaster cried that an old Nobodaddy was in his cups it was muchwhat indifferent and he would not lag behind his lead. But this was only to dye his desperation as cowed

he crouched in Horne's hall. He drank indeed at one draught to pluck up a *heart* of any grace for it thundered long rumblingly over all the heavens so that Master Madden, being godly certain whiles, knocked him on his ribs upon that crack of doom and Master Bloom, at the braggart's side, spoke to him calming words to slumber his great fear, advertising how it was no other thing but a hubbub noise that he heard, the discharge of fluid from the thunderhead, look you, having taken place, and all of the order of a natural phenomenon" (323; emphasis mine).

5

"Circe"

Ulysses is a writerly text, a text that cannot be consumed by readers unwilling to help prepare its meaning. Because *Ulysses* is Joyce's encyclopedia, this is no easy task—the list of ingredients seems to go on forever. "Oxen of the Sun" and "Circe" are particularly loaded with echoes and allusions, the former as a compendium of literary styles and the latter as a phantasmagorical repetition of all the episodes that precede it. Luckily for the reader struggling to find her way, these episodes are not only encyclopedic but also reflexive— "Oxen of the Sun" is a warped mirror of literary manners and "Circe" is a kaleidoscopic recomposition of *Ulysses*.[1]

The reflexiveness of "Circe" and "Oxen of the Sun" is in keeping with Stephen's notion of poesis: "As we, or mother Dana, weave and unweave our bodies . . . from day to day, their molecules shuttled to and fro, so does the artist weave and unweave his image" (159). Although every episode of *Ulysses* weaves and unweaves its creator's image, the circular pattern that results is particularly visible in "Oxen of the Sun" and "Circe." In "Oxen of the Sun," the narrator passes through different styles only to end in an anticipation of style, a belated infancy; the cacophony of the closing passages confirms the vast circularity of literary procreation. In "Circe," the narrator recedes, assigning most of the costume changes to Bloom,[2] and the spectacle that follows is a surrealistic pantomime of *Ulysses*.[3]

Circularity notwithstanding, the reader of "Circe" is not granted an easy passage home. In "Oxen of the Sun," the promise of organic unity is withheld; in "Circe," the reader's expectation of dramatic unity is systematically thwarted. Despite the fact that the episode is written in play form, language never becomes mimetic here, but takes on a hyperactive life of its own.[4] The crucial difference between the two episodes is that "Circe" finally does end in an uncanny homecoming, a vivid imagining of harmony that occurs when we no longer expect it. What accounts for Bloom's escape from the fractured world of Nighttown? What accounts for our willingness to believe, if only for a moment, in Bloom's vision of Rudy? What accounts for the satisfaction afforded by the inconclusive symmetries of "Circe"?

According to Joyce, experience is circular whether we know it or not. As Stephen puts it, "Every life is many days, day after day. We walk through ourselves, meeting robbers, ghosts, giants, old men, brothers-in-love, but always meeting ourselves" (175). Recognizing that circularity instead of becoming its victim depends on a continuous act of memory. Remembering the past becomes particularly important in "Oxen of the Sun" and "Circe," two of the most disorienting episodes in *Ulysses*. In "Oxen of the Sun," literary history is commemorated in a series of parodies and pastiches; in "Circe," memories achieve the force of hallucinations and a massive recycling of episodes takes place. In both episodes, memory enables Joyce to unweave and reweave his image of experience, conceived as perpetual exile and homecoming. As I will show in the following discussion of "Circe," it is memory that makes Bloom provisionally whole, leading the way from paralysis to epiphany. It is also memory that provides the reader with a parting glimpse of the circular structure of her own wanderings, releasing her from the obscurity of Nighttown.

In "Scylla and Charybdis," Stephen indicates that an artist must both act and be acted upon (173–74). In "Circe," he and Bloom share this twofold labor, reenacting the past and allowing the past to act on them. Joyce does the same, using Bloom to act out censored fantasies and, at the same time, allowing what he has already written to guide his pen. These encounters take place during Bloom's second descent into hell; the first, in "Hades," was far less comprehensive, affecting Bloom only. "Circe" precipitates the reader into a cartoonish underworld where Bloom's sexual peccadilloes, Stephen's family romance, mythological correspondences, and the nightmares of Irish history intersect. The narrative itself encounters ghosts of deceased episodes; not content with merely echoing himself, Joyce makes a ritual of his reliance upon the familiarity of the past:

THE DAUGHTERS OF ERIN

Kidney of Bloom, pray for us
Flower of the Bath, pray for us
Mentor of Menton, pray for us
Canvasser for the Freeman, pray for us
Charitable Mason, pray for us
Wandering Soap, pray for us
Sweets of Sin, pray for us
Music without Words, pray for us
Reprover of the Citizen, pray for us
Friend of all Frillies, pray for us
Midwife Most Merciful, pray for us
Potato Preservative against Plague and Pestilence,
    pray for us. (407)

As these lines suggest, the descent that takes place in "Circe" is extraordinarily complete.

The commotion in Nighttown is only natural, given the fact that Nighttown is the fictional site of the novel's unconscious.[5] Identities dissolve here, leaking into each other; the familiar protagonists emerge as characters in a dream, shadows of their creator. Thus, Bloom and Stephen overlap several times, forming composite images of Joyce. The poetics behind this fusion, which has already been formulated in "Scylla and Charybdis," is restated in the course of a conversation between Stephen and Lynch's cap:

STEPHEN

You remember fairly accurately all my errors, boasts, mistakes. How long shall I continue to close my eyes to disloyalty? Whetstone!

THE CAP

Ba!

STEPHEN

Here's another for you. (*he frowns*) The reason is because the fundamental and the dominant are separated by the greatest possible interval which ....

THE CAP

Which? Finish. You can't.

STEPHEN

(*with an effort*) Interval which. Is the greatest possible ellipse. Consistent with. The ultimate return. The octave. Which.

THE CAP

Which?

(*Outside the gramophone begins to blare* The Holy City.)

STEPHEN

(*abruptly*) What went forth to the ends of the world to traverse not itself, God, the sun, Shakespeare, a commercial traveller, having itself traversed in reality itself becomes that self. Wait a moment. Wait a second. Damn that fellow's noise in the street. Self which it itself was ineluctably preconditioned to become. *Ecco!*[6] (411–12)

Stephen's speech, with its closing "Ecco!" is a mock epiphany, an imitation of epiphany on the level of theory. Epiphanies, according to Stephen, are the fruit of cross-fertilizations of self and world. The exile understands that he has become the world that he has traversed, and in that moment, the vagaries of his flight become significant. Stephen affirms the possibility of a reciprocity of past and present, of loss and desire, that Bloom realizes at the end of the episode, confirming the epiphanic movement of the episode as a whole. Stephen's reflective anticipation of Bloom's vision marks a moment at which their performances become part of a single action.

At another point, both Bloom and Stephen play the part of author, calling attention to Joyce's intimacy with his fictional counterparts. Stephen uses a minor coincidence to link his life to Bloom's, and Bloom responds by imitating the act of writing:

BLOOM

(*points to his hand*) That weal there is an accident. Fell and cut it twentytwo years ago. I was sixteen.

ZOE

I see, says the blind man. Tell us news.

STEPHEN

See? Moves to one great goal. I am twentytwo. Sixteen years ago he was twentytwo too. Sixteen years ago I twentytwo tumbled. Twentytwo years ago he sixteen fell off his hobbyhorse. (*he winces*) Hurt my hand somewhere. Must see a dentist. Money?

(*Zoe whispers to Florry. They giggle. Bloom releases his hand and writes idly on the table in backhand, pencilling slow curves.*) (459)

The weal on Bloom's hand hardly warrants Stephen's observation that all things "move toward one great goal." Nevertheless, he uses it as an occasion to exercise his craft, passing off the exaggeration as ironic hyperbole and, at the same time, citing the numerical correspondence as evidence of an entelechy that relates him to Bloom. In this moment, as in many others, Stephen has authorial access to the inner logic of the plot, yet it is Bloom who backhandedly pencils slow, subliminal curves. Both the dreamer and his censor are presented here; taken together, they produce a comically refracted image of the author.

Another instance of fusion occurs after Bloom plays the masochistic voyeur:

LYNCH

(*points*) The mirror up to nature. (*he laughs*) Hu hu hu hu hu!

(*Stephen and Bloom gaze in the mirror. The face of William Shakespeare, beardless, appears there, rigid in facial paralysis, crowned by the reflection of the reindeer antlered hatrack in the hall.*)

SHAKESPEARE

(*in dignified ventriloquy*) 'Tis the loud laugh bespeaks the vacant mind. (*to Bloom*) Thou thoughtest as how thou wastest invisible. Gaze. (*he crows with a black capon's laugh*) How my Oldfellow chokit his Thursdaymornun. Iagogogo! (463)

This passage not only fuses the identities of Joyce, Bloom, and Stephen but condenses several themes that are central to the episode as well. Shakespeare's face reflects the paralysis of Dublin. Nighttown is rife with the literal corollary of Dublin's disease, namely syphilitic paralysis, or what the prostitutes call "locomotor ataxy." Stephen and Bloom see their own styles of paralysis reflected in the mirror that is held up to their fallen natures. Bloom, as masochistic participant in his own betrayal, is a crippled Othello, cuckolded in fact rather than avenged in fantasy. Stephen, like Hamlet, is paralyzed by a patriarchy that eats away at his nascent manhood. Like Shakespeare, Bloom is "the hornmad Iago ceaselessly willing that the moor in him shall suffer" (174), deriving masochistic pleasure from Molly's infidelities.[7] Like Shakespeare's Hamlet, Stephen is the unliving son looking forth through the ghost of his father: he embodies the potentialities of his creator which are actualized by the emerging text. Bloom and Stephen lose their reflections the instant they look into the mirror: identified as images of Joyce, they become semi-invisible, dissolving into his creation. Bloom, Stephen, and Joyce are father, son, and holy ghost, unified in the image of Shakespeare, "rigid in facial paralysis." Artistic conception, which depends, as "Oxen" tells us, on appropriating the creations of the father and thereby destroying the authority of those creations, is personified in Shakespeare's reinvented and compromised image.[8]

The last instance of fusion occurs at the end of the episode. Rudy returns to rejuvenate his father; Bloom responds by exchanging attributes with Stephen and returning to himself. Bloom's homecoming at the end of "Circe" depends on love; Nighttown, in its polymorphous perversity, has put that love to the test. Before we analyze the episode's closing epiphany, let us see how memory enables Bloom to survive his own refraction.

The costume changes that refract Bloom's image in Nighttown serve to dramatize desire.[9] The play, as it turns out, is not the thing—Bloom's wardrobe is far more revealing. The stage is set for its display by Stephen's opening gesture: "He flourishes his ashplant, shivering the lamp image, shattering light over the world" (353). Refraction is consummated in the parlor, which is appropriately equipped: "A shade of mauve tissuepaper dims the light of the chandelier. Round and round a moth flies, colliding, escaping. The floor is covered with an oilcloth mosaic of jade and azure and cinnabar rhomboids. Footmarks are stamped over it in all senses, heel to heel, heel to hollow, toe to toe, feet locked, a morris of shuffling feet without body phantoms, all in a scrimmage higgledypiggledy" (409–10).

Bloom, as a mock-heroic figure, is a perfect subject for refraction; his first appearance in Nighttown proves his knack for split-

ting iconic images by his mere presence: "Under the railway bridge
Bloom appears, flushed, panting, cramming bread and chocolate
into a side-pocket. From Gillen's hairdresser's window a composite
portrait shows him gallant Nelson's image. A concave mirror at the
side presents to him lovelorn longlost lugubru Booloohoom. Grave
Gladstone sees him level, Bloom for Bloom. He passes, struck by
the stare of truculent Wellington but in the convex mirror grin un-
struck the bonham eyes and fatchuck cheekchops of jollypoldy the
rixdix doldy" (354).[10]

Another crack in Bloom's identity is exposed by his father, who
scolds him for straying from his Jewish origins. Admonished for
consorting with gentiles, Bloom turns into an overassimilated Jew,
a besmirched dandy "(*in youth's smart blue Oxford suit with white
vestslips, narrowshouldered, in brown Alpine hat, wearing gent's sterling
silver Waterbury keyless watch and double curb Albert with seal attached,
one side of him coated with stiffening mud*)" (358). But his father's
scolding only serves to activate his displacement as a husband and
to whet his appetite for the illicit pleasures urged on him by his
wife: "Go and see life. See the wide world" (359).

Bloom in Nighttown is as cunning as Odysseus because he has
learned how to play the part of no man through his losses. He surrenders his identity quite naturally there, proceeding to flirt with a
series of half-repressed desires; it is no accident that he meets two
groups of old amours almost right away. The first group consists
of Bridie Kelley, Mrs. Breen, and Gerty MacDowell, an old flame
insofar as she is already "damaged goods" in Bloom's eyes. The
second group is a shade more glamorous, consisting of three upper-
class British pen pals, Mrs. Yelverton Barry, Mrs. Bellingham, and
Mrs. Mervyn Talboys. Bloom's sexual encounters in Nighttown are
the most dangerous encounters he has there; although he is incin-
erated after his stump speech by the man in the macintosh (who
draws attention to the fact that identities are expendable wherever
he goes), he promptly rises from his own ashes; he never really
meets his match until he encounters Bella Cohen, whose charms
lead him from fetishism to emasculation and enslavement. It is Bello
who sees to it that he not only acts but is vigorously acted upon.
Bloom meets Stephen's artistic requirements on the music room
floor, fully exploiting his own contradictions. He survives only be-

cause he has some protection against himself; memory saves him from bestialization.

Bloom becomes perfectly heterogeneous by forgetting himself; refraction is the narrative equivalent of his condition. Bello tortures him by equating his forgetfulness with impotence:

BELLO

(*sarcastically*) I wouldn't hurt your feelings for the world but there's a man of brawn in possession there. The tables are turned, my gay young fellow! He is something like a fullgrown outdoor man. Well for you, you muff, if you had that weapon with knobs and lumps and warts all over it. He shot his bolt, I can tell you! Foot to foot, knee to knee, belly to belly, bubs to breast! He's no eunuch. A shock of red hair he has sticking out of him behind like a furzebush! Wait for nine months, my lad! Holy ginger, its kicking and coughing up and down in her guts already! That makes you wild, don't it? Touches the spot? (*he spits in contempt*) Spittoon!

BLOOM

I was indecently treated, I ..... inform the police. Hundred pounds. Unmentionable. I ....

BELLO

Would if you could, lame duck. A downpour we want not your drizzle.

BLOOM

To drive me mad! Moll! I forgot! Forgive! Moll .... We .... Still .....

BELLO

(*ruthlessly*) No. Leopold Bloom, all is changed by woman's will since you slept horizontal in Sleepy Hollow your night of twenty years. Return and see. (441–42)

Bloom accepts Bello's challenge, tiptoeing back to the past "in tattered moccassins with a rusty fowlingpiece" to find Eccles Street transformed into the "Cuckoo's Rest" (442), a haven for adulterers. Eccles Street is renovated with the aid of a household deity, the nymph who has presided over Bloom's nuptial bed. Her coy reproaches for being forced to witness everything that has taken place on that bed, from fornication to the administering of enemas, enables Bloom to recover his lost identity as Molly's husband. Eventually he is strong enough to chase the nymph away and accuses her of deriving sadistic pleasure from her own virginity:

BLOOM

(*starts up, seizes her hand*) Hoy! Nebrakada! Cat o' nine lives! Fair play, madam. No pruningknife. The fox and the grapes, is it? What do you lack with your barbed wire? Crucifix not thick enough? (451)

Memory gives Bloom a modicum of control over refraction. He receives two antidotes to the drug that is Nighttown in the course of the episode, both of which are designed to fortify memory, namely mnemotechnic and moly. Mnemotechnic is a therapy that Virag recommends:

BLOOM

(*reflecting*) Wheatenmeal with lycopodium and syllabax. This searching ordeal. It has been an unusually fatiguing day, a chapter of accidents. Wait. I mean, wartsblood spreads warts, you said ...

VIRAG

(*severely, his nose hardhumped, his side eye winking*) Stop twirling your thumbs and have a good old thunk. See, you have forgotten. Exercise your mnemotechnic. *La causa è santa.* Tara. Tara. (*aside*) He will surely remember.

BLOOM

Rosemary also did I understand you to say or willpower over parasitic tissues. Then nay no I have an inkling. The touch of a deadhand cures. Mnemo?

VIRAG

(*excitedly*) I say so. I say so. E'en so. Technic. (*he taps his parchment-roll energetically*) This book tells you how to act with all descriptive particulars. (419)

Although June 16 may be an "unusually fatiguing day" for Bloom, demanding an inordinate number of evasions, every day is a "chapter of accidents." Memory imposes order on experience, revealing its "retrospective arrangement" (337). When Virag urges

Bloom to exercise memory, Bloom agrees that "the touch of a dead-hand cures." Time turns the wounds that identity receives at the hands of experience into distinguishing marks. Forgetting, on the other hand, enforces the tyranny of experience. Those who blindly repeat the past suffer from paralysis, but those who shoulder the burden of their own history revive the possibility of emancipation. Memory finally enables Bloom to read the hallucinations of the present as signatures of the past. In this moment, Bloom gathers all the characters that he has encountered in Nighttown back into himself, enacting Stephen's notion of poesis.

Virag's mnemotechnic is more than a mechanical method of remembering things; it is a thematic reminder that memory is implicated in the hallucinations of "Circe." By drawing heavily on preceding episodes for the material that its dreams are made of, "Circe" relegates them to the past. "Circe" becomes the garbled memory of that past; the retrospective arrangement of *Ulysses* is illuminated by the epiphany that concludes the episode. Bloom's encounter with Rudy, idiosyncratic though it may be, attests to the revisionary power of subjective memory.

Bloom's second antidote is moly. Moly is associated with various qualities, including "sudden fastidiousness in some detail."[11] In "Circe," both Bloom and Joyce display this trait; both make a ritual of remembering. (Moreover, Joyce encourages the same behavior in us, rewarding the reader who has hoarded stray details from previous episodes by making them surface again pages later.) Bloom is Joyce's kind of collector; because he can remember all the customs occulted in Nighttown, he is able to rescue Stephen, coming up with the right word at the right time. This is not to say that moly is merely an aid to memory; it is also an aid to forgetting, a "hybrid of chance and laughter" that protects against immobility. Loss of memory is equivalent to loss of identity, but fixed identity results in paralysis. Fixity and proteanism, unity and multiplicity, remembering and forgetting are reconciled by love at the end of "Circe"; love makes it possible to discover a passional use for the vagrant meanings that compose life's chapter of accidents. The reconciliation that takes place is characteristically asymmetrical; Joyce's distribution of opposed yet overlapping qualities between Bloom and Stephen acts as an insurance against visionary closure.

The differences between Stephen and Bloom are intimately connected, as Stephen's performance in "Circe" proves. Stephen's proteanism is poetic and rarefied; Bloom's proteanism is vulgar, concrete, and theatrical. Bloom is most in danger when he forgets himself; Stephen is most in danger when he falls prey to his memories of the past. Thus in Nighttown Stephen's memories occasion a dance of death. The dance is framed by a quarrel over money and by a song that links the accidents of the present to the weight of the past. Stephen characteristically settles the quarrel by consenting to his own exploitation, both by the whores, who demand too much, and by Lynch, who donates too little toward the pleasures he claims. As Lynch rounds up the whores, Stephen sings a song that anticipates *their* imminent exploitation and his own meeting with his mother's ghost:

> The fox crew, the cocks flew,
> The bells in heaven
> Were striking eleven.
> 'Tis time for her poor soul
> To get out of heaven. (455)

The song is a rushed overture to the dance of death. As usual, Stephen is privy to the secrets of the narrative that creates him. Guilt prompts him to be self-destructively generous to his fellow debauchees; the extortion of his money by Lynch and the prostitutes is associated with the cannibalism of "holy Ireland." The devouring claims of Ireland are, in turn, personified by May Dedalus; her hunger for Stephen's soul is patriotic in the most primitive sense.

Stephen summons his father with adolescent rhetoric that reminds us of his bond to Icarus:

STEPHEN

No, I flew. My foes beneath me. And ever shall be. World without end. (*he cries*) *Pater!* Free! (466)

Simon incites his son to riot by adjuring him to think of his mother's people. Stephen will turn into the image of his father, a derelict Irishman with a fine singing voice, unless he cuts the cord that binds him to his mother.

May Dedalus comes back from the dead to poison Stephen's vocation with her voiceless calling: "(*Stephen's mother, emaciated, rises stark through the floor, in leper grey with a wreath of faded orange-*

blossoms and a torn bridal veil, her face worn and noseless, green with gravemould. Her hair is scant and lank. She fixes her bluecircled hollow eyesockets on Stephen and opens her toothless mouth uttering a silent word. A choir of virgins and confessors sing voicelessly)" (473). Stephen's mother is the site of a false omphalos; accordingly Buck Mulligan, usurper of the tower, conspires with her ghost. Stephen vainly attempts to redeem the false omphalos by making his mother give him back the word known to all men, a word that he knows full well, as Hans Gabler's emendation of "Scylla and Charybdis"[12] proves. He is not asking his mother to solve a mystery but to forgive him for refusing to grant her dying wish. By begging her forgiveness, he surrenders to the authority of love. At the close of *Portrait,* he is not yet capable of such humility, moving his mother to pray that he may learn "what the heart is and what it feels" (252). Since then, her prayers have been partially answered; he has been educated by her death. But her response to his prayer in Nighttown is a corruption of the word known to all men; by glorifying guilt as his true vocation, she betrays her symbolic identity. She represents the devouring claims of the past, claims that must be thrust aside if Stephen is to triumph over paralysis.

Bloom may be as cunning as his Greek precursor in Nighttown, but it is Stephen who matches Odysseus' infernal meeting with his mother's ghost. Paradoxically, Stephen's mother is to blame for his lack of Odyssean heroism in Nighttown. Suddenly she becomes the womb from which all history's nightmares spring, nightmares that can only be mastered with the aid of new creations.[13]

Stephen's hallucination of his mother coincides with the hanging of the Croppy Boy. These moments are joined by the theme of positive negation, which motivates the Wagnerian pun on *nothung,* nothing and not hung. Like Stephen among the prostitutes, the Croppy Boy is a victim of Catholic guilt. He confesses to a priest who turns out to be a British soldier, and the king rewards the patriotism that confession per se demonstrates by having him executed. Old Gummy Granny, bewailing the strangers in her house, is a casualty of the senility that nationalism breeds. The Croppy Boy is flowing over with ruined potentiality. The physical language that he splutters reeks of death: "Horhot ho hray hor hother's hest" (485). These syllables are metonymically related to the sterile sperm that shoots over the cobblestones of Dublin. The executioner of the

Croppy Boy kills all hope of locating the true omphalos. The "coiled and smoking entrails" (485) of his victim are mutilated forms of those "cords of all" that "link back," "strandentwining cable of all flesh" (32). Stephen must cut the umbilical cords that are choking him to gain control of his own voice. If he fails to cut himself loose, he will suffer the Croppy Boy's fate; his poetry will be licked up like dead sperm by sentimental admirers.

Given his plight, it is not surprising that Stephen enters Night-town looking anxiously behind him. Bloom, on the other hand, who is not tied to his mother's apron strings, falls headlong into hell. Once inside, Stephen dresses far more conservatively than Bloom, choosing only one costume calculated to offend:[14]

FLORRY

(*to Stephen*) I'm sure you're a spoiled priest. Or a monk.

LYNCH

He is. A cardinal's son.

STEPHEN

Cardinal sin. Monks of the screw.

(*His Eminence Simon Stephen Cardinal Dedalus, Primate of all Ireland, appears in the doorway, dressed in red soutane, sandals and socks. Seven dwarf simian acolytes, also in red, cardinal sins, uphold his train, peeping under it. He wears a battered silk hat sideways on his head. His thumbs are stuck in his armpits and his palms outspread. Round his neck hangs a rosary of corks ending on his breast in a corkscrew cross. Releasing his thumbs, he invokes grace from on high with large wave gestures and proclaims with bloated pomp.*) (427)

The costume of Simon Stephen Cardinal Dedalus is designed to shock devout Catholics and to delight serious drinkers. The Primate of all Ireland laughs in his chains in accordance with the custom of the country; in fact, his history is as confining as Conservio's dungeon. He presents himself as the defective product of his mother's adoration of the church and his father's adoration of the pub. The poem he recites (427) was a favorite of John Joyce's, serving as a cryptic reminder of the weight of the past. Stephen knows that paralysis is his birthright; accordingly he dishonors his father and mother by squandering it.

The personae in Bloom's repertoire are residues of his losses as lover, husband, and son; Stephen has only lost his mother, and her death has redoubled his need to father himself. Bloom endures through compromise; negotiating his position has become second nature to him. Stephen's art is predicated on rebellion; accordingly, he must always have his foes around him. One of the reasons that history is a nightmare for Stephen is that it is filled with invitations to regress. For Bloom, the past is less terrible and the future is less sublime. Stephen returns defiantly; Bloom knows that the touch of a deadhand cures. Memory finally delivers both Bloom and the reader from the maze of Nighttown, as Joyce's use of the color mauve there illustrates.

Mauve light dissolves the signatures of things into slovenly traces in the music room: "A shade of mauve tissuepaper dims the light of the chandelier. Round and round a moth flies, colliding, escaping" (409). The reader of these traces is drawn into a promiscuous dance that confounds all senses. The moth flying around the light distractedly commemorates the identities sacrificed in this celebration of forgetfulness. Mauve also enhances the flavor of the chocolate aphrodisiac that Bloom accepts back from Zoe:

BLOOM

(*takes the chocolate*) Aphrodisiac? Tansy and pennyroyal. But I bought it. Vanilla calms or? Mnemo. Confused light confuses memory. Red influences lupus. Colours affect women's characters, any they have. This black makes me sad. Eat and be merry for tomorrow. (*he eats*) Influence taste too, mauve. But it is so long since I. Seems new. Aphro. That priest. Must come. Better late than never. Try truffles at Andrews. (429)

Bloom is susceptible to the influence of color. His knowledge of the mnemotechnical tricks color can play is not complete enough to immunize him against its powers of suggestion. Unlike Stephen, whose senses are ordered by literary history, he wants to take his perceptions literally. (This quality often makes him the straight man in Joyce's comedy.) Bloom in Nighttown is like the woman whose character is a residue of the colors she wears. The costumes that caricature the parts that he has played attach themselves to memory and grow into a motley of second skins. At this particular moment, a touch of mauve suffices to turn him into an unusually forgetful man. Zoe's chocolates and the lozenges of mauve light that cover the music room belong to the same brand of imagery. On this floor, Bloom forgets the proprieties of his own gender.

But mauve itself is transformed by its inclusion in the portrait of Rudy:

STEPHEN

(*murmurs*)

.... shadows ... the woods
... white breast ... dim sea.

(*He stretches out his arms, sighs again and curls his body. Bloom, holding the hat and ashplant, stands erect. A dog barks in the distance. Bloom tightens and loosens his grip on the ashplant. He looks down on Stephen's face and form.*)

BLOOM

(*communes with the night*) Face reminds me of his poor mother. In the shady wood. The deep white breast. Ferguson, I think I caught. A girl. Some girl. Best thing could happen him. (*he murmurs*) ..... swear that I will always hail, ever conceal, never reveal, any part or parts, art or arts ...... (*he murmurs*) ..... in the rough sands of the sea ... a cabletow's length from the shore .... where the tide ebbs .... and flows .....

(*Silent, thoughtful, alert he stands on guard, his fingers at his lips in the attitude of secret master. Against the dark wall a figure appears slowly, a fairy boy of eleven, a changeling, kidnapped, dressed in an Eton suit with glass shoes and a little bronze helmet, holding a book in his hand. He reads from right to left inaudibly, smiling, kissing the page.*)

BLOOM

(*wonderstruck, calls inaudibly*) Rudy!

RUDY

(*gazes, unseeing, into Bloom's eyes and goes on reading, kissing, smiling. He has a delicate mauve face. On his suit he has diamond and ruby buttons. In his free left hand he holds a slim ivory cane with a violet bowknot. A white lambkin peeps out of his waistcoat pocket.*) (497)

The broken lines from Yeats that Stephen murmurs move Bloom to recite a pigeon poetry of his own. Stephen's text is flawed by the influence of his mother's ghost. Bloom, on the other hand, has never known the restraint that an internal editor imposes. His garbled verses identify him as a provincial relative of Prospero, the "secret master" that Stephen emulates. But Bloom can only be led through literary history as a docile tourist. It would never occur to him to balance a poetic creed against his losses. Accordingly, in Stephen's Dublin, a city swimming in literary signatures, Bloom's style of self-redemption is idiosyncratic; it simply cannot be abstracted from the details of his life. The reader, of course, spurred on by the critics, can trace those details back to Homer. Joyce does not prescribe Bloom's historical naiveté as a cure for paralysis. On the contrary, although Bloom is ignorant of his own literary genealogy, he escapes bestialization with the aid of memory. In the passage quoted above, mauve, a color made palpable by its repeated application, intensifies a mirage. The "delicate mauve face" of Rudy fulfills Kenner's definition of epiphany: "What a thing is when fully developed, we call its nature. *Ulysses* adheres to this Aristotelian precept. The epiphanies are achieved, as always, by allowing the introductory seeds to sprout. From the familiar, sensuous mask we move to the opacities of the underlying will" (*Dublin's Joyce* 243). The opacity of Joyce's will is mirrored in Rudy's face, a sentimental icon that chides its worshipper. Bloom's relationship to Rudy doubles Joyce's relationship to his past. The father unburies his son as Joyce fictionalizes his biography; each attempts to reinvent desire by rewriting the past that he has begotten.

Although Bloom is the subject and the object of this particular epiphany, its real beneficiary is the reader. Similarly, the hallucinations that Nighttown is made of peel away from their sources; neither Bloom nor Stephen is given time to contemplate his projections, leaving this task to us. Kenner was right to call "Circe" a psychoanalysis without an analyst ("Circe" 360); the episode lacks the transcendental referent that would allow Bloom and Stephen to decode their fantasies. This lack of a transcendental referent is, of course, key to the epiphanic movement of the episode as a whole, a movement that emancipates the reader not by affirming an absolute but by shedding light on narrative process itself.

The pleasure that Bloom takes in his vision is slight in comparison to the satisfaction it affords the reader. The vision is the most loaded instance of condensation to be found in the long dream of

"Circe." Rudy returns not only to redeem his own death but also to redeem the suicide of Bloom's father. Like Bloom's father, he reads "backwards," momentarily restoring the historical continuity that the former destroyed. The figure of Rudy forms an ideal point at which Rudy's promise, Stephen's vocation, Bloom's hereditary love of the Book, Stephen's epiphanic investigations, Bloom's sublunary speculations, and Stephen's expatriotic fervor intersect. Seen from this point, Nighttown is no longer a tangled Medusa; accordingly the reader is free to take his leave of her. Whereas Virag's mnemotechnic is an exercise of thrift, epiphany is the achievement of an economy of desire. Mnemotechnic is a way of ordering the details that clutter sublunary minds; epiphany is the discovery of a passional use for them.

Unity and multiplicity are brought together in Bloom's vision, which prefigures the act of creation that will free Stephen from the tyranny of the past. Stephen must father himself through his art; Bloom's invention of a visionary son affirms the possibility of literary procreation. Like "Oxen of the Sun," "Circe" is circular; unlike "Oxen of the Sun," which ends in raw potentiality, "Circe" ends in a garbled promise. For a moment, the retrospective arrangement of "Circe's" chapter of accidents seems clear. Stephen, the embryo philosopher or unliving son, looks forth from the unquiet ghost of a father (Bloom) betrayed by fate long ago. The closing of the circle does not obliterate loss; once again, it merely reopens the possibility of an act of creation.

In "Circe," paralysis is given a particularly human face. Bloom's vision of Rudy does not cancel out the possibility of paralysis. Judging from the power of the closing epiphany, epiphany thrives on the threat of paralysis, a disease that literally pervades Nighttown. Bloom triumphs over paralysis by rewriting his past, a task that throws his "real" identity into doubt. Although at several points Bloom's ability to survive his own fragmentation is in question, he is finally made provisionally whole by a faint, barely audible promise of emancipation.

Notes

1. Lawrence describes "Oxen" as "the last stand for literary plagiarism" in *Ulysses*, claiming that once Joyce had pushed appropriation to its limit, he began to "pillage" his own text (145).

2. The circular plot of "Circe" thickens when one recalls that Bloom, like Stephen, is made in Joyce's image; thus Joyce is enacting his own idea of experience by weaving and unweaving an image of himself. For a discussion of the autobiographical content of "Circe," see Gordon 108–9.

3. In Kenner's words, "As *Ulysses* is the *Odyssey* transposed and rearranged, 'Circe' is *Ulysses* transposed and rearranged" ("Circe" 356).

4. According to Rabaté, the language of "Circe" is indeed mimetic, specializing in the imitation of gestures: "The semantization of gestures—jerks, twitches, hops, Saint Vitus's dances, spasms, contortions and convulsions—is accompanied by a language that keeps gesticulating to parade its mimicry. Mimetism is conveyed by an alliterative and paragrammatic writing constantly verging on poetry. This is enhanced by the varying speed of the hallucinations, which fade quickly into one another. . . . The progressions have a dream-like quality, both unnaturally swift and nightmarishly difficult. The dream occurs on the stage, as it were, without any conscious interventions from the characters" (*Authorized Reader* 81). Rabaté would probably agree that a narrative that focuses exclusively on gestures and phantasmagoria is not mimetic in the usual sense. If the language of "Circe" has been made to "parade" its own mimetic qualities, this suggests that those qualities have been emphasized at the expense of external reality.

5. The fact that Joyce chose Nighttown as the site of the novel's unconscious is significant. The transgressive aspect of ventriloquism and impersonation become plainly visible here, conjuring up a far more compromised portrait of the artist than we have seen thus far. Admittedly, Stephen's visit to the prostitute is a crucial event in his discovery of his vocation, but Joyce does not fully expose the illicit side of fiction making until "Circe."

6. The ellipsis here and in all quotations to "Circe" are Joyce's and are rendered according to the Gabler edition of *Ulysses*.

7. The original quote is "[Shakespeare's] unremitting intellect is the hornmad Iago ceaselessly willing that the moor in him shall suffer" (174). Although Bloom has a touch of the perversity attributed to Shakespeare, he obviously does not possess his hyperconsciousness. Joyce allots that quality to Stephen, as is evidenced by Stephen's habit of mocking the inner logic of the plot.

8. Mahaffey notes that "the blending of Stephen and Bloom in Shakespeare is reflected not only through the mirror image, but through the allusion to *Othello. Othello* dramatizes the destructiveness of sexual jealousy, warning Bloom of the necessity of accepting his parity with other men. The implied alternative to the violence engendered by fear and jealousy is a double awareness of the identity of different men and of the differ-

ent identities that comprise a single man, an apprehension of individuality that is incompatible with jealousy and violence" (113). I would add that the humanizing properties of this particular double image depend upon its association with artistic sublimation.

9. If stylistic proteanism is the ruling principle of "Oxen," psychological proteanism is the ruling principle of "Circe."

10. For a provocative discussion of the three surfaces of the mirror in the hairdresser's window, see Mahaffey 112.

11. "*Moly* is a nut to crack. My latest is this. Moly is the gift of Hermes, god of public ways, and is the invisible influence (prayer, chance, agility, *presence of mind,* power of recuperation) which saves in case of accident. This would cover immunity from syphilis. . . . Hermes is the god of signposts: i.e. he is, especially for a traveller like Ulysses, the point at which roads parallel merge and roads contrary also. He is an accident of providence. In this special case his plant may be said to have many leaves, indifference due to masturbation, pessimism congenital, a sense of the ridiculous, sudden fastidiousness in some detail, experience. It is the only occasion on which Ulysses is not helped by Minerva but by her male counterpart or inferior" (*Selected Letters* 272).

12. "—Marina, Stephen said, a child of storm, Miranda, a wonder, Perdita, that which was lost. What was lost is given back to him: his daughter's child. *My dearest wife,* Pericles says, *was like this maid.* Will any man love the daughter if he has not loved the mother?

—The art of being a grandfather, Mr Best gan murmur. *L'art d'être grandp* .....

—Will he not see reborn in her, with the memory of his own youth added, another image?

Do you know what you are talking about? Love, yes. Word known to all men. *Amor vero aliquid alicui bonum vult unde et ea quae concupiscimus ...*" (160–61).

13. In "Oxen," Stephen is an "embryo philosopher," passively contained within a matrix of styles; in "Circe," he actively struggles with the specter of his mother, envisioned as the womb from which all the nightmares of history spring.

14. In his excellent discussion "*Ulysses:* Book of Many Turns," Fritz Senn notes that it is appropriate that Stephen "comes to grief" in "Circe," an episode that "hinges on the volatile mutability of all things": "for all the flexibility of Stephen's mind, he fails, or refuses, to be flexible enough to deal with a real situation and to evade a blunt danger. He is not trying to select a more opportune role, but rather continues a monologue that is unintelligible and must appear provoking to the soldiers, who of course

are equally inflexible. The physical altercation in Circe is between characters who are rigid and might be called 'monotropic'" (*Joyce's Dislocutions* 131–32). Senn contrasts the monotropism of Stephen to the polytropism of Bloom and of the episode as a whole, hinting that the readers who refuse to adapt to the proteanism to "Circe" may fall by the wayside, like Stephen.

6

"Penelope"

The epiphany at the end of "Circe" is an inspired act of memory; the same is true of the epiphany that closes *Ulysses*. Both are home-comings, moments of recognition expanded by absence. Like the epiphanies of Joyce's earlier works, they are grounded in everyday reality; unlike the epiphanies of the earlier works, they reveal the circularity of life's "retrospective arrangement." The epiphanies of *Dubliners* are analytical; each one is a disclosure of bad faith or a demonstration of entrapment. The epiphanies of *Portrait* are relativistic; taken together, they cancel each other out, dissolving into musical changes that compose a destiny. The epiphanies of *Ulysses* are neither analytical nor relativistic, tracing the circle of an odyssey that spans one day that is "many days, day after day."

Although the epiphanies of *Ulysses* are climactic, they do not settle anything,[1] nor do they release the reader from narrated time. Bloom's vision of Rudy and Molly's closing assent are compre-hensive articulations of desire. At these points, the reader sees the shape of an odyssey that has no end; both Bloom and Molly return to the origin of all journeys by half remembering and half invent-ing the answers to their needs. The beginning of Joyce's odyssey is preserved in its closing epiphany; self-exile is not resolved but con-summated in homecoming, and infidelity rekindles broken vows.

In *Ulysses,* Joyce uses the artifice of epiphany to simulate the cir-cular movement of organic development described in "Oxen of the Sun": "And as the ends and ultimates of all things accord in some mean and measure with their inceptions and originals, that same multiplicit concordance which leads forth growth from birth accomplishing by a retrogressive metamorphosis that minishing and ablation towards the final which is agreeable unto nature so is it with our subsolar being" (322). Molly and Bloom give substance to this notion of circular metamorphosis or odyssey as return. The sources of their epiphanies are not hard to find; every episode of *Ulysses* contains the stuff that their waking dreams are made on.

The epiphanies of *Ulysses* mark points at which history is repeated with a difference. Like all Joycean epiphanies, they are narrative events, not communal ones; they change the position of the reader, not the lives of the characters. Stephen Dedalus describes epiphany as the intellectual reclamation of a sensuous object; Joyce replaces that object with narration, recasting epiphany as the emergence of pattern from process. From the vantage point of epiphany, the reader apprehends the circular course of her own exegetical journey. But even as her journey comes to an end, the desire that fueled it is voiced anew; as literal-minded as Molly may seem, her closing assent affirms the inseparability of eros and language, revealing her hunger for the "word known to all men."

Seen in retrospect, the reader's adventures bear witness to the self-referentiality of *Ulysses*. As we have seen, the shape of things to come is intimated in the opening episodes, which call attention to themselves as self-conscious artifacts. With "Aeolus," Joyce begins his inventory of the internal resources of the text, an investigation that culminates in the funhouse of "Circe." In "Penelope," Joyce toys with our desire for a "simple story," creating the illusion that we are returning to a unity of feeling that is somehow superior to language. And yet, as we will see, Molly never betrays narrative process; she performs the labor of creation by breathing new life into words spoken long ago.

How does Joyce assure the reader's subjection to narrated time? For one thing, the terms of the text rule out the possibility of a perfect resolution, rendering it impossible to subordinate narrative process to narrative structure. The incongruities built into *Ulysses* are particularly evident in "Ithaca." Throughout *Ulysses,* Stephen's lack of a spiritual father and Bloom's desire for a son is a source of dramatic tension. But when this "keyless couple" (546) speaks at last, it uses an alienated, authority-ridden language. Bloom's scientism and Stephen's Catholic upbringing intersect in the "mathematical catechism" of "Ithaca." Despite his penchant for Utopian scheming, Bloom reflects, in this cumbersome language, upon the impossibility of ideal homecomings, entertaining thoughts of formalizing his relationship to Stephen only to dismiss those thoughts again:

> What rendered problematic for Bloom the realisation of these mutually selfexcluding propositions?
> The irreparability of the past: once at a performance of Albert Hengler's circus in the Rotunda, Rutland square, Dublin, an intuitive particoloured clown in quest of paternity had penetrated from the ring to a place in the auditorium where Bloom, solitary, was seated and had publicly declared to an exhilarated audience that he (Bloom) was his (the clown's) papa. The imprevidibility of the future: once in the summer of 1898 he (Bloom) had marked a florin (2/-) with three notches on the milled edge and tendered it in payment of an account due to and received by J. and T. Davy, family grocers, 1 Charlemont Mall, Grand Canal, for circulation on the waters of civic finance, for possible, circuitous or direct, return.

> Was the clown Bloom's son?
> No.

> Had Bloom's coin returned?
> Never. (571)

The major epiphanies of *Ulysses* occur after the characters have revealed themselves to us by displaying the scars of experience. In all of Joyce's work, epiphany is implicated in the redundancy of self-knowledge. Stephen traces the hermeneutic circle of identity and self-knowledge with Maeterlink's aid: *"If Socrates leave his house today he will find the sage seated on his doorstep. If Judas go forth tonight it is to Judas his steps will tend"* (175). Pure victims of the "accidents" that recur in all their journeys are condemned to paralysis; diviners of the circle may be able to follow its curve home. The difference between the stasis of epiphany and the stasis of paralysis is that the former is associated with fictional self-knowledge, whereas the latter is a sign of its lack.

Although minor epiphanies are scattered throughout its pages, there are only two points at which the greater circle of *Ulysses* closes. Before the circle closes for the second and last time in "Penelope," it opens to admit the Other, which is to say that it closes upon a duality. Because that particular duality is primordial and procreative, *Ulysses* finally presents itself not as a closed circuit but as a single revolution in an endless series. Molly's monologue reminds us that the kind of odyssey mapped here is as self-perpetuating as any journey that originates in the "sexual myth." Stylistically, Joyce's reversion to unadulterated interior monologue, as opposed to the mixture of interior monologue, free indirect discourse, and quoted monologue that constitutes the initial style, confirms our understanding of *Ulysses* not as a perfect circle but as a circularity-in-process. The circle of our journey does not end in a sentimental return, nor does it prove to have been a linear journey in disguise. As "Oxen of the Sun" teaches us, Joyce's avoidance of linear narration has its corollary in a profound distrust of the myth of progress, a myth that he regards as decadent. His resistance to narrative closure, on the other hand, reflects his belief in the emancipatory potential of narrative process.

On the level of the characters, the hermeneutic circle of identity also opens and closes in "Penelope." By the end of the episode, Molly has remembered herself in Bloom. Before examining the language of "Penelope," I would like to discuss the parallactic meeting of Molly and Bloom that takes place here.

By giving Molly the "last word," Joyce makes the reader privy to a subliminal reunion, a cross-pollination of memories. The final epiphany, which renames Molly and Bloom, depends on Molly's recognition of her husband, who has found it advisable to conduct himself as "no man" throughout the day. Bloom's stealthy return from anonymity is encoded in the episode's flower theme. Molly's recollection of the florid suitor she invented to seduce her first lover anticipates the closing epiphany:

> he was the first man kissed me under the Moorish wall my sweetheart when a boy it never entered my head what kissing meant till he put his tongue in my mouth his mouth was sweetlike young I put my knee up to him a few times to learn the way what did I tell him I was engaged for for fun to the son of a Spanish nobleman named Don Miguel de la Flora and he believed me that I was to be married to him in 3 years time theres many a true word spoken in jest there is a flower that bloometh (625)

This early deception binds her to Bloom, who uses a floral name to win the heart of Martha. Later Molly uses a derivative of the same pseudonym to ridicule Bloom just before her full repossession of his name: "O move over your big carcass out of that for the love of Mike listen to him the winds that waft my sighs to thee so well he may sleep and sigh the great suggester Don Poldo de la Flora" (639).[2]

Before Molly can remember more intimate names, she must descend into her own version of hell, like Bloom and Stephen before her. Stephen, who reminds her of Rudy, leads her there:

> I saw him driving down to the Kingsbridge Station with his father and mother I was in mourning thats 11 years ago now yes hed be 11 though what was the good going into mourning for what was neither one thing nor the other the first cry was enough for me I heard the deathwatch too ticking in the wall of course he insisted hed go into mourning for the cat I suppose hes a man now by this time he was an innocent boy then and a darling little fellow in his lord Fauntleroy suit and curly hair like a prince on the stage[3] (637)

Molly's recollection of seeing Stephen as an "innocent boy" when she was in mourning echoes Bloom's vision of Rudy; both see Stephen as a changeling, stolen away years ago and, miraculously, returned again.

The poetic promise embodied in Stephen draws Molly and Bloom closer, mitigating their memory of pain. Like Bloom, Molly romanticizes Stephen's vocation:

> they all write about some woman in their poetry well I suppose he wont find many like me where softly sighs of love the light guitar where poetry is in the air the blue sea and the moon shining so beautifully coming back on the nightboat from Tarifa the lighthouse at Europa point the guitar that fellow played was so expressive will I ever go back there again all new faces two glancing eyes a lattice hid Ill sing that for him theyre my eyes if hes anything of a poet two eyes as darkly bright as loves own star arent those beautiful words as loves young star (637–38)

Both Molly and Bloom are moved to verse by a calling that they conceive of in purely romantic terms. Yet their own enactment of poesis, with Bloom playing the part of poet and Molly playing the part of muse, is not as sentimental as it may seem, demarcating poetry as everyman's domain. Their reunion is a poetic event insofar as it is strictly metaphorical and, at the same time, regenerative.

Molly's lyrical power over Bloom in the present is a residue of their reciprocity in the past; before recovering that intimacy, she encounters the accident that destroyed it:

> its a poor case that those that have a fine son like that theyre not satisfied and I none was he not able to make one it wasnt my fault we came together when I was watching the two dogs up in her behind in the middle of the naked street that disheartened me altogether I suppose I oughtnt to have buried him in that little woolly jacket I knitted crying as I was but give it to some poor child but I knew well Id never have another our 1st death too it was we were never the same since O Im not going to think myself into the glooms about that any more (640)

She leaves the past the same way she reentered it, placing unwarranted faith in Stephen. Her hopes turn upon a confluence of eroticism and language, a point at which the imperfect present flows into an unspoiled past. Schemes of seduction mingle with plans to recover her mother tongue and attempts to internalize Stephen's name:

> Dedalus I wonder its like those names in Gibraltar Delapez Delagracia they had the devils queer names there Father Vilaplana of Santa Maria that gave me the rosary Rosales y OReilly in the Calle Las Siete Revueltas and Pisimbo and Mrs Opisso in Governor street O what a name Id go and drown myself in the first river if I had a name like her O my and all the bits of streets Paradise ramp and Bedlam ramp and Rodgers Ramp and Crutchetts ramp and the devils gap steps well small blame to me if I am a harumscarum I know I am a bit I declare to God I dont feel a day older than then I wonder could I get my tongue round any of the Spanish como esta usted muy bien gracias y usted see I havent forgotten it all I thought I had only for the grammar a noun is the name of any person place or thing[4] (640–41)

Fantasies of mortifying Bloom lead to an altar consecrated to Stephen's seduction. The altar is swimming in red and white roses, symbolizing the rejuvenation of the youthful complexion that Molly was wishing for pages ago. Cakes with "cherries in them" (642) and piano keys washed in milk reapportion the maternal milk that Bloom enjoyed before the death of Rudy.

The blossoming that now takes place silences all sophisticated cults of negativity with a simple pantheistic credo. Molly is ripe to be fertilized again by words that hold the secret of Bloom's androgynous potency:

> the sun shines for you he said the day we were lying among the rhododendrons on Howth head in the grey tweed suit and his straw hat the day I got him to propose to me yes first I gave him the bit of seedcake out of my mouth and it was leapyear like now yes 16 years ago my God after that long kiss I near lost my breath yes he said I was a flower of the mountain yes so we are flowers all a womans body yes that was one true thing he said in his life and the sun shines for you today yes that was why I liked him because I saw he understood or felt what a woman is and I knew I could always get round him and I gave him all the pleasure I could leading him on till he asked me to say yes (643)

With this, Molly leaves the realm of satire and crosses the threshold that leads into an epiphanic world that Martha, Bloom's illicit muse, is barred from. The artificial flowering that Bloom extrapolates from Martha's letter is the satirical antithesis of Molly's epiphany: "Angry tulips with you darling manflower punish your cactus if you dont please poor forgetmenot how I long violets to dear roses when we soon anemone meet all naughty nightstalk wife Martha's perfume" (64). The affirmation that follows breaks through the intricately corroded surface of the life that Bloom and Molly share. Bloom's name is metaphorically unfolded and Poldy is rescued from the anonymity of his longing recollection of the same moment episodes ago.

The reunion of Molly and Bloom is a consummation of unspoken language, sealed by the metaphors they unknowingly share. It is paralleled by the narrator's conversion to univocality; the primitive poetry of "Penelope" undercuts the stylistic experiments that have preceded it, celebrating the reader's homecoming. Joyce's imitation of simplicity is very convincing; self-conscious innovation seems to give way to pure intuition. Primordial expression is reinstated: Molly's thoughts cannot be separated from her physicality, and her physicality is a representation of nature. By speaking through that body, Joyce renews the trope of sympathetic nature, that is, a nature that is not foreign but fertilizable. Molly enables him to trace his own mythic ancestry back to Vico's primitive poets:

> The nature of our civilized minds is so detached from the senses, even in the vulgar, by abstractions corresponding to all the abstract

terms our languages abound in, and so refined by the art of writing, and as it were so spiritualized by the use of numbers, because even the vulgar know how to count and reckon, that it is naturally beyond our power to form the vast image of this mistress called "Sympathetic Nature." Men shape the phrase with their lips but have nothing in their minds; for what they have in mind is falsehood, which is nothing; and their imagination no longer avails to form a vast false image. It is equally beyond our power to enter into the vast imagination of those first men, whose minds were not in the least abstract, refined or spiritualized, because they were entirely immersed in the senses, buffeted by the passions, buried in the body. (Vico 76 [378])

Molly personifies the ignorance of the first poets:

Poetic wisdom, the first wisdom of the gentile world, must have begun with a metaphysics not rational and abstract like that of the learned men now, but felt and imagined as that of these first men must have been, who, without power of ratiocination, were all robust sense and vigorous imagination. This metaphysics was their poetry, a faculty born with them (for they were furnished by nature with their senses and imaginations); born of their ignorance of causes, for ignorance, the mother of wonder, made everything wonderful to men who were ignorant of everything. (Vico 75 [375])

Although Molly is far from being "ignorant of everything," she is limited, as Joyce himself noted.[5] (Stephen and Bloom indulge the encyclopedism of their creator; Molly will have nothing to do with it.) She cannot always sense the "wonder of everything," but when she does, her communion is not adulterated by reason. Through Molly, the narrator returns to the mythological simplicity of the Other. Penetrable yet irreducible, the Other is represented as the source to which all wanderers eventually return.[6] Bloom's odyssey ends in "das ewige Weibliche"; the narrator's odyssey through a series of writerly styles ends in an antistyle that emulates speech. But just as no amount of intimacy can tame "das ewige Weibliche," no amount of imitation can erase the boundary between writing and speech. The style of "Penelope" is not, as Riquelme has claimed, "an abandoning of language at the margin of narrative"[7] but a display of abandonment within narration, a rhapsodic quotation of unliterary, silent speech.

All homecomings after long separations have their ironies, and the reader's homecoming is no exception. Molly's language is deceptively simple; upon closer inspection, it proves to be less primitive than it seems. Her colloquial inner monologue duplicates speech. Although it is spoken silently, it is unabbreviated and emphatic, extroverted and complete. The following remarks by Roland Barthes on the difference between written and spoken language shed light on the intricacies of its status:

> All modes of writing have in common the fact of being "closed" and thus different from spoken language. Writing is in no way an instrument for communication, it is not an open route through which there passes only the intention to speak. A whole disorder flows through speech and gives it this self-devouring momentum which keeps it in a perpetually suspended state. Conversely, writing is a hardened language which is self-contained and in no way meant to deliver to its own duration a mobile series of approximations. It is on the contrary meant to impose, thanks to the shadow cast by its system of signs, the image of a speech which had a structure even before it came into existence. What makes writing the opposite of speech is that the former always appears symbolical, introverted, sensibly turned toward an occult side of language, whereas the second is nothing but the flow of empty signs, the movement of which alone is significant. The whole of speech is epitomized in this expendability of words, in this froth ceaselessly swept onwards, and speech is found only where language self-evidently functions like a devouring process which swallows only the moving crest of words. Writing, on the contrary, is always rooted in something beyond language, it develops like a seed, not like a line, it manifests an essence and holds the threat of a secret, it is an anti-communication, it is intimidating. (*Writing* 19–20)

Molly refuses to be cloistered in writing. Her monologue is bluntly musical, rushing the reader forward and denying him the pleasure of lingering over coy words. She broadcasts her secrets to herself and thereby dispenses with the formalities of voyeurism; consequently her erotic reveries are neither very "literary" nor very pornographic. Her silent speech casts no shadow; if it occults anything, it is the legal structure of language that preceded it. Her voice spends itself in a "flow of empty signs," veering away from the kind of lapidary fullness characteristic of Stephen's. And the continuousness of this flow, which builds into lyrical harangue, is in direct contrast to the accommodating banality and oblique discretion of Bloom's inner speech. But the fact remains that her monologue is a piece of writing. Moreover, it is a piece of writing designed to represent a language of desire that can never be fully articulated or answered. In fact, it turns out that "Penelope" is less open and informal than it seems. The syntax of the monologue is actually quite conventional. At first glance, it appears to be composed of several long, undifferentiated sentences. Molly seems to enjoy antinomian privileges in the realm of grammar; the reader is led to believe that she slays the suitors whenever she speaks by the completeness of her irreverence for the patriarchal order to which they belong. But in fact her monologue is not syntactically inviolate; grammar can be imposed on it without much difficulty.[8] Nor is the music of the monologue ruined when punctuation is reintroduced. Joyce deleted the punctuation to strengthen its flow, and the strategy is successful, but only because it provides a graphic corollary to a velocity inherent in the words themselves.

Thus the narrator's return to a simplicity that he has never known, the legendary simplicity of the Other, depends on stylistic sophistication. In the course of reviving romantic traditions that he seemed eager to reject in "Aeolus" and the episodes that follow, he avails himself of the poetic convenience of a muse. Because the muse that he chooses is more earthbound than most, her contribution is bound to be problematic. Her nature is entirely adversarial; she is an expression of her creator's distaste for ethereal art. The same antipathy compels Bloom to chase away the nymph, one of Molly's foils, in "Circe":

THE NYMPH

(*eyeless, in nun's white habit, coif and hugewinged wimple, softly, with remote eyes*) Tranquilla convent. Sister Agatha. Mount Carmel. The apparitions of Knock and Lourdes. No more desire. (*she reclines her head, sighing*) Only the ethereal. Where dreamy creamy gull waves o'er the waters dull.

(*Bloom half rises. His back trouserbutton snaps.*)

THE BUTTON

Bip!

(*Two sluts of the Coombe dance rainily by, shawled, yelling flatly.*)

THE SLUTS

O, Leopold lost the pin of his drawers
He didn't know what to do,
To keep it up,
To keep it up.

BLOOM

(*coldly*) You have broken the spell. The last straw. If there were only
ethereal where would you all be, postulants and novices? Shy but
willing like an ass pissing.

THE YEWS

(*their silverfoil leaves precipitating, their skinny arms aging and swaying*)
Deciduously! (450–51)

The nymph serves Molly by looking lifeless beside her. As soon
as her coy insinuations enable Bloom to reconstruct his intimacy
with Molly, the nymph becomes repugnant to him. Molly is "a perfectly sane full amoral fertilizable untrustworthy engaging shrewd
limited prudent indifferent Weib" (*Selected Letters* 285); the nymph
is none of these things. Worst of all, from Joyce's point of view,
she is not fertilizable. Molly's fertility is not only biological but
literary. She is receptive to the written word, longing for a lyrical wooer. Her monologue, which ends in poetry, dramatizes the
resources of poetic language, the other or dialectical partner of writing. By contrast, the nymph is associated with the disembodied and
therefore formless poetics of the ethereal school summed up by the
image of A. E. expounding his theosophical theories to a slovenly
female admirer. Molly, who negates or affirms life according to her
pleasure, lives close to poetry's source; the repressed nymph does
not. Through Molly, Joyce attempts to lead the reader back to that
source; her monologue grounds artistic sublimation in the passions
of the body by imitating the inchoate speech of desire.

But although Molly is more earthy than ethereal, she is an idealized being nonetheless, as all muses must be. Bloom is not the only
one who mystifies her; Joyce is infatuated with her as well. His
weakness is betrayed by the kind of narcissism he lavishes on her.
Molly's self-presence is formidably complete. Because she is not a
part of Joyce but truly other, he barely qualifies the coherence he

concedes to her. She seems to exist in a state of erotic abundance, whether she is sexually fulfilled or not. Unlike Bloom, who has more than a touch of the scopophiliac about him, she takes total narcissistic pleasure in her own body. Her self-sufficiency exposes the reductive fondness of her creator. Boylan, who is full of himself and prefers nakedness to garters, would seem to be the perfect partner for her. But Boylan lacks the poetry of a fetishist. And whereas Boylan, for all his animal magnetism, merely bolts through her, Bloom manages to remain. Bloom's infatuation is shared by Joyce, who commits the masculine error of having Molly take a lover's pleasure in her own body. Molly's erotic self-absorption is that of a woman seen through the eyes of a man; Joyce is mirrored in her narcissism, his pleasure filling the mirror in which she admires herself.

But when it comes to linguistic pleasure, Molly exists in a state of lack. She needs to be inseminated by language; she cannot fertilize herself. (It is only by remembering Bloom's words to her on Howth Head that she brings forth her own involuntary poetry.) Her relationship to language is erotic; in keeping with her function as muse, she equates poetry with potency. The fact that Boylan prefers nakedness to garters is, finally, a shortcoming; although Bloom the fetishist is less well-endowed than his rival, he "knows how to take a woman" and probably "has more spunk in him" (611). Molly wants to be courted with amorous words; she believes that men should write long extravagant love letters to women, but women should write brief replies, "not those long crossed letters Atty Dillon used to write to the fellow that was something in the four courts that jilted her after out of the ladies letterwriter when I told her to say a few simple words he could twist how he liked" (624). Sexually, she may know how to act and be acted on, but her relationship to language is purely receptive:

> O thanks be to the great God I got somebody to give me what I badly wanted to put some heart up into me youve no chances at all in this place like you used long ago I wish somebody would write me a loveletter his wasn't much and I told him he could write what he liked yours ever Hugh Boylan in old Madrid stuff silly women believe love is sighing I am dying still if he wrote it I suppose thered be some truth in it true or no it fills up your whole day and life always something to think about every moment and see it all around you like a new world (624)

Molly's linguistic lack makes her the perfect muse. By virtue of that lack, she calls poetry into being. The fact that she is an antithetical muse is to Joyce's advantage: he can call on her without fear of metaphysical compromise.

Molly's attributes are part of a religious argument. Gerty Mac-Dowell, another one of her handmaidens, serves to identify her mistress as an anti-Catholic muse, as a glance at "Nausicaa" demonstrates. Catholicism and sexuality are hopelessly entangled in Gerty's mind, producing a sentimental eroticism.[9] Molly's monologue opens with a curse of Catholic morality, embodied by Mrs Riordan: "she had too much old chat in her about politics and earthquakes and the end of the world let us have a bit of fun first God help the world if all women were her sort down on bathingsuits and lownecks of course nobody wanted her to wear them I suppose she was pious because no man would look at her twice I hope Ill never be like her a wonder she didnt want us to cover our faces" (608). Gerty sublimates her desire, refining it into sugary longing; as a result of this displacement, the paraphernalia associated with her sexuality develops a will of its own:

> As for undies they were Gerty's chief care and who that knows the fluttering hopes and fears of seventeen (though Gerty would never see seventeen again) can find it in his heart to blame her? She had four dinky sets with awfully pretty stitchery, three garments and nighties extra, and each set slotted with different coloured ribbons, rosepink, pale blue, mauve and peagreen and she aired them herself and blued them when they came home from the wash and ironed them and she had a brickbat to keep the iron on because she wouldnt trust those washerwomen as far as she'd see them scorching the things. She was wearing the blue for luck, hoping against hope, her own colour and lucky too for a bride to have a bit of blue somewhere on her because the green she wore that day week brought grief because his father brought him in to study for the intermediate exhibition and because she thought perhaps he might be out because when she was dressing that morning she nearly slipped up the old pair on her inside out and that was for luck and lovers' meeting if you put those things on inside out or if they got untied that he was thinking about you so long as it wasn't of a Friday. (288)

Molly, on the other hand, has always lived in the chaos that Stephen enters upon rejecting the spiritual virginity enforced by

Catholicism in *Portrait*. She knows full well that she is subject to
the whimsical rules of this world; accordingly, she leaves fetishism
to her suitors:

> in any case if its going to go on I want at least two other good
> chemises for one thing and but I dont know what kind of drawers he
> likes none at all I think didnt he say yes and half the girls in Gibraltar
> never wore them either naked as God made them that Andalusian
> singing her Manola she didnt make much secret of what she hadnt
> yes and the second pair of silkette stockings is laddered after one days
> wear I could have brought them back to Lewers this morning and
> kicked up a row and made that one change them only not to upset
> myself and run the risk of walking into him and ruining the whole
> thing and one of those kidfitting corsets Id want advertised cheap
> in the Gentlewoman with elastic gores on the hips he saved the one
> I have but thats no good what did they say give a delightful figure
> line 11/6 obviating that unsightly broad appearance across the lower
> back to reduce flesh my belly is a bit too big Ill have to knock off
> the stout at dinner or am I getting too fond of it [10] (617–18)

Gerty has been taught to fear her own physicality. Her body has
already confirmed her suspicions; at eighteen, she is already lame,
a defect that may prevent her from escaping the dreariness of her
Irish girlhood. Molly is afraid of growing old and unattractive, but
she has always been at home with herself; accordingly, Catholicism
leaves no obvious imprint on her narcissism: "he said I could pose
for a picture naked to some rich fellow in Holles street when he lost
the job in Helys and I was selling the clothes and strumming in the
coffee palace would I be like that bath of the nymph with my hair
down yes only shes younger or Im a little like that dirty bitch in
that Spanish photo he has" (620).

Gerty could have been Stephen's muse in *Portrait,* serving as a
distant symbol of his own aspiration. His idealization of her would
have been a natural extension of his own solipsism. In *Ulysses,*
Gerty's redeeming feature is the scar that makes her human. Molly
is all too human, the perfect muse for "dear dirty Dublin." The
epiphany that she engenders is dimly anticipated at the end of "Nausicaa," confirming our impression that she possesses powers that
Gerty will always lack: "O sweety all your little girlwhite up I saw
dirty bracegirdle made me do love sticky we too naughty Grace darling she him half past the bed met him pike hoses frillies for Raoul

de perfume your wife black hair heave under embon *señorita* young
eyes Mulvey plump bubs me breadvan Winkle red slippers she rusty
sleep wander years return tail end Agendath swoony lovey showed
me of dreams her next year in drawers return next in her next her
next" (312). Bloom's thoughts drift beyond Gerty, a port in the
storm, to Molly. Molly's body, never virginal, always inseminated
before Bloom reaches it, is Joyce's version of the East. At the end
of "Ithaca," Bloom kisses "the plump mellow yellow smellow mel-
ons" of her "rump, on each plump melonous hemisphere" (604);
the "creamfruit melon" (179), as we know from Stephen's dream
and from Bloom's visions of Agendath Netaim (49), is associated
with the Orient and the Promised Land.

Bloom returns to the East again in the closing epiphany of
Molly's monologue; the wanderer is cast back upon the feminine
source of all being, a homeland that is at once foreign and familiar:

> I was thinking of so many things he didnt know of Mulvey and
> Mr Stanhope and Hester and father and old captain Groves and the
> sailors playing all birds fly and I say stoop and washing up dishes
> they called it on the pier and the sentry in front of the governors
> house with the thing round his white helmet poor devil half roasted
> and the Spanish girls laughing in their shawls and their tall combs
> and the auctions in the morning the Greeks and the jews and the
> Arabs and the devil knows who else from all the ends of Europe and
> Duke street and the fowl market all clucking outside Larby Sharons
> and the poor donkeys slipping half asleep and the vague fellows in
> the cloaks asleep in the shade on the steps and the big wheels of the
> carts of the bulls and the old castle thousands of years old yes and
> those handsome Moors all in white and turbans like kings asking you
> to sit down in their little bit of a shop and Ronda with the old win-
> dows of the posadas 2 glancing eyes a lattice hid for her lover to kiss
> the iron and the wineshops half open at night and the castanets and
> the night we missed the boat at Algeciras the watchman going about
> serene with his lamp and O that awful deepdown torrent O and the
> sea the sea crimson sometimes like fire and the glorious sunsets and
> the figtrees in the Alameda gardens yes and all the queer little streets
> and pink and blue and yellow houses and the rosegardens and the jes-
> samine and geraniums and cactuses and Gibraltar as a girl where I
> was a Flower of the mountain yes when I put the rose in my hair
> like the Andalusian girls used or shall I wear a red yes and how he
> kissed me under the Moorish wall and I thought well as well him as

another and then I asked him with my eyes to ask again yes and then
he asked me would I yes to say yes my mountain flower and first I
put my arms around him yes and drew him down to me so he could
feel my breasts all perfume yes and his heart was going like mad and
yes I said yes I will Yes. (643–44)

Molly recognizes Bloom not as her middle-aged husband but as her
betrothed; paradoxically, she honors him by confusing him with
Mulvey, her first love. Mulvey, killed in battle years ago, is the other
Ulysses, the Ulysses who leaves Ithaca never to return again. Thus
Bloom's circular journey is bisected by a line that extends to infinity.
The circle, after all, can never be completely closed; the past can
never be recovered, only repeated with a difference. By extension,
the wanderer invariably returns to herself, but she is always haunted
by the Other, the object of desire that has affected her indelibly and
that she has never been able to possess.

Stephen believes that in order to create, the artist must be able to
inseminate himself, becoming at once active and passive, aggressive
and receptive, masculine and feminine. (The equations are Joyce's,
not mine.) Bloom, with the aid of Molly, bears Stephen out. Both
husband and wife have a touch of the androgyne about them; their
union engenders poetry. Joyce honors Vico by presenting poetry
as our first language, giving Molly and Bloom access to it when
they encounter their strongest desires. Molly loves Bloom for the
same reason she cheats on him; he is not a "real man" like Blazes
Boylan; in his femaleness, he understands "what a woman is," thus
releasing her from the solitude of her mystified gender. Despite his
tendency to mystify his muse, Joyce shares Bloom's androgynous
compassion. In *Portrait,* his ambition is to record the "individuating rhythm" of his own past; in *Ulysses,* he wills his attributes to
Bloom and Stephen and uses Molly to approximate a language that
can be intuited but not known. Although in both cases, poetry
comes from the "striving to know what the heart is and what it
feels," the later attempt makes it possible to pass from the irony
consummated in the fine ethereal vagaries of Stephen's villanelle
to the living pages of "Penelope," where Joyce's muse is made of
ambivalent flesh and blood.

As readers, we have come full circle, ending close to where we
began. If the stylistic ventures of *Ulysses* took us farther and farther

away from the mimesis of consciousness accomplished by the initial style, "Penelope" returns us to familiar ground. And yet Molly's hunger for potent words prevents us from sinking into satiety and repose. By exposing the linguistic longing of his earthbound muse, Joyce provides for the replenishment of authorial will and reminds us that our own journey was motivated by a primary and indestructible need.

Notes

1. In his excellent chapter "The Dynamics of Corrective Unrest in *Ulysses*," Fritz Senn warns against clutching at "correct terminal solutions or ultimate formulae" when confronted with the ambiguities of Joyce's epic (*Joyce's Disclocutions* 69). The temptation to do precisely this is particularly strong at the close of "Circe" and "Penelope," and it has led many critics astray.

2. Molly's use of a floral name to seduce her first lover draws attention to the belatedness of Bloom's arrival on the scene. The fact that Molly invents an imaginary lover whose name anticipates that of Bloom, and that when Bloom embarks on a double life he unwittingly takes his pseudonym from Molly, is significant. As embodiment of "das ewige Weibliche," Molly possesses an authority that Bloom lacks. Suzette Henke comments on Joyce's deference to the female principle: "Joyce ends up by using the transcendental phallic signifier to inscribe the name of the *mother* even more prominently than that of the father throughout his fiction. The patriarchal signature is ubiquitous: inscribed everywhere in the body of the text, it is everywhere impotent. Consider the powerlessness of males in *Dubliners;* the ironic Icarian flight of Stephen Dedalus; the sexual dysfunction of Leopold Bloom; and the fall, both literal and figurative, of Humphrey Chimpden Earwicker in *Finnegans Wake*. . . . Joyce both fears and worships woman as erotic temptress and maternal procreator. Even Molly Bloom . . . offers motherly solicitude to the spouse who exults in the pleasures of polymorphous perversity. And she eventually returns, at the end of 'Penelope,' to an amorous reverie that immortalizes her own 'mother-love' for her husband Leopold. In a moment of sexual *jouissance,* she gives him her breasts to suck and nurtures him with a pabulum of seedcake and spittle. The male, returning to the womb of woman, is nourished and reborn" ("Re-visioning" 148–49).

3. It seems unlikely that a mother would refer to her fully formed infant as being "neither one thing nor the other." The oddness of the phrase points to the connection between Rudy's fictional death and the actual miscarriage suffered by the Joyces.

4. Jennifer Wicke notes that Molly's Gibraltar is not the "utopian space beyond all commodity exchange . . . profuse with oranges and dark-eyed women" envisioned by Bloom but a "colonized zone, as its British street-names remind us" (4).

5. "'Penelope' is the *clou* of the book. The first sentence contains 2,500 words. There are eight sentences in the episode. It begins and ends with the female word *Yes*. It turns like the huge earth ball slowly surely and evenly round and round spinning, its four cardinal points being the female breasts, arse, womb and cunt expressed by the words *because, bottom* (in all senses bottom button, bottom of the class, bottom of the sea, bottom of his heart), *woman, yes.* Though probably more obscene than any other episode, it seems to me to be perfectly sane full amoral fertilizable untrustworthy engaging shrewd limited prudent indifferent *Weib. Ich bin der* [*sic*] *Fleisch der stets bejaht*" (*Selected Letters* 285).

Elaine Unkeless maintains that Molly Bloom's limitations correspond to conventional sexist notions of female nature, arguing that if Molly is a memorable creation, it is Joyce's language that makes her so. As a character, Unkeless finds Molly to be illogical, inconsistent, inarticulate, ineducable, frustrated (150–68). Unkeless's distinction between Molly's defective character and Joyce's vital language is problematic. For one thing, the vitality of Molly's monologue depends on a poetics of contradiction. An archival study of Molly's monologue shows that Joyce's determination to incorporate contradiction went far beyond his choice of phrases, extending itself to his distribution of prepositions on a given page (see Card). Given the fact that much of the poetic force of Molly's monologue is derived from a poetics of contradiction, what does it mean to draw a distinction between the weakness of Molly's character and the strength of Joyce's language? Moreover, Unkeless's description of Molly as illogical, inconsistent, inarticulate, ineducable, and frustrated suffers from what Card refers to as the "selective fallacy." Molly can be all these things, but she can also be canny, resourceful, expressive, receptive to language, affirmative.

6. Not surprisingly, the simplicity of Molly's monologue is deceptive. The reader's repose in the univocality of "Penelope" is complicated by the fact that the episode is a tissue of contradictions.

7. "The substance of the book is and will remain beyond the horizon of writing and reading, always in the realm of the yet-to-be-written, the yet-to-be-formulated, because it is inaccessible to writing. The final style, the end of wandering, in *Ulysses* is also the end of writing as its teleology: to present as style what no style can actually present. We abandon ourselves to a narration that finishes with the abandoning of language at the margin of narrative" (Riquelme, *Teller* 228).

8. Lawrence emphasizes the comparative conventionality of "Penelope": "Upon first encounter, 'Penelope' seems very unconventional; the unpunctuated, unbroken 'sentences,' and the representation of thought as if it were continuous speech distinguish it from the earlier chapters of interior monologue. But however radical the monologue first appears on the page, its underlying conventionality becomes apparent. First, in reforging the link between character and style in 'Penelope,' Joyce returned to one of the stylistic conceptions that dominates the early chapters of the book. And, second, once we learn how to read the continuous rhythms of the prose, the style seems much less radical than it first appears. . . . As A. Walton Litz says, 'Penelope does not contribute to the sequence of styles which is one of our chief interests in *Ulysses*'" (204). In the course of the same discussion, Lawrence states that "however beautifully and powerfully Joyce presented the return to a single voice in 'Penelope,' he gives us a kind of closure that the rest of the book seems to subvert" (208). In my view, "Penelope" *is* subversive insofar as it overturns the precedent set by the episodes that come before it. It is Molly, and not Bloom, who disposes of all suitors, here conceived as all the episodes that presume to describe her, to anticipate her, to name her, by virtue of the stylistic imperviousness of her monologue.

9. For an excellent discussion of Gerty's ecstasy as an ironic revision of Stephen's rapture on the beach in *Portrait,* see Senn 165–70.

10. Wicke argues that Molly Bloom displays a kind of genius in the sphere of consumption: "The general movement of 'Penelope' . . . is not so much the random exhalation and inhalation of female circularity, or the utterly formless and fluid stream of menstrualized consciousness named the feminine. Instead, my reading of 'Penelope' shows me an arc repeated again and again, a mental passage to Gibraltar or back from Gibraltar, mediated by the act of consumption. . . . Molly uses consumption to think through, to produce a situated analysis, of the relations of Gibraltar to Ireland, Gibraltar to England, England to Ireland. She is metempsychosed from one to another, on wings of consumer memory which displace, enter, and refract a cultural experience as profound as the meditations launched by Stephen in the 'Nestor' episode or by Bloom in his colloquies with the Citizen" (760). Wicke's delineation of critical choices—"Penelope" as random expression of feminine circularity, "Penelope" as formless stream of menstrualized consciousness, "Penelope" as arc of the complex labor of consumption—is self-serving. Moreover, it is not clear from Wicke's argument whether we should ascribe the "situated analysis" referred to above to Molly, as creative consumer, or to Joyce, who makes poetic use of the act of consumption.

Conclusion

Joyce's narratives are structured like palimpsests; if those narratives seem formidably complete, it is because they are founded on a series of thematic and formal antinomies. Paralysis and epiphany constitute one of the dialectical pairs that Joyce used to structure his work: taken together, these terms provide a key to his artistic development.

The epiphanies of *Dubliners* are negative, bringing paralysis to light. As we have seen, they are not revelatory in a metaphysical sense, nor do they simply confirm an absence of meaning, but rather they function within a highly evolved rhetoric of paralysis. Post-structuralists often treat the semantic gaps of *Dubliners* as insoluble riddles that prefigure the obscurity of *Finnegans Wake*. I have attempted to show that the silences of *Dubliners* are resonant, enabling the reader to contemplate the deadly work of paralysis.

The epiphanies of *Portrait* are affirmative but contradictory, canceling each other out. The absoluteness of epiphany in *Portrait* is in keeping with Stephen's religion of art; that absoluteness is ironically undercut by the relativism and polyphony of the text itself. To believe in the fiction of Stephen Dedalus is to hope that, in the fullness of time, he will become less absolute. To see the dialectic of decadence and emancipation at work is to understand that Stephen's absoluteness has its counterpart in the relativism of his creator's voice.

The epiphanies of *Ulysses* are textual, shedding light on the shape of the reader's journey. Post-structuralists have celebrated the disjunctiveness of *Ulysses* at the expense of its unifying elements. I have attempted to show the unity concealed within the psychological proteanism of "Circe" and within the stylistic proteanism of "Oxen of the Sun." In keeping with the premise that *Ulysses* is a self-reflexive text, I have also argued that the univocality of "Penelope" is less simple than it seems, and that the reader's homecoming does not constitute a domestication of narrative process.

Epiphany loses its force in *Finnegans Wake,* no longer illuminating the structure of the whole. Describing his conception of *Finnegans Wake* to the French writer Edmond Jaloux, Joyce said that it would be composed "to suit the aesthetic of the dream, where the forms prolong and multiply themselves, where the visions pass from the trivial to the apocalyptic, where the brain uses the roots of vocables to make others from them which will be capable of naming its phantasms, its allegories, its allusions" (Losey 612). In the course of fleshing out the "aesthetic of the dream," Joyce abandoned the device of epiphany, a decision that seems inevitable if we consider the difference between *Finnegans Wake* and his earlier work. The negative epiphanies of *Dubliners* functioned within a scrupulously mean rhetoric of paralysis, a rhetoric that has no place in the proteiform and polyglot universe of *Finnegans Wake.* The absolute yet contradictory epiphanies of *Portrait* were turning points in the development of Stephen's character, but characters are replaced by clusters of names, deeds, and attributes in Joyce's "marryvoised moodmoulded cyclewheeling history" (*Finnegans Wake* 186). The textual epiphanies of *Ulysses* constituted revelatory condensations of meaning, but condensation is so constant in the dream script of *Finnegans Wake* that the possibility of a textual epiphany is ruled out.

This is not to say that epiphany is forgotten in *Finnegans Wake.* Several of the manuscript epiphanies resurface here, but although some of their features are preserved, they no longer function as "sudden spiritual manifestations" that can be isolated from the surrounding text. Manuscript epiphany 34 is a case in point:

> She comes at night when the city is still; invisible, inaudible, all unsummoned. She returns from her ancient seat to visit the least of her children, mother most venerable, as though he had never been alien to her. She knows the inmost heart; therefore she is gentle, nothing exacting; saying, I am susceptible of change, an imaginative influ-

ence in the hearts of my children. Who has pity for you when you are sad among the strangers? Years and years I loved you when you lay in my womb. (Scholes and Kain 44)

As the reader will recall, this epiphany is echoed in "Circe":

THE MOTHER

Who saved you the night you jumped into the train at Dalkey with Paddy Lee? Who had pity for you when you were sad among the strangers? Prayer is allpowerful. Prayer for the suffering souls in the Ursuline manual and forty days' indulgence. Repent, Stephen.

STEPHEN

The ghoul! Hyena!

THE MOTHER

I pray for you in my other world. Get Dilly to make you that boiled rice every night after your brainwork. Years and years I loved you, O, my son, my firstborn, when you lay in my womb. (474)

Epiphany 34 makes its last appearance in Book 1, chapter 7 of *Finnegans Wake,* finding its way into Mercius' reply to the accusations of Justius. Although something of the mood of the original is preserved, its actual words are only echoed by a few phrases, such as Mercius' reference to conspiring with his own usurpation ("I who oathily forswore the womb that bore you and the paps I sometimes sucked") and ALP's "because ye left me, because ye laughed on me, because, O me lonly son, ye are forgetting me!" (193–94). More importantly, the passage in question does not constitute a moment of narrative arrest, instead forming a ripple within a vast flow of punning, polyglot, protean language.

Joyce's continued commitment to the *idea* of epiphany is evidenced by the debate between Saint Patrick and the Archdruid that takes place in the closing chapter of *Finnegans Wake.* The Archdruid Balkelly, a composite of Bishop Berkeley and Shem, argues for a "hueful panepiphanal world" available to the senses of a "numpa one paraduxed seer," affirming the possibility of "savvying" the "inside true inwardness of reality," an assertion that Saint Patrick, a "patholic" manifestation of Shaun, dismisses as "aposteriorioprismically apatstrophied and paralogically periparolysed" (612).

Saint Patrick's ideologically overdetermined colorblindness transforms King Leary, or Laoghaire, high king of Ireland, into a con-
glomeration of greens, proving that Saint Patrick is closed to the
"hueful panepiphanal world" of which the Archdruid speaks. Like
Stephen Dedalus, the Archdruid resists the Catholic vision of Saint
Patrick, a monochromatic vision that is predicated on spiritual servi-
tude and blind faith.

Many a reader has been convinced by the Archdruid's argument,
maintaining that all of *Finnegans Wake* is an epiphany. Unfortu-
nately, such "panepiphanal" readings destroy the original meaning of epiphany as a "sudden spiritual manifestation,"[1] changing it
into something else entirely. The suddenness of epiphany in Joyce's
earlier works is a function of its static character: even in *Ulysses,*
epiphany marks a point at which the reader can see her journey in
retrospect. *Finnegans Wake,* the densest of Joyce's "piously forged
palimpsests" (182), doesn't allow for moments of narrative arrest;
all roads converge in the "book of Doublends Jined," and the reader
can never stop struggling if she is to make her way through its
imploded landscape.

Although *Finnegans Wake* does not contain epiphanies, it does
contain climactic moments. ALP's closing monologue is a case in
point. I would like to turn to her monologue in order to clarify the
difference between narrative climax and epiphany.

The power of ALP's monologue depends on a double movement
that fuses death and desire. Acting on the desire attached to her
memory of HCE, ALP does everything in her power to resurrect
and reerect him. She reminds him of the names that he coined for
her long ago: "I am leafy, your goolden, so you called me, may me
life, yea your goolden, silve me solve, exsogerraider!" (619). She
forgives his vagrancies, comparing him to Captain Van Der Decken,
Sinbad the Sailor, and Magellan: "You make me think of a wonder-
decker I once. Or somebalt that sailor, the man megallant, with the
bangled ears" (620). She tries to raise him up by mothering him:
"And stand up tall! Straight. I want to see you looking fine for
me" (620). She dismisses his indiscretions as "old mutthergoosip"
(623) and tries to remember him as a "youth in his florizel, a boy in
innocence, peeling a twig, a child beside a weenywhite steed. The
child we all love to place our hope in for ever" (621). She lingers
over the memory of their passion: "And one time you'd rush upon

me, darkly roaring, like a great black shadow with a sheeny stare to perce me rawly. And I'd frozen up and pray for thawe" (626). She suggests a sentimental journey to the top of Howth Hill in a passage that recalls the parallactic reunion of Molly and Bloom: "We can sit us down on the heathery benn, me on you, in quolm unsconsciounce. To scand the arising. . . . Ourselves, oursouls alone. At the site of salvocean" (623).

With every utterance of desire, ALP moves closer to death. Her longing for recognition leads to a loss of identity, her own and HCE's: "But you're changing, acoolsha, your changing from me, I can feel. Or is it me is? I'm getting mixed" (627). Her maternal ministrations deteriorate into an acceptance of her sonhusband's union with his daughterwife (627). The image of HCE in his youthful innocence gives way to the realization that he is "only a bumpkin" (627). Her memory of their passion is reduced to a phantasmal kiss bestowed in passing as she surrenders to the terrible embrace of her "cold mad feary father" (627).

The tension between ALP's expression of yearning and her involuntary surrender to death produces a powerful climax, but it does not yield an epiphany. Although ALP gives up her keys in parting (628), she does not show us to the door of *Finnegans Wake;* she sends us back to the first page with her dying breath.

The "languo of flos" (621) that Joyce invented in *Finnegans Wake* is even more protean than the language of *Ulysses.* Joyce's long-suffering reader is privy to an endless stream of rumors, legends, tours, interviews, pseudo-histories, lessons, and reports, joining the community of "abcedminded" inquisitors (18) that has been called into being by a self-interrogating text. Kimberly Devlin has argued that the *Wake* is "an essentially kinetic text," maintaining that it is "impelled by what Stephen calls the 'kinetic emotions,' desire and loathing, longing and fear." According to Devlin, the rich obscurity of *Finnegans Wake* "is a function of not only the literal darkness of sleep but also the figurative psychic darkness of dreams. Messages from the unconscious are often formally obfuscated because their content is either profoundly disturbing or embarrassingly egotistical. By looking at some of the oppositions found along the horizontal axis of the dreamtext, one can see the wishes and anxieties, the dialectics of kinetic emotion, that govern Wakean representation" (19). Devlin's description of the *Wake* as a kinetic text is founded on a misreading of Stephen's words. Stephen doesn't place any restrictions on the kinds of emotions that "proper art" can represent; he simply asserts that the emotions *excited* by "improper art" are kinetic, basing his aesthetic judgment on the success or failure of artistic sublimation. The art of *Finnegans Wake* is indeed kinetic, but not because it excites desire or loathing, the emotions aroused by pornographical or didactic art (*Portrait* 205). Joyce's "traumscrapt" is kinetic insofar as it is composed of riddles, with every riddle presenting itself as a fragment of a world that "is, was, and will be writing its own runes for ever" (*Finnegans Wake* 19). The ideal reader of *Finnegans Wake* is in perpetual motion, ruling out the form of attention of which Stephen speaks when he refers to a mind "arrested and raised" (*Portrait* 295) in nonkinetic contemplation.

Joyce's abandonment of epiphany in *Finnegans Wake* is a reflection of his growing preoccupation with narrative process. If he begins by holding the mirror up to paralysis in *Dubliners* and ends by holding the mirror up to narration in *Ulysses* and *Finnegans Wake,* he invents a new kind of narrative in *Finnegans Wake,* a "present tense integument" (186) whose every cell repeats the history of the human race. In *Ulysses,* Joyce dramatized the relativism of literary style, treating individual styles as moments within a circular history. In *Finnegans Wake,* Joyce creates an Irishman's version of esperanto, reviving old myths and "meanderthalltales" with the "lifewand" of etymology. As in *Ulysses,* Joyce resorts to linguistic play as a means of redistributing the dead weight of the past; as in *Ulysses,* he counters the threat of paralysis with the spectacle of human history conceived as perpetual recirculation.

Narrative process is the stage upon which the dialectic of decadence and emancipation is played out in *Finnegans Wake,* and that stage has been cleared of everything that might distract us from the circular pageant of history, including conventional characters. As we have seen, Joyce begins to dissolve the boundaries of character in *Ulysses,* willfully confounding the attributes of Stephen and Bloom. There are no characters in the usual sense in *Finnegans Wake;* characters are replaced by acronyms, and the spelling out of those acronyms yields phrases, sentences, or entire tales. Uniqueness of character is subordinated to narrative process; thus Shem and Shaun, insofar as they represent the "dialytically separated elements of precedent decomposition," serve "the very petpurpose of recomposition" (614) without ever becoming fully three-dimensional. Characters are reduced to names, and those names are played against each other in a way that evokes the "heroticisms, catastrophes and eccentricities transmitted by the ancient legacy of the past" (614). Joyce's Vichian conviction that "the history of people is the history of language" (Mercanton) is written into every line of *Finnegans Wake,* a cartoonlike reenactment of the tragicomic history of humankind.

The "middenhide hoard of objects" (19) found in the first chapter of *Finnegans Wake* is a testimony to decadence and a site of emancipation. The detritus of history is evidence of our chronic belatedness; rummaging through the trash heap, we may accidentally come upon "a bone, a pebble, a ramskin" that yield "Gutenmorg with his Crogmagnon Charter" (20). What is the purpose of forging fragments of letters from an imaginary past? What is the purpose of reviving the crippled giants of legendary times? By creating a palimpsest that forces us to decode layers upon layers of half-erased texts, Joyce revitalizes the present. For the "paraduxed seer," those "hides and hints and misses in print" (20) are potentially emancipatory, revealing the living connection between postmodernity (for Joyce anticipated the babel of the present age as no other author did) and the mythic childhood of human expression.

Note

1. Expanding on Stephen's definition of epiphany in *Stephen Hero* (211), Morris Beja provides a useful working definition of *epiphany* as a "sudden spiritual manifestation, whether from some object, scene, event, or memorable phase of mind—the manifestation being out of proportion to the strictly logical relevance of whatever produces it" (*Epiphany* 18). *Epiphany* as defined by Beja has no chance of surviving in *Finnegans Wake.* Conflating the trivial and the apocalyptic, Wakean dream logic undermines the sense of proportion upon which epiphany depends.

Epilogue

Naturalism Spiritualized

Robert Musil's journals contain a provocative misinterpretation of Joyce's *Ulysses:* "Naturalism spiritualized.—A step that was mature even in 1900. His punctuation is naturalistic. With this also goes 'indecency.' Attraction: how does a man live in cross-section? Compared to this I think I practise a heroic conception of art. Question: how does one think? His abbreviations are: short formulas for linguistically orthodox forms. They copy the . . . speech process. Not the thinking process" (584).

Joyce would probably have agreed with some of Musil's observations. The association of naturalism and "indecency" is a case in point: Joyce made a similar connection in the course of a conversation with Arthur Powers:

> For you must be caught up in the spirit of your times, and you admit that the best authors have always been the prophets: the Tolstoys, the Dostoievskis, the Ibsens—those who brought something new into literature. As for the romantic classicism you admire so much, *Ulysses* has changed all that; . . . in *Ulysses* I have opened the new way, and you will find that it will be followed more and more. In fact from it you may date a new orientation in literature—the new realism. . . . The modern theme is the subterranean forces, those hidden tides which govern everything and run humanity counter to the apparent flood: those poisonous subtleties which envelop the soul, the ascending fumes of sex. (Power 53–54)

Although these statements are related, they are not identical. *Naturalism* is a compromised term in Musil's vocabulary; *realism* can have radical connotations in Joyce's. Musil had no use for the myth of nature; Joyce often seemed determined to make that myth into a reality. Musil's experiments in essayistic fiction evidently blinded him to the fact that Joyce's "indecency" was also part of a heroic conception; for Joyce, sexual candor was a way of resisting paralysis. As a young man, Joyce identified repression as the most widespread social disease of his time; his brother recorded his belief that all of Europe suffered from "an incurable contagion which he termed syphilitic" (qtd. in Ellmann 140). Tracing the theme of G.P.I. (General Paralysis of the Insane) in his writing, we find that he attributed that contagion to unnatural causes; his own defensive iconoclasm proves that for him the most insidious thing about Europe's disease was that it sprang not from indulgence but from repression.

Musil cites Joyce's attentiveness to the rhythm of spoken language as evidence of his naturalism. Although he admires him, he disapproves of his insistence on copying the "speech process" instead of the "thinking process." Like Lukács, he interprets naturalism as a form of softness or passivity expressed in indiscriminate, uncritical imitation. By classifying Joyce as a naturalist, Musil limits himself to a one-dimensional reading of *Ulysses*. Not only is he compelled to ignore Joyce's massive quotation of other writers but he is also pressed to undervalue the metaphorical density of Joycean language. If the author of *Ulysses* or *Finnegans Wake* strikes us as myriad minded, it is not because he has a good ear for spoken language but because those texts are echolands covered with a wild profusion of metaphors and puns.

Yet, from a Joycean perspective, Musil's description of *Ulysses* as an instance of "naturalism spiritualized" is perfectly appropriate. Both *Portrait* and *Ulysses* tempt us to think of spirit and form as interchangeable terms; assuming their equivalence, Musil's phrase simply acknowledges that *Ulysses* transforms traditional narration by infusing it with formal self-consciousness. In "Nestor," Stephen reflects that the soul is the form of forms (21), an Aristotelian idea that underlies his theory of epiphany, a theory which is, in turn, derived from Aquinas. Evidence of Joyce's early acceptance of Aristotle's equation of spirit and form can be found in the essay entitled "A Portrait of the Artist," in which he suggests that the inner life of an artist is articulated in his attempt "to liberate from the personalised lumps of matter that which is their individuating rhythm, the first or formal relation of their parts" (258). If Stephen dramatizes the search for an individuating rhythm, the eighteen episodes of *Ulysses,* in a less obvious way, do the same; the dialogical babel of *Ulysses* is "spiritualized" by this series of styles, each style representing a separate unit of authorial will and desire.

Epiphany may be said to "spiritualize" narration by arresting it, leaving the reader free to contemplate its form. Yet there is nothing Platonic about the form that epiphany lays bare. Like Stephen, Joyce attaches his loyalties to Aristotle; his narrative practice harmonizes with Stephen's theory that aesthetic idealism is merely literary talk, a theory revealed in the course of his definition of *claritas,* the second quality of beauty:

> The connotation of the word [*claritas*], Stephen said, is rather vague. Aquinas uses a term which seems to be inexact. It baffled me for a long time. It would lead you to believe that he had in mind symbolism or idealism, the supreme quality of beauty being a light from some other world, the idea of which the matter is but the shadow, the reality of which it is but the symbol. I thought he might mean that *claritas* is the artistic discovery and representation of the divine purpose in anything or a force of generalisation which would make the esthetic image a universal one, make it outshine its proper conditions. But that is literary talk. I understand it so. When you have apprehended that basket as one thing and have then analyzed it according to its form and apprehended it as a thing you make the only synthesis which is logically and esthetically permissible. You see that it is that thing which it is and no other thing. The radiance of which he speaks is the scholastic *quidditas,* the *whatness* of a thing. (212–13)

Joyce endorses Stephen's rejection of idealism; if epiphany marks the moment at which narrative *process* is spiritualized, it also marks the moment at which narrative *form* is naturalized or presented as the provisional product of narrative process.

Natural Supernaturalism

Pursued long enough, the phrase *naturalism spiritualized* leads straight into a circular trap laid by Joyce; it turns out that his naturalism cannot really be distinguished from his formalism, because so many of his form-giving principles are derived from nature. M. H.

Abrams circumvents this trap in the following lines: "Emerson long ago said that to an 'aroused intellect', 'facts, dull . . . despised things' are an 'Epiphany of God.' It was James Joyce, however, who by deliberately transferring the theological term into a naturalistic aesthetic, affixed to the Moment what seems destined to become its standard name" (421). Both Musil and Lukács regret Joyce's naturalism, which they associate with promiscuous imitation; Abrams defers to his naturalistic aesthetic, acknowledging the formal discrimination that his naturalism entails.

Natural development plays a part in all the works we have discussed here. The stories that comprise *Dubliners* cover three ages of man, as Joyce explained in a letter to Grant Richards: "I have tried to present [Dublin] to the indifferent public under four of its aspects: childhood, adolescence, maturity and public life" (*Selected Letters* 83). Gestation is the ruling trope of *Portrait*. *Ulysses* is made in the image of the human body, each episode corresponding to a different part. In addition, literary history is associated with embryological development in "Oxen of the Sun" and nature is given the last word in "Penelope," an episode that was meant to turn "like the huge earth ball slowly surely and evenly round and round spinning, its four cardinal points being the female breasts, arse, womb and cunt" (*Selected Letters* 285). Joyce's habitual invocation of nature betrays a desire to structure his fictions like living things.

Yet, at the same time, Joyce's writing drowns out nature. There is no place in his work for phenomena that exist independently of man; the silence of inhuman things is swept away by language. This flood of words occurs in stages. In *Dubliners,* concise language is used to analyze inchoate states of being. Pound marveled over Joyce's ability to treat the ambiguities of inner life like so many cold facts: "Mr. Joyce writes a clear, hard prose. He deals with subjective things, but he presents them with such clarity of outline that he might be dealing with locomotives or builder's specifications" (27). Whereas *Dubliners* objectifies subliminal events, *Portrait* evokes the unspoken language of subjectivity. In *Ulysses,* the drama of authorial *Bildung* gives way to the drama of narrative process. If *Portrait* uses lexical and metrical changes to tabulate the inner growth of Stephen Dedalus, *Ulysses* employs a series of styles to dramatize the act of narration. The chimeras encountered in this third odyssey announce in no uncertain terms that they are made of language.

Although in the beginning of his career Joyce adopted a "style of scrupulous meanness," he eventually learned how to abandon himself to self-reflexive linguistic play. Given this development, it is misleading to refer to him as a naturalist unless we agree that nature dies into language and is reborn as narrative process in *Ulysses* and *Finnegans Wake*. Fritz Senn stresses the importance of process in *Ulysses*:

> It is against some assured metropolitan firmness that the book's metamorphotic fictions are played off. At some stage the illusion of specific reality will be recognized as perhaps the most cunning artifice among many. Ultimately there may be nothing but verbal imagination. In the end, as there was in the beginning, there may be nothing but the word—Joyce has a way of belaboring this point. The suggestion is here made very strongly that this verbum *in principio* is indeed a dynamic *verb*, rather than some material or abstract *noun*. It may be precisely the nominalizing tendency of our conceptualizing that gets in the way of our dealing with processes, processes that could be most appropriately served by verbs that express voices, moods, tenses, and engage in multiple conjugations. (*Joyce's Dislocutions* 200)

By dramatizing narrative process in *Ulysses,* Joyce makes language occupy center stage. It has been said that Dublin is the main character of that novel; in fact Dublin is only one of the many masks that language assumes in its enactment of emancipation. Perhaps Nature is another.

"A More Subtle Inquisitor"

Dubliners, Portrait, Ulysses, and *Finnegans Wake* confront us as cryptic worlds-unto-themselves; Joyce strengthens the illusion of their self-sufficiency by filling them with metaphors linking narrative to natural process and writing to sexual reproduction. Because these metaphors are so pervasive, sympathetic readers often find themselves using sexual terms to characterize Joyce's writing, as Fritz Senn does:

> Taking up Joyce's own, or Stephen Dedalus,' insistent metaphors, we can see literature as a process of conception and parturition. A quasibiological vocabulary suggests itself, which serves to describe an evolution of powerful, vital drives in a teeming world of luxuriant

growth. In fact, such a monstrosity as the Oxen of the Sun episode in *Ulysses* can be read as a hymn to fertility in its theme and by its very nature—a misbirth maybe, but the offshoot of some generative (perhaps too generative) force. If we were not trying to be so erudite about this chapter, we might be impressed by its sheer animal exuberance. It seems that all of Joyce's writings came into being through some analogous biological force and were subject to many changes during their prolonged periods of gestation. The works are not only separate, though related, but they all got out of hand in the workshop; they could not be contained within whatever groundplan there was. They proliferated into something never imagined at the instant of conception. (*Joyce's Dislocutions* 200)

To resort to another quasibiological metaphor, Joyce's language is polymorphously perverse, opening itself to a multiplicity of styles and interpretations. The protean characters of the later works are creatures of polymorphous language. Bloom and Stephen in particular seem to have inherited the perversity of Joycean language; both have a touch of the androgyne about them. In *Portrait,* Stephen conceives of poetic inspiration as self-insemination ("In the virgin womb of the imagination the Word was made flesh" [217]); in "Circe" Bloom discovers his own womb and is hailed as "a finished example of the new womanly man" (403); in "Scylla and Charybdis" Stephen argues that the artist begets himself in an endless process of acting and being acted upon (174).

Joyce's artistic androgyny expresses itself in language that Stephen Heath terms "ambiviolent," borrowing a neologism from *Finnegans Wake:*

> The writing opens out onto a multiplicity of fragments of sense, of possibilities, which are traced and retraced, colliding and breaking ceaselessly in the play of this text that resists any homogenization. As 'collideorscape' (F.W.143.28), *Finnegans Wake* is the space of writing-reading, of an ambiviolence ('Language this allsfare for the loathe of Marses ambiviolent . . .' (F.W.518.2), disturbing the categories that claim to define and represent literary practice, leaving the latter in ruins, and criticism too. ("Ambiviolences" 31–32)

Ambiviolence is a useful word because it conveys the aggressive indeterminacy of Joycean language. All of Joyce's fiction was written in a spirit of defiance; in fact, at times the specter of censorship seems to overstimulate his imagination. His rebellion began quietly enough, although even in the case of *Dubliners,* iconoclasm determined narrative form, resulting in an ironic interplay of literal and figurative levels of meaning. Joyce made a habit of anticipating the objections of his "idiot questioner," to use Blake's phrase. By fictionalizing his censors, he turned them into invaluable foes; he learned not to expect too much from actual censors early in his career, as the following lines, written in defense of *Dubliners,* suggest: "The printer denounces 'Two Gallants' and 'Counterparts.' A Dubliner would denounce 'Ivy Day in the Committee-Room.' The more subtle inquisitor will denounce 'An Encounter,' the enormity of which the printer cannot see because he is, as I said, a plain blunt man" (*Selected Letters* 83). Joyce's correspondence with his publishers indicates that he probably never encountered the "more subtle inquisitor" referred to here, but in a sense everything he wrote is dedicated to him: the satirical note that runs through all his writing is an acknowledgment of his presence.

In his later works, Joyce typically defies the censor by making daily life the object of his stylistic experiments, tampering with habits of perception. Throughout his career, he resists the temptation of becoming his own censor by periodically changing his method of narration. Seen in this light, the stylistic diversity of *Ulysses* seems almost obsessive. Yet although *Ulysses* is a writerly tour de force, it fulfills the classical requirements formulated by Stephen: "The feelings excited by improper art are kinetic, desire or loathing. Desire urges us to possess, to go to something; loathing urges us to abandon, to go from something. These are kinetic emotions. The arts which excite them, pornographical or didactic, are therefore improper arts. The esthetic emotion (I use the general term) is therefore static. The mind is arrested above desire and loathing" (*Portrait* 205). Joyce produces "nonkinetic" works of fiction by subjecting ambiviolent language to the discipline of narrative form. Because form does not simply dictate content, he never lapses into didactic experimentalism; conversely, formal rigor serves as a safeguard against rhetorical sensationalism. "Penelope," the most obscene episode in *Ulysses* by Joyce's estimation (*Selected Letters* 285) puts this marriage of formalism and iconoclasm to the test. At last Molly lies before us, revealed in disarmingly naked language, yet instead of merely titillating our sensibilities, her monologue closes the circle of our stylistic odyssey.

The Jesuit and the Greengrocer

Two methods of composition are played against each other to produce the vital stasis of *Ulysses*. The first is an art of assemblage; the second is an art of system building. Frank Budgen provides an account of the first method in *The Making of Ulysses:* "I have seen him collect in the space of a few hours the oddest assortment of material: a parody on *The House that Jack Built,* the name and action of a poison, the method of caning boys on training ships, the wobbly cessation of a tired unfinished sentence, the nervous trick of a convive turning his glass in inward-turning circles, a Swiss music-hall joke turning on a pun in Swiss dialect, a description of the Fitzsimmons shift" (172). Joyce recognized his own genius for assemblage, remarking that he was "quite content to go down in posterity as a scissors and paste man for that seems to me a harsh but not unjust description" (*Letters,* ed. Gilbert). In the same vein, he said he had a greengrocer's mind, an observation born out by the epic inventory of *Ulysses*. Bloom is the creature of that mind, indulging Joyce's passion for collecting wherever he goes.

The second method, that of system building, produces symbolic or mythological patterns that seem to be woven into a preexisting narrative; in fact, those patterns often served as scaffoldings that enabled Joyce to build sentences into paragraphs and paragraphs into episodes. Joyce's fear of allowing this method to run away with him is reflected in his comment to Beckett that he "may have oversystematized *Ulysses*" (qtd. in Ellmann 702). His fondness for analogical patterns in particular has led critics to speak of his medieval-mindedness. Stephen, in the guise of "jejune jesuit" (*Ulysses* 4), shares his rage for order. Bloom is Joyce's answer to its tyranny, introducing the mundane, the accidental, the incomplete.

Both *Portrait* and *Ulysses* present the longing for systematic closure as a sign of youth. We gather that the ironic author of *Portrait* is no longer a young man because he betrays the relative truth of Stephen's absolute convictions. Stephen has still not come out of his cocoon at the end of *Portrait,* as his replacement of Catholicism with "aesthetical Jesuitry" (Burke, "Definitions" 445) suggests. When he reappears in *Ulysses,* loss has tempered his otherworldliness; traces of it remain, however, in a spirit of negation. Stephen, as we noted earlier, takes a crucial left turn in *Portrait:*

"Bending to the left, he followed the lane which led up to his house. The faint sour stink of rotted cabbages came towards him from the kitchengardens on the rising ground above the river. He smiled to think that it was this disorder, the misrule and confusion of his father's house and the stagnation of vegetable life, which was to win the day in his soul" (162). Stephen's left turn is completed in the character of Bloom; for better or worse, Bloom is truly a citizen of this world. Having learned that life is governed by a capricious logic of its own, he has developed a knack for righting things, as Fritz Senn points out, reflecting his pessimistic solicitude for local symmetries (*Joyce's Dislocutions* 59–72).

Joyce combines the rigor of the Jesuit with the detail-mindedness of the greengrocer. As a "jejune Jesuit," Stephen grandiloquently evokes Daedalus, "divine Artificer," at the end of *Portrait;* as a lapsed Jesuit, Joyce produces overdetermined narratives that are structured like palimpsests. In contrast to Stephen, Bloom pays close attention to concrete facts, expanding his stock at every turn; like Bloom, Joyce has a spider's eye for particulars. In *Ulysses,* the greengrocer and the Jesuit occasionally unite to produce such strange hybrids as Stephen's hyperrealistic parable of the plums and Bloom's utopian hallucinations. Throughout Joyce's works, the collision of minutiae and master plans yields epiphanies. Epiphany dramatizes the difference between the concrete particularity of narrative process and the abstract generality of its underlying symbolic pattern by temporarily arresting movement.

The fact that Joyce divides his own writerly attributes between Stephen and Bloom should demonstrate the futility of isolating either pattern or process as the sole locus of meaning in his work. It has become fashionable, however, to exalt process over pattern, to promote the greengrocer and spurn the Jesuit. Thus Stephen Heath uses Stuart Gilbert's book on *Ulysses* as an example of the sterility of schematic readings: "[Gilbert's book] enumerates and lists; in response to questions (interrogations of sense) it catalogues, it gives, in other words, the beginnings of the series of elements that that writing of *Ulysses* perpetually unfolds. The aim of the writing of *Ulysses* is the achievement of a multiplicity of levels of narrative (of 'adventure') and inter-reference (the permutations available in the reading of correspondences) the interplay of which will be the fragmentation of every particular one" ("Ambiviolences" 38).

Admittedly, critics who devote all their energy to constructing a skeleton key to Joyce's works are taking a perpetual turn to the right. But by arguing that the final effect of a Joycean palimpsest is to destroy the meaning of its component parts, Heath implicitly denies the semantic richness of the palimpsest as a whole.

Heath's post-structuralist approach turns out to be doubly restrictive; not only does it confine our attention to narrative process but it also demands that we value only the "negativity" of that process. This second restriction betrays the familiar postmodernist prejudice against affirmation; operating on the assumption that all received truths are ideologically suspect, negation becomes the only legitimate aesthetic or interpretive practice. Stephen Heath's post-structuralist perspective compels him to ignore the affirmative elements found in *Portrait, Ulysses,* and *Finnegans Wake.* His emphasis on the negative aspect of epiphany comes as no surprise. According to Heath, epiphany begins as "the definition of a climactic point of banality by its copying down in writing," evolving, in *Dubliners,* into a "second, more general procedure within which it can be contained," namely

> the development of a kind of "colourless" writing . . . which can be held at the same level as the repetition of fragments of discourse, framing them in an absence of any principle or, more exactly, in the signification of its purpose to remain silent, outside commentary, interpretation, *parole.* . . . A further procedure, that of *A Portrait,* is to rend the blanket of sense through the production of the counter-text of the fiction of the artist and his "voluntary exile"; his paradoxical status forming a contra-position to the realm of the doxa within the interstices of which the writing can, hesitatingly, proceed. ("Ambiviolences" 35)

Heath's description of Joyce's early epiphanies is serviceable only if we disregard the lyrical epiphanies, which intimate subliminal meanings, and concentrate on the dramatic ones. His account of the epiphanies found in Joyce's fiction applies to *Dubliners* but not to *Portrait,* in which epiphany commonly marks a high point in the emotional curve of Stephen's *Bildung.* He also fails to acknowledge that the drama of vocation enacted in *Portrait* represents a hypothetical answer to the problem of paralysis epiphanized in *Dubliners.*

The epiphanies of *Ulysses* tend to be ambiguously affirmative,

suspending promises rather than fulfilling them. The epiphany at
the close of "Proteus" is a perfect example:

> My handkerchief. He threw it. I remember. Did I not take it up?
> His hand groped vainly in his pockets. No, I didn't. Better buy
> one.
> He laid the dry snot picked from his nostril on a ledge of rock,
> carefully. For the rest let look who will.
> Behind. Perhaps there is someone.
> He turned his face over a shoulder, rere regardant. Moving
> through the air high spars of a threemaster, her sails brailed up on
> the crosstrees, homing, upstream, silently moving, a silent ship. (42)

The three-masted schooner recalls Stephen's dream of ships at the
close of *Portrait,* ships that beckon him to embark on his new-
found vocation. Those visionary ships reverse the direction of his
childhood dream of a ship entering the harbor, carrying the body
of Parnell. Taken together, these three epiphanies retell a meander-
thalltale of maritime questing. The ambiviolence of Joycean language is never pointed enough to deconstruct that tale, as the post-
structuralists would have it. Our own willingness to set out on the
myriad quests that reading *Ulysses* requires is sustained by the hover-
ing presence of meaning as opposed to its continual retraction.

The pleasure afforded by these strenuous journeys is a function of
the vital medium through which we move. Post-structuralist readers
invariably fail to recognize that Joyce celebrates narrative process as
an end-in-itself, endorsing Stephen's claim that literature is an eternal affirmation of the human spirit (*Ulysses* 544). The superanimated
quality of Joyce's writing cannot be accounted for purely in terms
of negation or evasion. Post-structural critics also avoid imposing
metanarratives of progress or decline on Joyce's fiction; however,
Joyce had no qualms about appraising his own development, referring to *Portrait* as the work of his youth and *Ulysses* as the work
of his maturity (Power 36). Perhaps he regarded *Ulysses* as the riper
work because in *Ulysses* process is all. By telling an ordinary tale
in an extraordinary variety of ways, Joyce approximates the richness of the phenomenal world. The post-structuralists remind us
that our experience of that richness depends on displacement and
praise Joyce's victory over paralysis in purely negative terms. Yet
although *Ulysses* makes us into more sophisticated or self-conscious

travelers, it also inspires wonder. Joyce's iconoclasm prevents us from attaching that wonder to some higher principle, throwing us back upon narrative process. *Portrait* is still haunted by the ghost of a higher principle; Stephen's Icarian ambitions introduce a romance of consummation. In *Ulysses,* that particular romance is left behind. Molly's closing dream is faithful to process; her closing "yes" is not an answer but an ejaculation. The post-structuralists make much of the reader's displacement, and rightly so; but they neglect to account for the fruitfulness of her wanderings.

Bibliography

Abrams, M. H. *Natural Supernaturalism*. New York: W. W. Norton, 1971.

Adams, Robert Martin. *Surface and Symbol*. New York: Oxford University Press, 1972.

Anderson, Perry, Rodney Livingstone, and Francis Mulherne, eds. *Aesthetics and Politics*. London: New Left Books, 1977.

Atherton, J. S. "The Oxen of the Sun." In *"Ulysses": A Collection of Critical Essays*. Ed. Clive Hart and David Hayman. Berkeley: University of California Press, 1974. 313–39.

Attridge, Derek, ed. *The Cambridge Companion to James Joyce*. Cambridge: Cambridge University Press, 1990.

Attridge, Derek, and Daniel Ferrer, eds. *Post-Structuralist Joyce: Essays from the French*. Cambridge: Cambridge University Press, 1984.

Bakhtin, M. M. *The Dialogical Imagination*. Ed. Michael Holquist. Austin: University of Texas Press, 1981.

Barthes, Roland. *Critical Essays*. Evanston: Northwestern University Press, 1972.

———. *Writing Degree Zero*. Trans. A. Lavers and C. Smith. New York: Hill and Wang, 1968.

Beck, Warren. *Joyce's Dubliners: Substance, Vision, and Art*. Durham: Duke University Press, 1969.

Beckett, Samuel. "Dante . . . Bruno. Vico . . . Joyce." In *James Joyce/ "Finnegans Wake": A Symposium: Our Exagimination Round His Factification for Incamination of Work in Progress* by Samuel Beckett et al. Norfolk, Conn.: New Directions, 1962. 1–22.

Begnal, Michael H., and Fritz Senn, eds. *A Conceptual Guide to "Finnegans Wake."* University Park: Pennsylvania State University Press, 1974.

Beja, Morris. *Epiphany and the Modern Novel*. Seattle: University of Washington Press, 1971.

Beja, Morris, and Shari Benstock, eds. *Coping with Joyce: Essays from the Copenhagen Symposium.* Columbus: Ohio State University Press, 1989.

Beja, Morris, Phillip Herring, Maurice Harmon, and David Norris, eds. *James Joyce: The Centennial Symposium.* Urbana: University of Illinois Press, 1986.

Benjamin, Walter. "Conversations with Brecht." Trans. Anya Benstock. In *Aesthetics and Politics.* Ed. Perry Anderson, Rodney Livingstone, and Francis Mulherne. London: New Left Books, 1977.

———. *Illuminations.* Ed. Hannah Arendt. New York: Schocken Books, 1969.

———. "The Work of Art in the Age of Mechanical Reproduction." In *Illuminations.* Ed. Hannah Arendt. Trans. Harry Zohn. New York: Schocken Books, 1969. 217–51.

Benstock, Bernard. *James Joyce.* New York: Frederick Ungar, 1985.

———. *Joyce-Again's Wake: An Analysis of "Finnegans Wake."* Seattle: University of Washington Press, 1965.

———. *Narrative Con/texts in "Ulysses."* Urbana: University of Illinois Press, 1991.

———, ed. *Critical Essays on James Joyce's "Ulysses."* Boston: G. K. Hall, 1989.

———, ed. *James Joyce: The Augmented Ninth.* Syracuse: Syracuse University Press, 1988.

———, ed. *The Seventh of Joyce.* Bloomington: Indiana University Press, 1982.

Bishop, John. *Joyce's Book of the Dark: "Finnegans Wake."* Madison: University of Wisconsin Press, 1986.

Bosinelli, Rosa Maria, Paola Pugliatti, and Romana Zachi, eds. *Myriad-minded Man.* Bologna: Cooperative Libraria Universitaria Editrice Bologna, 1986.

Bowen, Zack. *"Ulysses" as a Comic Novel.* Syracuse: Syracuse University Press, 1989.

Brivic, Sheldon. *The Veil of Signs: Joyce, Lacan, and Perception.* Urbana: University of Illinois Press, 1991.

Budgen, Frank. *James Joyce and the Making of "Ulysses."* Bloomington: Indiana University Press, 1964.

Burgess, Anthony. *Re Joyce.* New York: W. W. Norton, 1965.

Burke, Kenneth. "Definitions." In *A Portrait of the Artist as a Young Man* by James Joyce. Ed. Chester G. Anderson. New York: Viking Critical Library, 1968. 440–45.

Campbell, Joseph, and Henry Morton Robinson. *A Skeleton Key to "Finnegans Wake."* New York: Viking Press, 1961.

Card, James Van Dyck. *An Anatomy of "Penelope."* London: Associated University Presses, 1984.

Cheng, Vincent J., and Timothy Martin, eds. *Joyce in Context.* Cambridge: Cambridge University Press, 1992.

Cixous, Hélène. *The Exile of James Joyce.* Trans. Sally Purcell. London: Calder, 1976.

———. "Joyce: The (R)Use of Writing." In *Post-Structuralist Joyce: Essays from the French.* Ed. Derek Attridge and Daniel Ferrer. Cambridge: Cambridge University Press, 1984.

Connolly, Thomas E. *The Personal Library of James Joyce.* State University of New York at Buffalo Studies 20, no. 1 (Apr. 1955).

Cross, Richard K. *Flaubert and Joyce.* Princeton: Princeton University Press, 1971.

Curran, C. P. *James Joyce Remembered.* London: Oxford University Press, 1968.

Dante Alighieri. *Vita Nuova.* Trans. Mark Musa. New Brunswick: Rutgers University Press, 1957.

Devlin, Kimberly. *Wandering and Return in "Finnegans Wake."* Princeton: Princeton University Press, 1991.

Dunleavy, Janet E., Melvin J. Friedman, and Michael Patrick Gillespie, eds. *Joycean Occasions: Essays from the Milwaukee James Joyce Conference.* London: Associated University Presses, 1991.

Eco, Umberto. *The Aesthetics of Chaosmos: The Middle Ages of James Joyce.* Trans. Ellen Esrock. Tulsa: University of Tulsa Press, 1989.

Eliot, T. S. "*Ulysses,* Order, and Myth." *Dial* 75 (Nov. 1923): 480–83.

Ellmann, Richard. *The Consciousness of Joyce.* New York: Oxford University Press, 1977.

———. *Eminent Domain: Yeats among Wilde, Joyce, Pound, Eliot, and Auden.* New York: Oxford University Press, 1972.

———. "The Growth of Imagination." In *A Portrait of the Artist as a Young Man* by James Joyce. Ed. Chester G. Anderson. New York: Viking Critical Library, 1968. 388–98.

———. *James Joyce.* New York: Oxford University Press, 1982.

———. *"Ulysses" on the Liffey.* New York: Oxford University Press, 1972.

Feshbach, Sidney. "Death in 'An Encounter.'" *James Joyce Quarterly* 2 (Winter 1965): 82–96.

French, Marilyn. *The Book as World: James Joyce's "Ulysses."* Cambridge, Mass.: Harvard University Press, 1976.

Gaiser, Gottlieb, ed. *International Perspectives on Joyce.* Troy, N.Y.: Whitson, 1986.

Gilbert, Stuart. *James Joyce's "Ulysses": A Study.* New York: Vintage Books, 1952.

Gillespie, Michael Patrick. *Reading the Book of Himself: Narrative Strategies in the Works of James Joyce.* Columbus: Ohio State University Press, 1989.

Glasheen, Adaline. *A Census of "Finnegans Wake."* Evanston: Northwestern University Press, 1956.

Goldberg, S. L. *The Classical Temper: A Study of James Joyce's "Ulysses."* London: Chatto and Windus, 1961.

Gordon, John. *James Joyce's Metamorphoses.* Dublin: Gill and Macmillan, 1981.

Groden, Michael. *"Ulysses" in Progress.* Princeton: Princeton University Press, 1977.

Guerra, Lia. "Fragmentation in *Dubliners* and the Reader's Epiphany." In *Myriadminded Man.* Ed. Rosa Maria Bosinelli, Paola Pugliatti, and Romana Zachi. Bologna: Cooperative Libraria Universitaria Editrice Bologna, 1986.

Habermas, Jürgen. "Modernity—An Incomplete Project." Trans. Seila Ben-habib. In *The Anti-Aesthetic: Essays on Postmodern Culture.* Ed. Hal Foster. Port Townsend, Wash.: Bay Press, 1983. 3–15.

Hart, Clive. *James Joyce's "Ulysses."* Sydney: Sydney University Press, 1968.

Hart, Clive, and David Hayman, eds. *"Ulysses": A Collection of Critical Essays.* Berkeley: University of California Press, 1974.

Hayman, David. "The Joycean Inset." *James Joyce Quarterly* 23 (1986): 137–55.

———. *"Ulysses": The Mechanics of Meaning.* Englewood Cliffs, N.J.: Prentice-Hall, 1970.

Heath, Stephen. "Ambiviolences: Notes for Reading Joyce." In *Post-Structuralist Joyce.* Ed. Derek Attridge and Daniel Ferrer. Cambridge: Cambridge University Press, 1984. 31–68.

Henke, Suzette. *James Joyce and the Politics of Desire.* New York: Routledge, 1990.

———. "Re-visioning Joyce's Masculine Signature." In *Joyce in Context.* Ed. Vincent Cheng and Timothy Martin. Cambridge: Cambridge University Press, 1992. 138–50.

Henke, Suzette, and Elaine Unkeless, eds. *Women in Joyce.* Urbana: University of Illinois Press, 1982.

Herring, Phillip. *Joyce's Uncertainty Principle.* Princeton: Princeton University Press, 1987.

———. "Structure and Meaning in Joyce's 'The Sisters.'" In *The Seventh of Joyce.* Ed. Bernard Benstock. Bloomington: Indiana University Press, 1982. 131–44.

Houston, John Porter. *Joyce and Prose: An Exploration of the Language of "Ulysses."* London: Associated University Presses, 1989.

Ingersoll, Earl G. "The Gender of Travel in 'The Dead.'" *James Joyce Quarterly* 30, no. 1 (Fall 1992): 41–50.

Iser, Wolfgang. *The Implied Reader: Patterns of Communication in Prose Fiction from Bunyan to Beckett.* Baltimore: Johns Hopkins University Press, 1974.

Jameson, Fredric. *Fables of Aggression: Wyndam Lewis, the Modernist as Fascist.* Berkeley: University of California Press, 1979.

———. "Magical Narratives: Romance as Genre." *New Literary History* 7, no. 3 (Spring 1976): 135–63.

———. "Reflections in Conclusion." In *Aesthetics and Politics.* Ed. Perry Anderson, Rodney Livingstone, and Francis Mulherne. London: New Left Books, 1977. 196–213.

———. "Ulysses in History." In *James Joyce and Modern Literature.* Ed. W. J. McCormack and Alistair Stead. London: Routledge and Kegan Paul, 1982. 126–41.

Jolas, Maria. *A James Joyce Yearbook.* Paris: Transition Press, 1949.

Joyce, James. *Dubliners.* Ed. Robert Scholes and Walton Litz. New York: Viking Critical Library, 1968.

———. *Finnegans Wake.* New York: Penguin, 1976.

———. "Ireland, Island of Saints and Sages." In *The Critical Writings of James Joyce.* Ed. Ellsworth Mason and Richard Ellmann. New York: Viking Press, 1959. 153–74.

———. *Letters of James Joyce.* Ed. Stuart Gilbert. London: Faber and Faber, 1957.

———. *Letters of James Joyce.* Vols. 2 and 3. Ed. Richard Ellmann. New York: Viking Press, 1966.

———. "A Portrait of the Artist." In *A Portrait of the Artist as a Young Man* by James Joyce. Ed. Chester G. Anderson. New York: Viking Critical Library, 1968. 257–66.

———. *A Portrait of the Artist as a Young Man.* Ed. Chester G. Anderson. New York: Viking Critical Library, 1968.

———. *Scribbledehobble: The Ur-Workbook to Finnegans Wake.* In the Buffalo Collection, cited in John J. Slocum and Herbert Cahoon, *A Bibliography of James Joyce: 1882–1941.* New Haven: Yale University Press, 1953.

———. *Selected Joyce Letters.* Ed. Richard Ellmann. New York: Viking Press, 1975.

———. *Stephen Hero.* New York: New Directions, 1963.

———. *Ulysses.* Ed. Hans Gabler. New York: Random House, 1986.

Joyce, Stanislaus. "The Background to *Dubliners.*" *Listener* (25 Mar. 1954).

———. *The Complete Dublin Diary of Stanislaus Joyce.* Ithaca: Cornell University Press, 1971.

————. *My Brother's Keeper*. New York: Viking, 1958.

Kenner, Hugh. "Circe." In *"Ulysses": A Collection of Critical Essays*. Ed. Clive Hart and David Hayman. Berkeley: University of California Press, 1974. 341–62.

————. *Dublin's Joyce*. Boston: Beacon Press, 1962.

————. *Joyce's Voices*. Berkeley: University of California Press, 1978.

————. *Ulysses*. London: George Allen and Unwin, 1980.

Kershner, R. B. *Joyce, Bakhtin, and Popular Literature: Chronicles of Disorder*. Chapel Hill: University of North Carolina Press, 1989.

Lawrence, Karen. *The Odyssey of Style in "Ulysses."* Princeton: Princeton University Press, 1981.

Lernout, Geert. *The French Joyce*. Ann Arbor: University of Michigan Press, 1990.

Levin, Harry. *James Joyce: A Critical Introduction*. New York: New Directions, 1960.

Litz, A. Walton. *The Art of James Joyce: Method and Design in "Ulysses" and "Finnegans Wake."* New York: Oxford University Press, 1964.

Losey, Jay B. "Dream Epiphanies in *Finnegans Wake*." *James Joyce Quarterly* 26, no. 4 (Summer 1989): 611–16.

Lukács, Georg. "Grösse und Verfall des Expressionismus." In *Marxism und Literatur*. Ed. Fritz J. Raddatz. Reinbeck bei Hamburg: Rowohlt, 1969. 1:7–42.

————. *The Meaning of Contemporary Realism*. Trans. John Mander and Necke Mander. London: Merlin Press, 1963.

Lyotard, Jean Francois. *The Postmodern Condition: A Report on Knowledge*. Trans. Geoff Bennington and Brian Massumi. Minneapolis: University of Minnesota Press, 1984.

MacCabe, Colin. *James Joyce and the Revolution of the Word*. London: Macmillan, 1978.

————, ed. *James Joyce: New Perspectives*. Bloomington: Indiana University Press, 1982.

Macdonald, Michael Bruce. "The Strength and Sorrow of Young Stephen: Toward a Reading of the Dialectic of Dissonance and Harmony in Joyce's *Portrait*." *Twentieth Century Literature: A Scholarly and Critical Journal* 37 (Winter 1991): 368–74.

Magalaner, Marvin. *Time of Apprenticeship: The Fiction of Young James Joyce*. London: Abelard-Schuman, 1959.

————, and Richard Kain. *Joyce: The Man, the Work, the Reputation*. Westport, Conn.: Greenwood Press, 1979.

Mahaffey, Vicki. *Reauthorizing Joyce*. Cambridge: Cambridge University Press, 1988.

Manganiello, Dominic. *Joyce's Politics*. London: Routledge, 1980.

McCormack, W. J., and Alistair Stead. *James Joyce and Modern Literature*. London: Routledge and Kegan Paul, 1982.

McMichael, James. *Ulysses and Justice*. Princeton: Princeton University Press, 1991.

Mercanton, Jacques. "Les heures de James Joyce." [Souvenirs Lausanne] Editions l'Age d'Homme [1967]. Series: Merveilleuse Collection, 5.

Moretti, Franco. "Ulysses and the End of Liberal Capitalism." In *Signs Taken for Wonders*. Trans. Susan Fischer. London: New Left Books, 1983. 182–208.

Musil, Robert. *Tagebücher, Aphorismen, Essays, und Reden*. Ed. Adolf Frisé. Hamburg: Rowohlt Verlag, 1955.

O'Grady, Thomas B. "Conception, Gestation, and Reproduction: Stephen's Dream of Parnell." *James Joyce Quarterly* 27 (Winter 1990): 253–59.

Parrinder, Patrick. *James Joyce*. Cambridge: Cambridge University Press, 1984.

Peake, C. H. *James Joyce: The Citizen and the Artist*. Stanford: Stanford University Press, 1977.

Peterson, Richard, Alan Cohn, and Edmund Epstein. *Joyce Centenary Essays*. Carbondale: Southern Illinois University Press, 1983.

Poe, Edgar Allan. *Marginalia*. In *The Complete Works of Edgar Allan Poe*, vol. 26. Ed. James A. Harrison. New York: AMS Press, 1965.

Potts, Willard. *Portrait of the Artist in Exile: Recollections of Joyce by Europeans*. Seattle: University of Washington Press, 1979.

Pound, Ezra. *Pound/Joyce: The Letters of Ezra Pound to James Joyce*. Ed. Forrest Read. London: Faber, 1968.

Power, Arthur. *Conversations with James Joyce*. London: Millington, 1974.

Rabaté, Jean-Michel. *James Joyce, Authorized Reader*. Baltimore: Johns Hopkins University Press, 1991.

———. *Joyce upon the Void: The Genesis of Doubt*. London: Macmillan, 1991.

Restuccia, Frances L. *Joyce and the Law of the Father*. New Haven: Yale University Press, 1989.

Reynolds, Mary T. *Joyce and Dante: The Shaping Imagination*. Princeton: Princeton University Press, 1981.

Riquelme, John Paul. *Teller and Tale in Joyce's Fiction: Oscillating Perspectives*. Baltimore: Johns Hopkins University Press, 1983.

Robinson, David. " 'What Kind of a Name Is That?': Joyce's Critique of Names and Naming in *A Portrait*." *James Joyce Quarterly* 27 (Winter 1990): 325–35.

Roughley, Alan. *James Joyce and Critical Theory: An Introduction*. Ann Arbor: University of Michigan Press, 1991.

Ruggieri, Franca. "Forms of Silence in *Dubliners*." In *Myriadminded Man*. Ed. Rosa Maria Bosinelli, Paola Pugliatti and Romana Zachi. Bologna: Cooperative Libraria Universitaria Editrice Bologna, 1986.

Sailer, Susan Shaw. *On the Void of to Be: Incoherence and Trope in "Finnegans Wake."* Ann Arbor: University of Michigan Press, 1993.

Scholes, Robert. *In Search of James Joyce*. Urbana: University of Illinois Press, 1992.

Scholes, Robert, and Richard Kain. *The Workshop of Daedalus*. Evanston, Ill.: Northwestern University Press, 1965.

Schutte, William M. *Joyce and Shakespeare*. New Haven: Yale University Press, 1957.

Scott, Bonnie Kime. *James Joyce*. New Jersey: Humanities Press International, 1987.

———. *Joyce and Feminism*. Bloomington: Indiana University Press, 1984.

Segall, Jeffrey. *Joyce in America: Cultural Politics and the Trials of "Ulysses."* Berkeley: University of California Press, 1993.

Senn, Fritz, ed. *Joyce's Dislocutions*. Baltimore: Johns Hopkins University Press, 1984.

———. *New Light on Joyce from the Dublin Symposium*. Bloomington: Indiana University Press, 1972.

Shechner, Mark. *Joyce in Nighttown: A Psychoanalytic Inquiry into "Ulysses."* Princeton: Princeton University Press, 1976.

Silverman, A. O. Introductory note to section 1, "The Epiphanies." In *The Workshop of Daedalus*. Ed. Robert Scholes and Richard Kain. Evanston, Ill.: Northwestern University Press, 1965. 3–7.

Staley, Thomas F., and Bernard Benstock, eds. *Approaches to "Ulysses": Ten Essays*. Pittsburgh: University of Pittsburgh Press, 1976.

Stevens, Wallace. "Men Made out of Words." *The Collected Poems of Wallace Stevens*. New York: Alfred A. Knopf, 1957. 355.

———. "The Noble Rider and the Sound of Words." *The Necessary Angel*. New York: Alfred A. Knopf, 1951. 3–36.

Sullivan, Kevin. *Joyce among the Jesuits*. New York: Columbia University Press, 1958.

Sultan, Stanley. *The Argument of "Ulysses."* Columbus: Ohio State University Press, 1964.

Theoharis, Theoharis Constantine. *Joyce's "Ulysses."* Chapel Hill: University of North Carolina Press, 1988.

Thornton, Weldon. *Allusions in "Ulysses": A Line-by-Line Reference to Joyce's Complex Symbolism*. New York: Simon and Schuster, 1973.

Unkeless, Elaine. "The Conventional Molly Bloom." In *Women in Joyce*. Ed. Suzette Henke and Elaine Unkeless. Urbana: University of Illinois Press, 1982. 150–68.

Verene, Donald Phillip, ed. *Vico and Joyce*. Albany: State University of New York Press, 1987.

Vico, Giambattista. *The New Science*. Trans. Thomas Goddard Bergin and Max Harold Fisch. Ithaca: Cornell University Press, 1970.

Wicke, Jennifer. "'Who's She when She's at Home?': Molly Bloom and the Work of Consumption." *James Joyce Quarterly* 28 (Summer 1991): 749–63.

Williams, Trevor L. "Dominant Ideologies: The Production of Stephen Dedalus." In *James Joyce: The Augmented Ninth*. Ed. Bernard Benstock. Syracuse: Syracuse University Press, 1988. 312–22.

Wilson, Edmund. *Axel's Castle*. London: Fontana, 1961.

Wolf, Christa. *No Place on Earth*. Trans. Jan Van Huerk. New York: Farrar, Straus, and Giroux, 1982.

Woolf, Virginia. *A Writers Diary*. Ed. Leonard Woolf. New York: Harcourt Brace Jovanovich, 1953.

Index

Abrams, M. H., 168
Addison-Steele: style of, 107
Adorno, Theodor, 1, 2, 9
Adrian IV, 101, 109
A. E., 148
"Aeolus," 82–84, 147
"After the Race," 32
Anna Livia Plurabelle, 159–61
Aquinas, 10–11, 113, 166
"Araby," 15, 17, 33, 43, 44
Aristotle, 133, 166, 167
"Arrayed for Bridal," 36
Atherton, J. S., 102
Attridge, Derek, 95–97
Autonomy: of the work of art, 2, 9, 62;
    of the artist, 27, 48, 62

Bakhtin, M. M., 95
Balfe, 21
Barry, Mrs. Yelverton, 124
Barthes, Roland, 19, 42, 74, 146
Baudelaire, Charles, 61
Beau Mount and Lecher, 102, 103
Beckett, Samuel, 43, 97
Beja, Morris, 163
Bellingham, Mrs., 124
Benjamin, Walter, 1, 2, 6–7, 73
Benstock, Bernard, 80
Blake, William, 107, 171
Bloom, Leopold, 9, 79, 82–85, 88, 90,

91–94, 97, 100, 103, 106, 108, 110,
    112, 114, 117, 119–29, 131–34,
    138–45, 147–49, 152–54, 170, 172,
    173
Bloom, Molly, 9, 16, 22, 74, 93–94,
    97, 103, 106, 110, 123, 125, 126,
    138–56, 171, 176
Bloom, Rudy, 91, 97, 100, 119, 127,
    132–34, 138, 142, 143, 144
Bowen, Zack, 114
Boylan, Blazes, 149, 153
Brecht, Bertolt, 1, 9
Breen, Mrs., 124
Browne, Mr., 35
Browne, Thomas, 107, 110, 113, 115
Browning, Robert, 45
Budgen, Frank, 75, 99, 172
Bunyan, John, 100, 107, 113
Burke, Edmund, 108
Burke, Kenneth, 58–59, 172
Bushe, Seymour, 83

"Calypso," 81–82
Capitalism, 1, 5, 7, 13
Card, James Van Dyck, 155
Carlyle, Thomas, 108, 116
Catholicism, 10, 26, 42, 50, 52, 58, 66–
    68, 70–72, 94, 100–101, 103, 129,
    130, 139, 150–51, 160
Christ, 6, 37, 103

"Circe," 8, 9, 41, 79, 90–91, 92, 114,
    118–37, 138, 139, 147, 154, 158,
    159, 170
Cixous, Hélène, 42
"Clay," 19–22, 42, 44
Cocytus, 40
Conmee, Father, 87
Conrad, Joseph, 42
Conroy, Gabriel, 8, 34–41, 45, 46,
    48–50, 55
Conroy, Gretta, 35, 36, 38, 39, 45, 46
Corley, 16
Cotter, 29, 31
Cranly, 6, 71–72
Critical realism, 17
Croppy Boy, 114, 129–30
"Cyclops," 88–89

Daedalus, 4, 54, 75, 76, 173
Dana, 12, 118
Dante, 57
Dante Alighieri, 17–19, 27, 40, 43, 44
D'Arcy, Bartell, 36
Darwinianism, 10, 105–6
Davin, 51, 54
Dawson, 84
"The Dead," 13, 33–41, 48–49
Deasy, Mr., 80–81, 103, 115
Decadence, 1–6, 9, 11, 47, 78, 86, 95,
    98, 106, 112, 157, 163
Dedalus, May, 66–67, 74, 103, 128–29
Dedalus, Simon, 51–53, 65, 130
Dedalus, Stephen, 3, 5, 6, 14, 16, 17,
    32, 43, 47–77, 78, 79, 80, 81, 82, 86,
    90, 93, 97, 99, 100, 101–3, 108, 111,
    112, 113, 114, 115, 119–25, 127–34,
    135, 136, 139, 140, 142, 143, 145,
    146, 152, 156, 157, 158, 160, 161,
    162, 163, 169–70, 173, 175, 176
De Quincey, Thomas, 105, 108
Des Esseintes, 67
Dickens, Charles, 109
Divine Comedy, 18
Dowie, Alexander, 114–15
Dublin by Lamplight Laundry, 19
Dubliners, 3–11, 13–46, 47, 54, 56, 77,

138, 154, 157, 158, 162, 168, 169,
    171, 172, 175
Duffy, Mr., 39
Dumas, Alexandre, 64

Earwicker, Humphrey Chimpden, 40,
    154, 160–61
Eccles Street, 80, 125
Eliot, T. S., 78, 114
Eliza, 15, 30, 31
Ellipsis, 14, 30–32
Ellmann, Richard, 55–57, 76
Emancipation, 1, 3–5, 6, 8–9, 11, 41,
    47, 78, 86, 94, 95, 98, 127, 133, 141,
    162, 163
Epiphany, 5–9, 11, 13–17, 19–22, 26,
    30, 32–33, 39–41, 42, 45, 49, 54, 55,
    56, 61, 62, 70, 77, 94, 104, 119, 121,
    123, 127, 133, 134, 138–41, 144,
    152, 153, 157–63, 166–68, 173–76
Erin, 16, 120
"Eumaeus," 9, 91–92
"Eveline," 32

"Fergus' Song," 115
Ferrer, Daniel, 95–97
Feshbach, Sidney, 23
Finnegans Wake, 3, 8, 11, 12, 14, 17,
    45, 76, 80, 90, 111, 114, 115, 154,
    158–63, 166, 169, 174
Fionnula, 16
Flaubert, Gustave, 60, 61
Flynn, Father, 27–32
Frankfurt School, 3
Freud, Sigmund, 44
Fuga per canonem, 88, 94
Furey, Michael, 39, 46

Gabler, Hans, 129, 135
Gaelic language, 53, 54
Gaelic League, 54
Genesis, 86
Gibbon, Edward, 108, 109
Gibraltar, 143, 152–53, 155, 156
Gilbert, Stuart, 97, 173
Gnomon, 27–30, 32, 37, 39, 45

Goldberg, S. L., 88
Goldsmith, Oliver, 109
Gordon, John, 115–16
Gospels, 28
"Grace," 18

Habermas, Jürgen, 2, 9, 10
"Hades," 119
Haines, 103, 108, 115
Hamlet, 86, 123
Hauptmann, Gerhart, 71
Hayman, David, 75–76
Heath, Stephen, 41, 42, 173–74
Heidegger, Martin, 50
Henke, Suzette, 154
Henry II, 101
Hermes, 136
Herring, Phillip, 29–30, 43
Hodgson's *Book of Errors,* 109
Homer, 89, 99, 133
Horne's lying-in hospital, 106, 111, 114, 117
Houston, John Porter, 113, 116
Huysmans, Joris-Karl, 67

Iago, 122, 123, 135
Ibsen, Henrik, 71
Icarus, 4, 59, 128, 154, 176
Inferno, 18, 40
Ingersoll, Earl G., 45, 46
Interior monologue, 15, 87, 141
"Ireland, Island of Saints and Sages," 110
Irish nationalism, 34, 66
"Ithaca," 8, 92–93
Ivors, Molly, 34–37, 45

Jaloux, Edmund, 158
Jameson, Fredric, 5, 7, 11, 13
Jesuit habits of mind, 58, 59, 172–73
Joyce, John, 130
Joyce, Stanislaus, 18
Junius, 109
Justius, 159

Kafka, Franz, 39
Kain, Richard, 19, 44, 159

Kelley, Bridie, 124
Kenner, Hugh, 7–8, 115, 133, 135
Keon, Father, 44
Kershner, R. B., 75, 94

Lamb, Charles, 109
Lambert, Ned, 87
Landor, Walter Savage, 109, 113
Lawrence, Karen, 87, 114, 115, 134, 156
Lenehan, 16, 102, 107, 113, 116
"Lestrygonians," 84–85
Lily, 36
Lir, 16
Litany of the Virgin, 89
Little Review, 82
Litz, A. Walton, 156
Logos, 105
Lukács, Georg, 17, 47–48, 50, 60–62, 166, 168
Lunn, Eugene, 60–61, 72
Lynch, 74, 116, 128
Lyotard, Jean-François, 2–3, 10

Macaulay, Thomas, 108, 109
Macdonald, Michael Bruce, 76
Madonna, 46
Maeterlink, Maurice, 140
Magalaner, Marvin, 19, 44
Magi, 6, 37
Mahaffey, Vicki, 75–77, 135–36
Mahony, 24, 26, 27, 45, 94
Mananaan MacLir, 83, 94
Mandeville, Sir John, 107, 113
Manx Parliament, 83
Maria, 19–22, 25, 44
Mariolatry, 58, 72
Martha, 141, 144
Mary, 19, 58
Mercedes, 64
Mercius, 159
Michelangelo's Moses, 84
Milton, John, 113
Modernism, 1–12, 17, 47, 53, 60, 61, 66, 96
Moly, 126, 127, 136

Moretti, Franco, 7
Morkan sisters, 34
Mulligan, Buck, 80–81, 101, 108, 129
Murphy, 91–92, 95
Musil, Robert, 165–66, 168

Nannetti, Joseph P., 83
Narrator, omniscient, 60, 94
Naturalism, 61–62, 167–69, 170
"Nausicaa," 89–90, 150–52, 156
Neoconservatism, 2
"Nestor," 79–80, 97, 102, 166
Newman, John Henry Cardinal, 70, 71,
    108, 113
Nighttown, 91, 112, 118–37
Norman Invasion of 1156, 110

O'Callaghan, Miss, 36
Odysseus, 25, 78, 84, 96, 124, 129
O'Grady, Thomas B., 77
Othello, 123, 135
"Oxen of the Sun," 90, 95–117, 118,
    119, 138, 141, 168, 170

"A Painful Case," 39
Paralysis, 4, 5, 6, 7, 8, 9, 11, 13, 14, 17–
    19, 21, 22, 23, 27, 29, 30, 35, 40, 41,
    44, 47, 51, 52, 54–56, 59, 62, 64, 65,
    66, 77, 100, 111, 119, 122, 127, 129,
    130, 133, 134, 140, 157, 158, 162,
    166
Parnell, Charles Stewart, 19, 33, 57, 66,
    77, 175
Parody, 18, 36, 48, 105–9, 115, 116
Pastiche, 106–9, 115, 116
Pater, Walter, 47, 108, 113
Patrick, Saint, 159–60
"Penelope," 8, 9, 93–94, 138–56, 158,
    171
Pepys, Samuel, 107, 113
Pigeon House, 25
Poe, Edgar Allan, 36
"A Portrait of the Artist," 166–67
A Portrait of the Artist as a Young Man, 4,
    5, 8, 9, 11, 41, 47–77, 78–80, 95–97,

129, 138, 151, 153, 157, 166, 168,
    169, 170, 172–76
Postmodernism, 1–3, 10
Post-structuralism, 3, 95–96, 174–76
Power, Arthur, 165, 175
Protestantism, 10
"Proteus," 7, 75, 80–81, 99, 175
Purefoy, Mina, 98
Purefoy, Mortimer Edward, 99, 106

Rabaté, Jean-Michel, 2–3, 40–41, 43–
    44, 135
Realism, 2, 17, 47, 61, 67, 87
Repetition, 23–31, 42, 46, 52, 56, 98,
    105, 119
Restuccia, Frances L., 77
Reynolds, Mary T., 43
Richards, Grant, 168
Riordan, 150
Riquelme, John Paul, 80, 145, 155
Robinson, David, 75, 76
Romans, 67
Rousseau, Jean-Jacques, 60
Ruggieri, Franca, 42, 43, 46
Ruskin, John, 108

Scholes, Robert, 159
Scribbledehobble, 11
"Scylla and Charybdis," 85–86, 170
Senn, Fritz, 136–37, 155, 156, 169–70,
    173
Shakespeare, 41, 86, 100, 122, 123, 135
Shaun, 159, 162
Shelley, Percy Bysshe, 11
Shem, 159, 162
"Silent, O Moyle," 16
Silverman, A. O., 14
Simony, 27–29, 77
"Sirens," 88–89
"The Sisters," 15, 27–32, 43, 44, 75
Smith, 25
Solipsism, 5, 47, 48, 61–62, 66, 67,
    69–72, 151
Stasis, 5, 7–9, 73, 77, 140
Stephen Hero, 6, 14, 77

Sterne, Laurence, 108, 113
Stevens, Wallace, 65
Swift, Jonathan, 101, 107, 109–11, 113
Symbolism, 67, 74

Talboys, Mrs. Mervyn, 124
Taylor, John F., 83
Telemachiad, 79–81
"Telemachus," 80–81
Temple, 60
"Two Gallants," 15–16, 33, 37

Ulysses, 3, 5, 7–9, 11, 12, 16, 18, 22, 41,
    49, 61, 62, 74–76, 79–156, 157, 160,
    162, 165–76
Unkeless, Elaine, 155

Vico, Giambattista, 10, 144–45
Virag, 126–27, 134
Virgil, 70
Vita Nuova, 18, 43

"Wandering Rocks," 87, 88, 89
Weaver, Harriet Shaw, 78–79, 104–5
Weber, Max, 9
Wicke, Jennifer, 155, 156
Wilde, Oscar, 47
Williams, Trevor L., 76
Wolf, Christa, 55
Woolf, Virginia, 78

Yeats, William Butler, 107, 132

Zoe, 122, 131

Vivian Heller has taught English literature at the New School for Social Research and at Bennington College. She is currently completing a collection of short stories.